The Low Fat
Cook's Companion

First published in 1998 by Lorenz Books

© Anness Publishing Limited 1998

Lorenz Books is an imprint of
Anness Publishing Limited
Hermes House
88–89 Blackfriars Road
London SE1 8HA

This edition distributed in Canada by Raincoast Books
8680 Cambie Street, Vancouver, British Columbia V6P 6M9

ISBN 1 85967 794 0

A CIP catalogue record for this book is available from the British Library

Publisher: Joanna Lorenz
Senior Cookery Editor: Linda Fraser
Project Editor: Sarah Ainley
Photographers: James Duncan, Michelle Garrett, Ferguson Hill,
David Jordan, Don Last, Peter Reilly
Recipes: Catherine Atkinson, Christine France, Silvana Franco,
Shehzad Husain, Sue Maggs, Annie Nichols, Anne Sheasby, Liz Trigg
Jacket Design: Bobbie Colgate Stone
Nutritionalist: Helen Daniels

For all recipes, quantities are given in both metric and imperial measures,
and, where appropriate, measures are also given in standard cups and spoons.
Follow one set, but not a mixture, because they are not interchangeable.

The material in this book previously appeared as individual titles in the *Step-by-Step* series.

Printed and bound in Indonesia

3 5 7 9 10 8 6 4 2

The Low Fat Cook's Companion

OVER 300 DELICIOUS RECIPES
FOR HEALTHY EATING

LORENZ BOOKS

CONTENTS

INTRODUCTION

So much has been written in the past decade about what we should and should not eat, it's hardly surprising we're sceptical about dietary advice – it seems that everything we enjoy is bad for us. Often nutritionalists are vague and simply suggest eating a "balanced diet". However, when it comes to avoiding serious medical conditions such as heart disease, recommendations are loud are clear: reduce your intake of fat (especially saturated) and you'll considerably reduce the risks.

But what does this mean when you are shopping in the supermarket, faced with confusingly labelled foods? What exactly is saturated fat and how do we begin to limit the amount of fat we eat? These are the questions that are answered in this book.

Cutting down on fat does not mean sacrificing taste, and it's easy to follow a healthy eating plan without becoming a faddist. There's no need to forgo all your favourite foods, as the recipes in this book illustrate, but you may need to alter your approach to cooking, choose ingredients that are naturally lower in fat and prepare them using little – if any – additional fat. This is not as limiting as it sounds – you can still enjoy hearty main courses and desserts so delicious it's hard to believe they're good for you. With this in mind, it won't be long before you develop a preference for lower fat versions of everyday foods.

Do we need fat in our diet?

We only need 10 g/¼ oz fat in our daily diet for our bodies to function properly. A totally fat-free diet would be almost impossible to achieve, since some fat is present in virtually every food.

A certain amount of essential fatty acids are necessary in our diet to help our bodies absorb vitamins A, D, E and K as they are fat-soluble and cannot be made by the body. Fat is also needed to make hormones. Recent research has proved that we all eat far too much fat. Doctors now recommend that we limit our fat intake to no more than 30% of our total daily calorie intake, even as low as 25% for a really healthy diet. Some fats in the diet are a contributory factor in heart disease and cancers, such as breast, prostate and colon.

Types of fat in foods

Saturated fats are hard fats found in meat, most dairy products, such as butter, cream, dripping, hard margarines, cheeses and animal fats. Palm and coconut oil are also high in saturated fats. Saturated fats can raise the blood cholesterol level and clog up the arteries. The way we prepare and cook foods can limit the amount of saturated fat that we consume.

Polyunsaturated fats are soft fats such as sunflower, safflower, grapeseed, soya and corn oils, and fish such as mackerel, salmon or herring and nuts, seeds, cereals, lean meats and green vegetables. These fats may help to reduce our cholesterol levels.

Mono-unsaturated fats should make up most of the fat in our diet. They appear to have a protective effect and help lower cholesterol levels. Olive oil, rapeseed oil, peanut oil and avocados are all rich sources of mono-unsaturated fats.

A selection of foods containing the three main types of fat found in foods.

Eating a healthy low-fat diet

Eat a good variety of different foods every day to make sure you get all the nutrients you need.

1 Skimmed milk contains the same amount of calcium, protein and B vitamins as whole milk, but a fraction of the fat.
2 Natural low-fat yogurt, cottage cheese and fromage frais are all high in calcium and protein, and are good substitutes for cream.
3 Starchy foods such as rice, bread, potatoes, cereals and pasta should be eaten at every meal. These foods provide energy and some vitamins, minerals and dietary fibre.
4 Vegetables, salads and fruits should form a major part of the diet, and about 450 g/1 lb should be eaten each day.
5 Eat meat in moderation but eat plenty of fish, particularly oily fish such as mackerel, salmon, tuna, herring and sardines.

A few simple changes to a normal diet can reduce fat intake considerably. The following tips are designed to make the change to a healthier diet as easy as possible.

Meat and poultry
Red meats such as lamb, pork and beef are high in saturated fats, but chicken and turkey contain far less fat. Remove the skin before cooking and trim off any visible fat. Avoid sausages,

burgers, patés, bacon and minced beef. Buy lean cuts of meat and skim any fat from the surface of stocks and stews.

Dairy products
Replace whole milk with skimmed or semi-skimmed and use low-fat yogurt, low-fat crème fraîche or fromage frais instead

of cream. Eat cream, cream cheese and hard cheeses in moderation. There are reduced-fat cheeses on the market with 14% fat content which is half the fat content of full fat cheese. Use these wherever possible.

Spreads, oils and dressings
Use butter, margarine and low-fat spreads sparingly. Try to avoid using fat and oil for cooking. If you have to use oil, choose olive, corn, sunflower, soya, rapeseed and peanut oils, which are low in saturates. Look out for oil-free dressings and reduced fat mayonnaise.

Hidden fats
Biscuits, cakes, pastries, snacks and processed meals and curries all contain high proportions of fat. Get into the habit of reading food labels carefully and looking for a low-fat option.

Cooking methods
Grill, poach and steam foods whenever possible. If you do fry foods, use as little fat as possible and pat off the excess after browning, with kitchen paper. Make sauces and stews by first cooking the onions and garlic in a small quantity of stock, rather than frying in oil.

A selection of foods for a healthy low-fat diet.

The Fat and Calorie Contents of Food

This chart shows the weight of fat and the energy content of 115 g/4 oz of various foods.

FRUIT AND NUTS	Fat	Energy
Apples, eating	0.1 g	47 Kcals/197 kJ
Avocados	19.5 g	190 Kcals/795 kJ
Bananas	0.3 g	95 Kcals/397 kJ
Dried mixed fruit	1.6 g	227 Kcals/950 kJ
Grapefruit	0.1 g	30 Kcals/125 kJ
Oranges	0.1 g	37 Kcals/155 kJ
Peaches	0.1 g	33 Kcals/138 kJ
Almonds	55.8 g	612 Kcals/2560 kJ
Brazil nuts	68.2 g	682 Kcals/2853 kJ
Peanut butter, smooth	53.7 g	623 Kcals/2606 kJ
Pine nuts	68.6 g	688 Kcals/2878 kJ

DAIRY PRODUCE, FATS AND OILS	Fat	Energy
Cream, double	48.0 g	449 Kcals/1897 kJ
Cream, single	19.1 g	198 Kcals/828 kJ
Cream, whipping	39.3 g	373 Kcals/1560 kJ
Milk, skimmed	0.1 g	33 Kcals/130 kJ
Milk, whole	3.9 g	66 Kcals/276 kJ
Cheddar cheese	34.4 g	412 Kcals/1724 kJ
Cheddar-type, reduced-fat	15.0 g	261 Kcals/1092 kJ
Cream cheese	47.4 g	439 Kcals/1837 kJ
Brie	26.9 g	319 Kcals/1335kJ
Edam cheese	25.4 g	333 Kcals/1393 kJ
Feta cheese	20.2 g	250 Kcals/1046 kJ
Parmesan cheese	32.7 g	452 Kcals/1891 kJ
Greek yogurt	9.1 g	115 Kcals/481 kJ
Low fat yogurt, natural	0.8 g	56 Kcals/234 kJ
Butter	81.7 g	737 Kcals/308 kJ
Lard	99.0 g	891 Kcals/3730 kJ
Low fat spread	40.5 g	390 Kcals/1632 kJ
Margarine	81.6 g	739 Kcals/3092 kJ
Coconut oil	99.9 g	899 Kcals/3761 kJ
Corn oil	99.9 g	899 Kcals/3761 kJ
Olive oil	99.9 g	899 Kcals/3761 kJ
Safflower oil	99.9 g	899 Kcals/3761 kJ
Eggs (2, size 4)	10.9 g	147 Kcals/615 kJ
Egg white	Trace	36 Kcals/150 kJ
Egg yolk	30.5 g	339 Kcals/1418 kJ

OTHER FOODS	Fat	Energy
Sugar	0	94 Kcals/648 kJ
Chocolate, milk	30.3 g	529 Kcals/2213 kJ
Honey	0	88 Kcals/1205 kJ
Jam	0	61 Kcals/1092 kJ
Marmalade	0	61 Kcals/1092 kJ
Lemon curd	5.1 g	283 Kcals/1184 kJ

The Lowdown on Low Fat

Reduce your fat intake simply by switching to lower fat foods.

0.2 g fat
5 ml/1 tsp whole milk
200 ml/7 fl oz/scant 1 cup skimmed milk

1.0 g fat
115 g/4 oz/½ cup low fat natural yogurt
15 g/½ oz Greek yogurt
1 thin slice (1/20) avocado pear
3 bananas
9 apples, apricots, peaches, pears,
oranges or small bunches of grapes

2.5 g fat
¼ back bacon rasher
8 turkey rashers

10 g/¼ oz fat
115 g/4 oz/½ cup fat reduced cocoa powder
50 g/2 oz/¼ cup cocoa powder

12 g fat
15 g/½ oz butter
25 g/1 oz low fat spread

15 g/½ oz fat
50 g/2 oz Cheddar cheese
65 g/2½ oz Edam cheese
75 g/3 oz feta cheese
100 g/4 oz fat reduced cheddar
200 g/7 oz cottage cheese

WEIGHING NOTE
The weights given here have been
rounded slightly up or down to make
measuring portions easier.

Choosing Foods

The amount of fat, particularly saturated fat, is affected by two main factors – the type of foods we eat most often and the way in which we prepare and cook them.

Low fat doesn't mean no fat. It's misleading to start thinking simply of 'good' and 'bad' foods, it's really how much we eat of them that matters.

If you are going to cut down your fat intake, you'll need to make other alterations to your diet to compensate. High-fibre fruit, vegetables and cereals will help fill the gap. You should aim to increase your intake of carbohydrate foods to provide more than half your energy requirements. This will not only make your diet healthier, but you will also gradually lose weight, should you need to do this.

Fresh Foods and Ingredients

Fresh Beans and other Pulses

There are many varieties of fresh beans and pulses available, including peas, broad beans and runner beans and more unusual ones such as fresh flageolet beans, black-eyed beans and butter beans.

Fresh corn on the cob and baby sweetcorn are also popular, as are mangetouts, sugar-snap peas and green beans.

All are good sources of dietary fibre and contain other nutrients including vitamins and minerals. Beans and pulses are very versatile and can be used in many dishes including salads, stir-fries, casseroles, pasta sauces, soups and curries. Some varieties, such as sugar-snap peas and mangetouts, can be eaten either raw or cooked.

Fresh Fruit

Fresh fruit plays an important part in a healthy, balanced, high fibre diet. Choose fruits that contain useful amounts of fibre such as apples, pears, bananas, berries such as raspberries, blackberries and gooseberries, guava, mangoes, oranges, peaches and pears.

Fruits are very versatile and can be enjoyed raw or cooked, on their own or as part of a recipe. They are also good sources of vitamins and minerals, particularly vitamin C. A piece of fresh fruit makes a quick and easy, nutritious snack at any time of the day. Try topping wholewheat breakfast cereals with some fruit such as raspberries for a tasty and nutritious start to the day.

Fresh Herbs

In cookery, herbs are used mainly for their flavouring and seasoning properties, as well as for adding colour and texture. They have a great deal to offer and by simply adding a single herb or a combination of herbs to foods, everyday dishes can be transformed into delicious meals.

Herbs are also very low in fat and calories and those such as parsley provide a useful balance of vitamins and minerals. Many people grow their own herbs and a wide selection is readily available in supermarkets, greengrocers and market stores.

Potatoes

Potatoes are one of the most commonly eaten vegetables in the world and are valuable in terms of nutrition. They are high in carbohydrate, low in fat and contain some vitamin C and dietary fibre. Potatoes contain more dietary fibre when eaten with their skins on. Wash old and new potatoes thoroughly and cook them with their skins on – for example baked, boiled and roasted. The flavour will be just as delicious and you will be getting extra fibre.

Potatoes are very versatile and are used in many dishes. Mashed potatoes (with their skins left on, of course!) make an ideal topping for pies and bakes. For roast potatoes use a minimum amount of oil, and if you need to make chips, leave the skins on and cut the chips

thickly using a knife. With baked and mashed potatoes avoid adding high fat butter, soured cream or cheese and instead use skimmed milk, reduced-fat hard cheese and herbs to add flavour.

Fresh Vegetables

Fresh vegetables, like fresh fruit, play an important part in a healthy, balanced diet. We are now encouraged to eat at least five portions of fruit and vegetables each day for a healthy diet. Vegetables are nutritious and are valuable sources of vitamins and minerals, some being especially rich in vitamins A, C and E. Vegetables also contain some dietary fibre and those that are particularly good sources include broccoli, Brussels sprouts, cabbage, carrots, fennel, okra, parsnips, spinach, spring greens and sweetcorn.

Vegetables are also very versatile and many can be eaten either raw or cooked. Add vegetables to dishes such as soups, stews, casseroles, stir-fries, salads, burgers and meatloaves, or simply serve them on their own, raw or lightly cooked and tossed in a little lemon juice.

Wholemeal Bakes

Bakes such as wholemeal pitta breads, scones, muffins and teacakes make a good, high fibre snack or treat. Choose wholemeal or whole grain varieties whenever possible or make your own bakes at home using wholemeal flour and adding extra dried fruit. Serve bakes such as scones or muffins plain or with a little low fat spread, honey or reduced-sugar jam for a delicious, filling snack.

Wholemeal Bread

Bread has been an important part of the diet in many countries for thousands of years and nowadays continues to contribute to a healthy, balanced diet. Bread is available in many varieties and is a good source of carbohydrate as well as being low in fat. It also contains some calcium, iron and B vitamins and wholemeal varieties are high in fibre.

Make delicious sandwiches and toasted sandwiches using wholemeal bread and low fat fillings. Use wholemeal breadcrumbs in recipes such as stuffings, coatings and toppings and serve thick slices of wholemeal bread at mealtimes for a filling, healthy and high fibre accompaniment to many dishes.

Equipment

There are only a few essentials for low fat recipes – accurate measuring and weighing equipment and a non-stick frying pan. There are, however, many gadgets which make cooking with the minimum of fat a lot easier.

Baking sheet
A flat, rigid, non-stick baking sheet ensures even cooking.

Baking tray
A shallow-sided non-stick tray that won't buckle at high temperatures is ideal for roasting.

Bowls
A set of bowls is useful for mixing, whisking and soaking. A non-porous material such as glass or stainless steel is essential when whisking egg whites.

Chopping board
A hygienic nylon board is recommended for chopping and cutting.

Colander
This is useful for draining cooked pasta and vegetables quickly.

Cook's knife
A large all-purpose cook's knife is essential for chopping, dicing and slicing.

Filleting knife
A thin, flexible-bladed knife is useful for filleting fish.

Frying pan
A non-stick surface is vital for 'frying' and browning meat and vegetables.

Large spoon
Use this for folding in, stirring and basting.

Measuring cups or weighing scales
Use these for accurately measuring both dry and wet ingredients.

Measuring spoons
Essential for measuring small quantities accurately.

Non-stick coated fabric sheet
This re-usable non-stick material can be cut to size, and used to line cake tins, baking sheets or frying pans. Heat resistant up to 290°C/550°F and microwave-safe, it will last up to 5 years.

Non-stick baking paper
Ideal for lining cake tins and baking sheets without the need for greasing.

Non-stick baking tins
For easy removal of low fat bakes and sponge cakes.

Perforated spoon
Useful for lifting cooked food out of cooking liquid.

Ridged grill pan
For giving grilled meat and vegetables characteristic 'char lines'.

Sieve
For sifting dry ingredients and draining yogurt.

Small grater
For finely grating fresh Parmesan cheese and nutmeg.

Vegetable peeler
For preparing fruit and vegetables.

Whisk
Essential for whisking egg whites and for thorough mixing.

non-stick baking paper

non-stick baking tins

ridged grill pan

non-stick baking tins

non-stick coated
fabric sheet

sieve

large spoon

baking sheet

chopping boards

measuring cups

vegetable peeler

Healthy Cooking Techniques

The aims of cooking for a healthy heart are to avoid adding fat to food, to reduce the saturated fat content of the ingredients where possible, to use techniques that retain the vitamins and minerals and, of course, to ensure that the food is delicious by preserving or enhancing its flavour, colour and texture.

STIR-FRYING

This method means that food cooks quickly to retain maximum nutritional value, colour and texture.

Slivers of meat can be marinated in savoury mixtures of, for example, soy sauce, fruit juice, tomato purée and vinegar, or similar sauces before cooking to tenderize them and add flavour.

Foods need to be cut into small pieces, so that they cook quickly and evenly.

2 Add garlic to flavour a stir-fry for a few seconds, then add the meat.

1 Preheat the wok, then dribble only 5–10ml/1–2 tsp oil around the rim. Cut meat into thin slivers or cubes to minimize cooking time.

3 Once the meat is almost cooked add the other ingredients.

STEAMING

Food is cooked over boiling liquid (usually water) but it does not touch the liquid. As a result most of the vitamins and minerals are retained.

Browning is not part of the process, so fat need never be added.

Steaming preserves the texture of foods and is a good cooking method for those who prefer their vegetables with a bit of bite. It is also very useful for fish, poultry and puddings.

1 Prepare ingredients as for stir-frying. Expandable steamers will fit a range of saucepan sizes. Add food straight into the steamer and cover.

2 If using a bamboo steamer over either a wok or pan of boiling liquid, place the food in a bowl first, then cover.

MICROWAVING

This is a quick and useful way of cooking vegetables, fruit and fish.

Naturally moist foods are cooked without additional liquid, and only a small amount of liquid is added to other foods. As a result, vitamins and minerals do not leach out into cooking water which is then thrown away.

Fat is not required for cooking, and microwaved food can be seasoned with fresh chopped herbs instead of salt. The flavour can be sharpened by adding a little lemon juice.

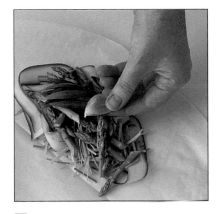

1 Place food in a microwave-proof dish, or wrap in a paper parcel. Refer to the manufacturer's handbook for information on power levels and cooking times.

CASEROLING

One-pot meals are good for stress-free entertaining. They also have the advantage that vitamins and minerals are retained in the stock, which is served alongside the other ingredients.

Use only the minimum amount of fat for cooking and make the casserole a day ahead, then cool and chill it. Any fat will solidify on the surface and can easily be lifted off before the casserole is re-heated.

1 Trim visible fat from meat or remove skin from poultry.

PRESSURE COOKING

This method cuts cooking time dramatically, which encourages the frequent consumption of beneficial low-fat foods (brown rice cooks in 7 minutes, potatoes in 6). Like steaming, pressure cooking retains more nutrients because the food is not in contact with the cooking water.

GRILLING

There's no need to add fat when grilling meat, fish or vegetables. Use a rack and any fat that runs from the meat can easily be drained. Brush the rack with oil before cooking to prevent the food from sticking. Cook under a preheated grill and baste with lemon juice, if necessary.

POACHING

This is an excellent way of cooking delicate white fish (plaice) or whole oily fish (mackerel, salmon, trout). Fish steaks, particularly cod, halibut, salmon and tuna also cook well by either method and there is no need to add any fat.

Poaching can be done either in the oven or on top of the cooker.

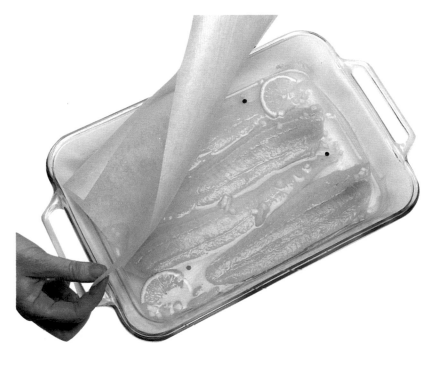

1 To oven-poach fish, pour in boiling liquid to barely cover the fish, add any flavourings and cover with buttered greaseproof paper. Cook in a pre-heated oven to 180°C/350°F/Gas 4.

2 To poach on top of the cooker, suspend the fish in the poaching liquid, either in a muslin hammock or on a rack. Cover with liquid, bring to the boil and simmer gently until cooked.

Puréeing Soup

1 Allow the cooked soup to cool slightly, then ladle it into a blender or food processor.

2 Process the mixture until smooth. If there is a large quantity of soup, blend or purée it in a couple of batches.

3 Rinse the saucepan, then pour the blended soup back into it. Adjust the seasoning and reheat the soup gently before serving.

Peeling Tomatoes

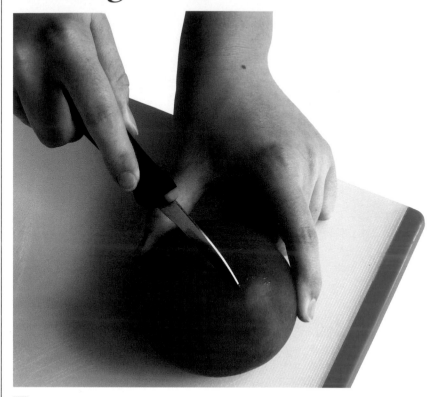

1 Using a sharp knife, cut a small cross in the base of each tomato.

2 Place the tomatoes in a bowl and cover them with boiling water. Leave them for 30 seconds, then using a slotted spoon, transfer them to a bowl of cold water.

3 Remove the tomatoes from the water and peel off the skins. Slice or chop the tomatoes and use as required in the recipe.

Chicken Stock

This classic, flavourful stock forms the base for many soups and sauces.

Makes 1.5 litres/2½ pints/6¼ cups

INGREDIENTS
1 kg/2¼ lb chicken wings or thighs
1 onion
2 whole cloves
1 bay leaf
1 sprig of thyme
3–4 sprigs of parsley
10 black peppercorns

1 Cut the chicken into pieces and put into a large, heavy-based saucepan. Peel the onion and stick with the cloves. Tie the bay leaf, thyme, parsley and peppercorns in a piece of muslin and add to the saucepan together with the onion.

2 Pour in 1.75 litres/3 pints/7½ cups of cold water. Slowly bring to simmering point, skimming off any scum which rises to the surface with a slotted spoon. Continue to simmer very gently, uncovered, for 1½ hours.

3 Strain the stock through a sieve into a large bowl and leave until cold. Remove any fat from the surface with a slotted spoon. Keep chilled in the refrigerator until required, or freeze in usable amounts.

Vegetable Stock

A vegetarian version of the basic stock.

Makes 1.5 litres/2½ pints/6¼ cups

INGREDIENTS
2 carrots
2 celery sticks
2 onions
2 tomatoes
10 mushroom stalks
2 bay leaves
1 sprig of thyme
3–4 sprigs of parsley
10 black peppercorns

1 Roughly chop the carrots, celery, onions, tomatoes and mushroom stalks. Place them in a large heavy-based saucepan. Tie the bay leaves, thyme, parsley and peppercorns in a piece of muslin and add to the pan.

2 Pour in 1.75 litres/3 pints/7½ cups cold water. Slowly bring to simmering point. Continue to simmer very gently, uncovered, for 1½ hours.

3 Strain through a sieve into a large bowl and leave until cold. Keep chilled in the refrigerator until required, or freeze in usable amounts.

Sautéed Onions

Fried onions form the basis of many savoury recipes. This is a fat free version.

INGREDIENTS
2 medium onions, sliced
175 ml/6 fl oz/¾ cup chicken or
    vegetable stock
15 ml/1 tbsp dry red or white wine or
    wine vinegar

1 Put the onions and stock into a non-stick frying pan. Cover and bring to the boil. Simmer for 1 minute.

2 Uncover and boil for about 5 minutes, or until the stock has reduced entirely. Lower the heat and stir the onions until just beginning to colour.

3 Add the wine or vinegar and continue to cook until the onions are dry and lightly browned.

Whipped 'Cream'

Serve this sweet 'cream' instead of whipped double cream. It isn't suitable for cooking, but freezes very well.

Makes 150 ml/¼ pint/⅔ cup

INGREDIENTS
2.5 ml/½ tsp powdered gelatine
50 g/2 oz/¼ cup skimmed milk
    powder
15 ml/1 tbsp caster sugar
15 ml/1 tbsp lemon juice

1 Sprinkle the gelatine over 15 ml/1 tbsp cold water in a small bowl and leave to 'sponge' for 5 minutes. Place the bowl over a saucepan of hot water and stir until dissolved. Leave to cool.

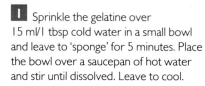

2 Whisk the skimmed milk powder, caster sugar, lemon juice and 60 ml/4 tbsp cold water until frothy. Add the dissolved gelatine and whisk for a few seconds more. Chill in the refrigerator for 30 minutes.

3 Whisk the chilled mixture again until very thick and frothy. Serve within 30 minutes of making.

Making Wholemeal Shortcrust Pastry

1 Put the flour and salt in a bowl and add the fat. Rub the fat into the flour between your finger tips until the mixture resembles breadcrumbs.

2 Using a round-bladed knife, keep stirring in small amounts of cold water until the mixture begins to stick together in lumps.

3 Collect the dough together and knead lightly to form a smooth, soft ball. Wrap in greaseproof paper or foil and leave to rest in the fridge for 30 minutes before rolling out and using as required.

Preventing Fruit Discoloration

Use this method for bananas, apples and pears.

1 Choose firm, ripe fruit (bananas in this instance). Peel, slice and put the fruit into a bowl.

2 Sprinkle lemon juice liberally all over the fruit.

3 Remove the fruit from the bowl using a slotted spoon to drain off any excess lemon juice and use as required, as soon as possible. Discard any remaining lemon juice.

Soups & Starters

Melon and Basil Soup

A deliciously refreshing, chilled fruit soup, just right for a hot summer's day.

Serves 4–6

INGREDIENTS
2 Charentais or rock melons
75 g/3 oz/⅓ cup caster sugar
175 ml/6 fl oz/¾ cup water
finely grated rind and juice of 1 lime
45 ml/3 tbsp shredded fresh basil
fresh basil leaves, to garnish

basil

caster sugar

lime

Charentais melon

NUTRITIONAL NOTES
PER PORTION:

ENERGY 63Kcals/268KJ PROTEIN 0.28g
FAT 0.09g SATURATED FAT 0g
CARBOHYDRATE 16g
FIBRE 0.25g SUGAR 16.2g
SODIUM 17.3mg

1 Cut the melons in half across the middle. Scrape out the seeds and discard. Using a melon baller, scoop out 20–24 balls and set aside for the garnish. Scoop out the remaining flesh and place in a blender or food processor.

2 Place the sugar, water and lime zest in a small pan over a low heat. Stir until dissolved, bring to the boil and simmer for 2–3 minutes. Remove from the heat and leave to cool slightly. Pour half the mixture into the blender or food processor with the melon flesh. Blend until smooth, adding the remaining syrup and lime juice to taste.

COOK'S TIP
Add the syrup in two stages, as the amount of sugar needed will depend on the sweetness of the melon.

3 Pour the mixture into a bowl, stir in the basil and chill. Serve garnished with basil leaves and melon balls.

Leek, Parsnip and Ginger Soup

A flavoursome winter warmer, with the added spiciness of fresh ginger.

Serves 4–6

INGREDIENTS

30 ml/2 tbsp olive oil
225 g/8 oz leeks, sliced
25 g/1 oz fresh ginger root, finely chopped
675 g/1½ lb parsnips, roughly chopped
300 ml/½ pint/1¼ cups dry white wine
1.1 litres/2 pints/5 cups vegetable stock or water
salt and freshly ground black pepper
low-fat fromage blanc, to garnish
paprika, to garnish

1 Heat the oil in a large pan and add the leeks and ginger. Cook gently for 2–3 minutes, until the leeks start to soften.

2 Add the parsnips and cook for a further 7–8 minutes.

NUTRITIONAL NOTES
PER PORTION:

ENERGY 165Kcals/692KJ PROTEIN 3.4g
FAT 6.5g SATURATED FAT 0.99g
CARBOHYDRATE 16.4g
FIBRE 6g SUGAR 8.2g
SODIUM 17mg

ginger

parsnips

vegetable stock

leek

3 Pour in the wine and stock or water and bring to the boil. Reduce the heat and simmer for 20–30 minutes or until the parsnips are tender.

4 Purée in a blender until smooth. Season to taste. Reheat and garnish with a swirl of fromage blanc and a light dusting of paprika.

Broccoli and Almond Soup

The creaminess of the toasted almonds combines perfectly with the slight bitterness of the taste of broccoli.

Serves 4–6

INGREDIENTS

50 g/2 oz/⅔ cup ground almonds
675 g/1½ lb broccoli
850 ml/1½ pints/3¾ cups vegetable
  stock or water
300 ml/½ pint/1¼ cups skimmed
  milk
salt and freshly ground black pepper

ground almonds

skimmed milk

broccoli

1 Preheat the oven to 180°C/350°F/ Gas 4. Spread the ground almonds evenly on a baking sheet and toast in the oven for about 10 minutes, or until golden. Reserve ¼ of the almonds and set aside for the garnish.

2 Cut the broccoli into small florets and steam for 6–7 minutes or until tender.

NUTRITIONAL NOTES

PER PORTION:

ENERGY 104Kcals/436KJ PROTEIN 8.36g
FAT 5.7g SATURATED FAT 0.66g
CARBOHYDRATE 5.1g
FIBRE 3.5g SUGAR 4.5g
SODIUM 37.2mg

3 Place the remaining toasted almonds, broccoli, stock or water and milk in a blender and blend until smooth. Season to taste.

4 Reheat the soup and serve sprinkled with the reserved toasted almonds.

Pea, Leek and Broccoli Soup

A delicious and nutritious soup, ideal for warming those chilly winter evenings.

Serves 4–6

INGREDIENTS
1 onion, chopped
225 g/8 oz/2 cups leeks
  (trimmed weight), sliced
225 g/8 oz unpeeled potatoes, diced
900 ml/1½ pints/3¾ cups
  vegetable stock
1 bay leaf
225 g/8 oz broccoli florets
175 g/6 oz/1½ cups frozen peas
30–45 ml/2–3 tbsp chopped
  fresh parsley
salt and ground black pepper
parsley leaves, to garnish

onion

leeks

potatoes

vegetable stock

bay leaf

broccoli

peas

parsley

salt

black pepper

NUTRITIONAL NOTES
PER PORTION:

ENERGY 125Kcals/528KJ PROTEIN 8.11g
FAT 1.92g SATURATED FAT 0.26g
CARBOHYDRATE 19.94g
FIBRE 6.31g ADDED SUGAR 0.04g
SODIUM 0.52g

COOK'S TIP
If you prefer, cut the vegetables finely and leave the cooked soup chunky rather than puréeing it.

1 Put the onion, leeks, potatoes, stock and bay leaf in a large saucepan and mix together. Cover, bring to the boil and simmer for 10 minutes, stirring.

2 Add the broccoli and peas, cover, return to the boil and simmer for a further 10 minutes, stirring occasionally.

3 Set aside to cool slightly and remove and discard the bay leaf. Purée in a blender or food processor until smooth.

4 Add the parsley, season to taste and process briefly. Return to the saucepan and reheat gently until piping hot. Ladle into soup bowls and garnish with parsley leaves.

Italian Vegetable Soup

The success of this clear soup depends on the quality of the stock, so use home-made vegetable stock rather than stock cubes.

Serves 4

INGREDIENTS
1 small carrot
1 baby leek
1 celery stick
50 g/2 oz green cabbage
900 ml/1½ pints/3¾ cups
   vegetable stock
1 bay leaf
115 g/4 oz/1 cup cooked cannellini
   beans
25 g/1 oz/⅕ cup soup pasta, such as
   tiny shells, bows, stars or elbows
salt and freshly ground black pepper
snipped fresh chives, to garnish

stock

cabbage

bay leaf

chives

baby leek

celery

carrot

pasta

1 Cut the carrot, leek and celery into 5 cm/2 in long julienne strips. Slice the cabbage very finely.

2 Put the stock and bay leaf into a large saucepan and bring to the boil. Add the carrot, leek and celery, cover and simmer for 6 minutes.

NUTRITIONAL NOTES
PER PORTION:
ENERGY 126 Kcals/529 KJ **FAT** 2.2 g
SATURATED FAT 0.6 g
CHOLESTEROL 19 mg

3 Add the cabbage, beans and pasta shapes. Stir, then simmer uncovered for a further 4-5 minutes, or until the vegetables and pasta are tender.

4 Remove the bay leaf and season to taste. Ladle into four soup bowls and garnish with snipped chives. Serve immediately.

Sweetcorn and Chicken Soup

This popular classic Chinese soup is very easy to make.

Serves 4-6

INGREDIENTS

1 chicken breast fillet, about
 115 g/4 oz, cubed
10 ml/2 tsp light soy sauce
15 ml/1 tbsp Chinese rice wine
5 ml/1 tsp cornflour
60 ml/4 tbsp cold water
5 ml/1 tsp sesame oil
30 ml/2 tbsp groundnut oil
5 ml/1 tsp grated fresh root
 ginger
1 litre/1¾ pints/4 cups chicken
 stock
425 g/15 oz can cream-style
 sweetcorn
225 g/8 oz can sweetcorn kernels
2 eggs, beaten
2-3 spring onions, green parts
 only, cut into tiny rounds
salt and ground black pepper

cornflour

chicken stock

cream-style sweetcorn

chicken

sweetcorn kernels

Chinese rice wine

egg

sesame oil

ginger

NUTRITIONAL NOTES
PER PORTION:

ENERGY 163 Kcals/686 KJ **FAT** 4.6 g
SATURATED FAT 1.1 g
CHOLESTEROL 72.4 mg

1 Mince the chicken in a food processor, taking care not to over-process. Transfer the chicken to a bowl and stir in the soy sauce, rice wine, cornflour, water, sesame oil and seasoning. Cover and leave for about 15 minutes to absorb the flavours.

2 Heat a wok over a medium heat. Add the groundnut oil and swirl it around. Add the ginger and stir-fry for a few seconds. Add the stock, creamed sweetcorn and sweetcorn kernels. Bring to just below boiling point.

3 Spoon about 90 ml/6 tbsp of the hot liquid into the chicken mixture until it forms a smooth paste and stir. Return to the wok. Slowly bring to the boil, stirring constantly, then simmer for 2–3 minutes until cooked.

4 Pour the beaten eggs into the soup in a slow steady stream, using a fork or chopsticks to stir the top of the soup in a figure-of-eight pattern. The egg should set in lacy shreds. Serve immediately with the spring onions sprinkled over.

Red Onion and Beetroot Soup

This beautiful vivid ruby-red soup will look stunning at any dinner party.

Serves 4–6

INGREDIENTS

15 ml/1 tbsp olive oil
350 g/12 oz red onions, sliced
2 garlic cloves, crushed
275 g/10 oz cooked beetroot, cut into sticks
1.1 litres/2 pints/5 cups vegetable stock or water
50 g/2 oz/1 cup cooked soup pasta
30 ml/2 tbsp raspberry vinegar
salt and freshly ground black pepper
low-fat yogurt or fromage blanc, to garnish
snipped chives, to garnish

garlic

red onion

beetroot

pasta

chives

1 Heat the olive oil and add the onions and garlic.

2 Cook gently for about 20 minutes or until soft and tender.

3 Add the beetroot, stock or water, cooked pasta shapes and vinegar and heat through. Season to taste.

4 Ladle into bowls. Top each one with a spoonful of yogurt or fromage blanc and sprinkle with chives.

COOK'S TIP

Try substituting cooked barley for the pasta to give extra nuttiness.

NUTRITIONAL NOTES

PER PORTION:

ENERGY 104 Kcals/436 KJ **FAT** 1.4 g
SATURATED FAT 0.1 g

Cauliflower, Flageolet and Fennel Seed Soup

The sweet, anise-liquorice flavour of the fennel seeds gives a delicious edge to this hearty soup.

Serves 4–6

INGREDIENTS
15 ml/1 tbsp olive oil
1 garlic clove, crushed
1 onion, chopped
10 ml/2 tsp fennel seeds
1 cauliflower, cut into small florets
2 × 400 g/14 oz cans flageolet beans,
   drained and rinsed
1.1 litres/2 pints/5 cups vegetable
   stock or water
salt and freshly ground black pepper
chopped fresh parsley, to garnish
toasted slices of French bread, to
   serve

flageolet beans

French bread

onion

garlic

cauliflower

fennel seeds

parsley

1 Heat the olive oil. Add the garlic, onion and fennel seeds and cook gently for 5 minutes or until softened.

2 Add the cauliflower, half of the beans and the stock or water.

NUTRITIONAL NOTES
PER PORTION:

ENERGY 169 Kcals/710 KJ **FAT** 3.9 g
SATURATED FAT 0.7 g

3 Bring to the boil. Reduce the heat and simmer for 10 minutes or until the cauliflower is tender.

4 Pour the soup into a blender and blend until smooth. Stir in the remaining beans and season to taste. Reheat and pour into bowls. Sprinkle with chopped parsley and serve with toasted slices of French bread.

Spicy Chick-pea and Bacon Soup

This is a tasty mixture of chick-peas and bacon flavoured with a subtle mix of spices.

NUTRITIONAL NOTES
PER PORTION:

ENERGY 207Kcals/874KJ PROTEIN 15.56g
FAT 7.28g SATURATED FAT 1.43g
CARBOHYDRATE 22.40g
FIBRE 4.82g ADDED SUGAR 0.02g
SODIUM 1.17g

Serves 4–6

INGREDIENTS
10 ml/2 tsp sunflower oil
1 onion, chopped
2 garlic cloves, crushed
5 ml/1 tsp each garam masala,
  ground coriander, ground cumin
  and ground turmeric
2.5 ml/½ tsp hot chilli powder
30 ml/2 tbsp plain wholemeal flour
600 ml/1 pint/2½ cups
  vegetable stock
400 g/14 oz can chopped tomatoes
400 g/14 oz can chick-peas, rinsed
6 rashers lean smoked back bacon,
salt and ground black pepper
coriander sprigs, to garnish

1 Heat the oil in a large saucepan. Add the onion and garlic and cook for 5 minutes, stirring occasionally.

2 Add the spices and flour and cook for 1 minute, stirring.

3 Gradually add the stock, stirring constantly, then add the tomatoes and chick-peas.

sunflower oil

garlic

garam masala

ground coriander

onion

ground cumin

ground turmeric

hot chilli powder

wholemeal flour

vegetable stock

chopped tomatoes

chick-peas

back bacon

salt

black pepper

coriander

4 Bring to the boil, stirring, then cover and simmer for 25 minutes, stirring occasionally.

COOK'S TIP
Use other canned beans such as red kidney beans or flageolet beans in place of the chick-peas.

5 Meanwhile, grill the bacon for 2–3 minutes on each side.

6 Dice the bacon, then stir into the soup. Season to taste, reheat gently until piping hot and ladle into soup bowls to serve. Garnish each with a coriander sprig and serve immediately.

Fresh Tomato, Lentil and Onion Soup

This delicious wholesome soup is ideal served with thick slices of wholemeal or granary bread.

Serves 4–6

INGREDIENTS
10 ml/2 tsp sunflower oil
1 large onion, chopped
2 sticks celery, chopped
175 g/6 oz/¾ cup split red lentils
2 large tomatoes, skinned and roughly chopped
900 ml/1½ pints/3¾ cups vegetable stock
10 ml/2 tsp dried *herbes de Provence*
salt and freshly ground black pepper

sunflower oil
onion
celery
split red lentils
tomatoes
herbes de Provence
vegetable stock
salt
black pepper

NUTRITIONAL NOTES
PER PORTION:

ENERGY 202Kcals/856KJ PROTEIN 12.40g
FAT 3.07g SATURATED FAT 0.38g
CARBOHYDRATE 33.34g
FIBRE 4.27g ADDED SUGAR 0.04g
SODIUM 0.54g

1 Heat the oil in a large saucepan. Add the onion and celery and cook for 5 minutes, stirring occasionally. Add the lentils and cook for 1 minute.

2 Stir in the tomatoes, stock, herbs and seasoning. Cover, bring to the boil and simmer for about 20 minutes, stirring occasionally.

3 When the lentils are cooked and tender, set the soup aside to cool slightly.

4 Purée in a blender or food processor until smooth. Adjust the seasoning, return to the saucepan and reheat gently until piping hot. Ladle into soup bowls to serve and garnish each with chopped parsley.

Chilled Fresh Tomato Soup

This effortless uncooked soup can be made in minutes.

Serves 4–6

INGREDIENTS

1.5 kg/3–3½ lb ripe tomatoes, peeled
   and roughly chopped
4 garlic cloves, crushed
30 ml/2 tbsp balsamic vinegar
freshly ground black pepper
4 slices wholemeal bread
low-fat fromage blanc, to garnish

wholemeal bread

garlic

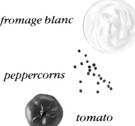

fromage blanc

peppercorns

tomato

COOK'S TIP
For the best flavour, it is important to use only fully ripened, flavourful tomatoes in this soup.

1 Place the tomatoes in a blender with the garlic and olive oil if using. Blend until smooth.

2 Pass the mixture through a sieve to remove the seeds. Stir in the balsamic vinegar and season to taste with pepper. Leave in the fridge to chill.

NUTRITIONAL NOTES
PER PORTION:

ENERGY 104Kcals/436KJ PROTEIN 5.42g
FAT 1.4g SATURATED FAT 0.1g
CARBOHYDRATE 19.22g
FIBRE 3.9g SUGAR 3.97g
SODIUM 160.33mg

3 Toast the bread lightly on both sides. Whilst still hot, cut off the crusts and slice in half horizontally. Place the toast on a board with the uncooked sides facing down and, using a circular motion, rub to remove any doughy pieces of bread.

4 Cut each slice into 4 triangles. Place on a grill pan and toast the uncooked sides until lightly golden. Garnish each bowl of soup with a spoonful of fromage blanc and serve with the melba toast.

Curried Celery Soup

An unusual combination of flavours, this warming soup is excellent served with warm wholemeal bread rolls or wholemeal pitta bread.

NUTRITIONAL NOTES

Per portion:

ENERGY 102Kcals/431KJ PROTEIN 3.72g
FAT 2.93g SATURATED FAT 0.25g
CARBOHYDRATE 16.11g
FIBRE 4.44g ADDED SUGAR 0.04g
SODIUM 0.62g

Serves 4–6

INGREDIENTS

10 ml/2 tsp olive oil
1 onion, chopped
1 leek, washed and sliced
675 g/1½ lb celery, chopped
15 ml/1 tbsp medium or hot curry powder
225 g/8 oz unpeeled potatoes, washed and diced
900 ml/1½ pints/3¾ cups vegetable stock
1 bouquet garni
30 ml/2 tbsp chopped fresh mixed herbs
salt
celery seeds and leaves, to garnish

olive oil

onion

leek

celery

curry powder

potatoes

vegetable stock

bouquet garni

fresh mixed herbs

salt

celery seeds

1 Heat the oil in a large saucepan. Add the onion, leek and celery, cover and cook gently for 10 minutes, stirring occasionally.

2 Add the curry powder and cook for 2 minutes, stirring occasionally.

3 Add the potatoes, stock and bouquet garni, cover, and bring to the boil. Simmer for 20 minutes, until the vegetables are tender

4 Remove and discard the bouquet garni and set the soup aside to cool slightly.

5 Purée in a blender or food processor until smooth.

6 Add the mixed herbs, season to taste and process briefly. Return to the saucepan and reheat gently until piping hot. Ladle into soup bowls and garnish each with a sprinkling of celery seeds and some celery leaves.

COOK'S TIP

For a tasty change, use celeriac and sweet potatoes in place of celery and standard potatoes.

Consommé with Agnolotti

Serves 4–6

INGREDIENTS
75 g/3 oz cooked peeled prawns
75 g/3 oz canned crab meat, drained
5 ml/1 tsp fresh root ginger, peeled
    and finely grated
15 ml/1 tbsp fresh white
    breadcrumbs
5 ml/1 tsp light soy sauce
1 spring onion, finely chopped
1 garlic clove, crushed
1 quantity of basic pasta dough
egg white, beaten
400 g/14 oz can chicken or
    fish consommé
30 ml/2 tbsp sherry or vermouth
salt and ground black pepper
50 g/2 oz cooked, peeled prawns
    and fresh coriander leaves,
    to garnish

root ginger   *crab meat*   *prawns*

spring onion   *fresh coriander*

garlic

chicken consommé

flour

fresh white breadcrumbs

basic pasta dough

1 Put the prawns, crab meat, ginger, breadcrumbs, soy sauce, onion, garlic and seasoning into a food processor or blender and process until smooth.

2 Roll the pasta into thin sheets. Stamp out 32 rounds 5 cm/2 in in diameter, with a fluted pastry cutter.

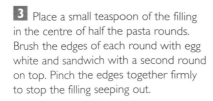

3 Place a small teaspoon of the filling in the centre of half the pasta rounds. Brush the edges of each round with egg white and sandwich with a second round on top. Pinch the edges together firmly to stop the filling seeping out.

4 Cook the pasta in a large pan of boiling, salted water for 5 minutes (cook in batches to stop them sticking together). Remove and drop into a bowl of cold water for 5 seconds before placing on a tray. (You can make these pasta shapes a day in advance. Cover with clear film and store in the fridge.)

5 Heat the chicken or fish consommé in a pan with the sherry or vermouth. When piping hot, add the cooked pasta shapes and simmer for 1–2 minutes.

6 Serve in a shallow soup bowl covered with hot consommé. Garnish with extra peeled prawns and fresh coriander leaves.

NUTRITIONAL NOTES
PER PORTION:

ENERGY 300Kcals/1265KJ **FAT** 4.6g
SATURATED FAT 1.1g **CHOLESTEROL** 148mg
CARBOHYDRATE 43g **FIBRE** 1.7g

Chicken Stellette Soup

Serves 4–6

INGREDIENTS

900 ml/1½ pints/3¾ cups
   chicken stock
1 bay leaf
4 spring onions, sliced
50 g/2oz soup pasta (stellette)
225 g/8 oz button
   mushrooms, sliced
115 g/4 oz cooked chicken breast
150 ml/¼ pint/⅔ cup dry
   white wine
15 ml/1 tbsp chopped parsley
salt and ground black pepper

stellette   *white wine*

stock

*cooked
chicken
breast*

*spring
onions*

parsley

bay leaf

mushrooms

1 Put the stock and bay leaf into a pan and bring to the boil.

2 Add the spring onions and mushrooms to the stock.

NUTRITIONAL NOTES

PER PORTION:

ENERGY 126Kcals/529KJ **FAT** 2.2g
SATURATED FAT 0.6g **CHOLESTEROL** 19mg
CARBOHYDRATE 11g **FIBRE** 1.3g

3 Remove the skin from the chicken and slice thinly. Transfer to a plate and set aside.

4 Add the pasta to the pan, cover and simmer for 7–8 minutes. Just before serving, add the chicken, wine and parsley, heat through for 2–3 minutes.

Vegetable Minestrone with Anellini

Serves 6–8

INGREDIENTS

large pinch of saffron strands
1 onion, chopped
1 leek, sliced
1 stick celery, sliced
2 carrots, diced
2–3 garlic cloves, crushed
600 ml/1 pint/2½ cups
    chicken stock
2 x 400 g/14 oz cans
    chopped tomatoes
50 g/2 oz/½ cup frozen peas
50 g/2 oz soup pasta (anellini)
5 ml/1 tsp caster sugar
15 ml/1 tbsp chopped fresh parsley
15 ml/1 tbsp chopped fresh basil
salt and ground black pepper

anellini *frozen peas* *onion*

saffron strands *basil* *stock*

parsley *chopped tomatoes*

carrot *celery*

garlic *leek*

1 Soak the pinch of saffron strands in 15 ml/1 tbsp boiling water. Leave to stand for 10 minutes.

2 Meanwhile, put the prepared onion, leek, celery, carrots and garlic into a pan. Add the chicken stock, bring to the boil, cover and simmer for 10 minutes.

NUTRITIONAL NOTES

PER PORTION:

ENERGY 87Kcals/367KJ **FAT** 0.7g
SATURATED FAT 0.1g **CHOLESTEROL** 0mg
CARBOHYDRATE 17g **FIBRE** 3.3g

3 Add the canned tomatoes, the saffron with its liquid, and the peas. Bring back to the boil and add the anellini. Simmer for 10 minutes until tender.

4 Season with salt, pepper and sugar to taste. Stir in the chopped herbs just before serving.

Beetroot Soup with Ravioli

Serves 4–6

INGREDIENTS
1 quantity of basic pasta dough
egg white, beaten, for brushing
flour, for dusting
1 small onion or shallot,
    finely chopped
2 garlic cloves, crushed
5 ml/1 tsp fennel seeds
600 ml/1 pint/2½ cups chicken or
    vegetable stock
225 g/8 oz cooked beetroot
30 ml/2 tbsp fresh orange juice
fennel or dill leaves, to garnish
crusty bread, to serve

FOR THE FILLING
115 g/4 oz mushrooms,
    finely chopped
1 shallot or small onion,
    finely chopped
1–2 garlic cloves, crushed
5 ml/1 tsp fresh thyme
15 ml/1 tbsp fresh parsley
90 ml/6 tbsp fresh white
    breadcrumbs
salt and ground black pepper
large pinch ground nutmeg

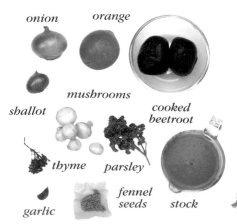

onion *orange*

shallot *mushrooms* *cooked beetroot*

thyme *parsley* *nutmeg*

garlic *fennel seeds* *stock* *basic pasta dough* *breadcrumbs*

dill

1 Process all the filling ingredients in a food processor or blender.

2 Roll the pasta into thin sheets. Lay one piece over a ravioli tray and put a teaspoonful of the filling into each depression. Brush around the edges of each ravioli with egg white. Cover with another sheet of pasta and press the edges well together to seal. Transfer to a floured dish towel and rest for 1 hour before cooking.

3 Cook the ravioli in a large pan of boiling, salted water for 2 minutes. (Cook in batches to stop them sticking together.) Remove and drop into a bowl of cold water for 5 seconds before placing on a tray. (You can make these pasta shapes a day in advance. Cover with clear film and store in the fridge.) Put the onion, garlic and fennel seeds into a pan with 150 ml/¼ pint/⅔ cup of the stock. Bring to the boil, cover and simmer for 5 minutes until tender. Peel and finely dice the beetroot (reserve 60 ml/4 tbsp for the garnish). Add the rest to the soup with the remaining stock. and bring to the boil.

4 Add the orange juice and cooked ravioli and simmer for 2 minutes. Serve in shallow soup bowls, garnished with the reserved, diced beetroot and fennel or dill leaves. Serve hot, with some crusty bread.

NUTRITIONAL NOTES

PER PORTION:

ENERGY 358Kcals/1504KJ **FAT** 4.9g
SATURATED FAT 1.0g **CHOLESTEROL** 110mg
CARBOHYDRATE 67g **FIBRE** 4.3g

Sweetcorn Chowder with Conchigliette

Serves 6–8

INGREDIENTS
1 small green pepper
450 g/1 lb potatoes, peeled
    and diced
350 g/12 oz/2 cups canned or
    frozen sweetcorn
1 onion, chopped
1 stick celery, chopped
a bouquet garni (bay leaf, parsley
    stalks and thyme)
600 ml/1 pint/2½ cups
    chicken stock
300 ml/½ pint/1¼ cups
    skimmed milk
50 g/2 oz small pasta shells
    (conchigliette)
150 g/5 oz smoked turkey
    rashers, diced
bread sticks, to serve
salt and ground black pepper

smoked turkey rashers   *sweetcorn*

potatoes

small pasta shells   *stock*

onion   *parsley*   *celery*

green pepper   *skimmed milk*   *bay leaf*   *thyme*

1 Halve the green pepper, remove the stalk and seeds. Cut the flesh into small dice, cover with boiling water and stand for 2 minutes. Drain and rinse.

2 Put the potatoes into a saucepan with the sweetcorn, onion, celery, green pepper, bouquet garni and stock. Bring to the boil, cover and simmer for 20 minutes until tender.

3 Add the milk, and season with salt and pepper. Process half of the soup in a food processor or blender and return to the pan with the conchigliette. Simmer for 10 minutes.

4 Fry the turkey rashers quickly in a non-stick frying pan for 2–3 minutes. Stir into the soup. Serve with bread sticks.

NUTRITIONAL NOTES
Per portion:

ENERGY 215Kcals/904KJ **FAT** 1.6g
SATURATED FAT 0.3g **CHOLESTEROL** 13mg
CARBOHYDRATE 41g **FIBRE** 2.8g

Tsatziki

Serve this classic Greek dip with strips of toasted pitta bread.

Serves 4

Ingredients

1 mini cucumber
4 spring onions
1 garlic clove
200 ml/7 fl oz/scant 1 cup Greek-style yogurt
45 ml/3 tbsp chopped fresh mint
fresh mint sprig, to garnish (optional)
salt and pepper

mini cucumber

spring onions

garlic

Greek-style yogurt

mint

1 Trim the ends from the cucumber, then cut it into 5 mm/¼ in dice.

2 Trim the spring onions and garlic, then chop both very finely.

3 Beat the yogurt until smooth, if necessary, then gently stir in the cucumber, onions, garlic and mint.

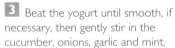

4 Transfer the mixture to a serving bowl and add salt and plenty of freshly ground black pepper to taste. Chill until ready to serve and then garnish with a small mint sprig, if you like.

Cook's Tip

Choose Greek-style yogurt for this dip – it has a higher fat content than most yogurts, but this gives it a deliciously rich, creamy texture.

Nutritional Notes

Per portion:

Energy 65 Kcals/275 KJ **Fat** 4.7 g
Saturated Fat 2.9 g **Protein** 3.9 g
Carbohydrate 2.1 g **Fibre** 0.3 g

Spiced Carrot Dip

This is a delicious low-fat dip with a sweet and spicy flavour. Serve wheat crackers or fiery tortilla chips as accompaniments for dipping.

Serves 4

INGREDIENTS
1 onion
3 carrots, plus extra, to garnish
grated rind and juice of 2 oranges
15 ml/1 tbsp hot curry paste
150 ml/¼ pint/⅔ cup low-fat
   natural yogurt
handful of fresh basil leaves
15–30 ml/1–2 tbsp fresh lemon
   juice, to taste
red Tabasco sauce, to taste
salt and pepper

onion

carrots

*orange
rind and juice*

curry paste

basil

*lemon
juice*

*low fat
natural yogurt*

*red Tabasco
sauce*

1 Finely chop the onion. Peel and grate the carrots. Place the onion, carrots, orange rind and juice and curry paste in a small saucepan. Bring to the boil, cover and simmer for 10 minutes, until tender.

2 Process the mixture in a blender or food processor until smooth. Leave to cool completely.

NUTRITIONAL NOTES
PER PORTION:

ENERGY 67 Kcals/281 KJ **FAT** 1.5 g
SATURATED FAT 1 g

3 Stir in the yogurt, then tear the basil leaves into small pieces and stir them into the carrot mixture.

4 Add the lemon juice, Tabasco, salt and pepper to taste. Serve within a few hours at room temperature. Garnish with grated carrot.

VARIATION
Greek-style yogurt or soured cream may be used in place of the natural yogurt to make a richer, creamy dip.

Garlic and Chilli Dip

This dip is delicious with fresh prawns and other shellfish. It will also spice up any kind of fish when used as an accompanying sauce.

Serves 4

INGREDIENTS
1 small red chilli
2.5 cm/1 in piece root ginger
2 garlic cloves
5 ml/1 tsp mustard powder
15 ml/1 tbsp chilli sauce
30 ml/2 tbsp olive oil
30 ml/2 tbsp light soy sauce
juice of two limes
30 ml/2 tbsp chopped fresh
    parsley
salt and pepper

mustard powder *parsley* *red chilli* *root ginger* *light soy sauce* *limes* *chilli sauce* *garlic*

1 Halve the chilli, remove the seeds, stalk and membrane, and chop finely. Peel and roughly chop the ginger.

2 Crush the chilli, ginger, garlic and mustard powder to a paste, using a pestle and mortar.

3 In a bowl, mix together all the remaining ingredients, except the parsley Add the paste and blend it in. Cover and chill for 24 hours.

4 Stir in the parsley and season to taste. It is best to serve in small individual bowls for dipping.

COOK'S TIP
Medium-sized Mediterranean prawns are ideal served with this sauce. Remove the shell but leave the tails intact so there is something to hold on to.

NUTRITIONAL NOTES
PER PORTION:

ENERGY 41 Kcals/171 KJ **FAT** 3.3 g
SATURATED FAT 0.4 g **PROTEIN** 1.2 g
CARBOHYDRATE 1.8 g **FIBRE** 0.4 g

Oriental Hoisin Dip

This speedy Oriental dip needs no cooking and can be made in just a few minutes – it tastes great with mini spring rolls or prawn crackers.

Serves 4

INGREDIENTS
4 spring onions
4 cm/1½ in piece root ginger
2 red chillies
2 garlic cloves
60 ml/4 tbsp hoisin sauce
120 ml/4 fl oz/½ cup passata
5 ml/1 tsp sesame oil (optional)

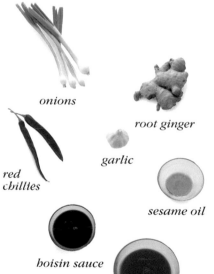

onions

root ginger

garlic

red chillies

sesame oil

hoisin sauce

passata

1 Trim off and discard the green ends of the spring onions. Slice the remainder very thinly.

2 Peel the ginger with a swivel-bladed vegetable peeler, then chop it finely.

COOK'S TIP
Hoisin sauce makes an excellent base for full-flavour dips, especially when combining crunchy vegetables and other Oriental seasonings.

NUTRITIONAL NOTES
PER PORTION:

ENERGY 33 Kcals/140 KJ **FAT** 0.9 g
SATURATED FAT 0.1 g **PROTEIN** 1.3 g
CARBOHYDRATE 5.3 g **FIBRE** 0.4 g

3 Halve the chillies lengthways and remove their seeds. Finely slice the flesh widthways into tiny strips. Finely chop the garlic.

4 Stir together the hoisin sauce, passata, spring onions, ginger, chilli, garlic and sesame oil, if using, and serve within 1 hour.

Fat-free Saffron Dip

Serve this mild dip with fresh vegetable crudités -
it is particularly good with florets of cauliflower.

Serves 4

INGREDIENTS
15 ml/1 tbsp boiling water
small pinch of saffron strands
200 g/7 oz/scant 1 cup fat-free
  fromage frais
10 fresh chives
10 fresh basil leaves
salt and pepper

saffron strands

fromage frais

basil leaves

chives

1 Pour the boiling water into a small container and add the saffron strands. Leave to infuse for 3 minutes.

2 Beat the fromage frais until smooth, then stir in the infused saffron liquid.

3 Use a pair of scissors to snip the chives into the dip. Tear the basil leaves into small pieces and stir them in.

4 Add salt and pepper to taste. Serve immediately.

VARIATION
Leave out the saffron and add a
squeeze of lemon or lime juice
instead.

NUTRITIONAL NOTES

PER PORTION:

ENERGY 30 Kcals/127.5 KJ **FAT** 0.1 g
SATURATED FAT 0.05 g

Guacamole with Crudités

This fresh-tasting spicy dip is made using peas instead of the traditional avocados.

Serves 4–6

INGREDIENTS
350 g/12 oz/2¼ cups frozen peas, defrosted
1 garlic clove, crushed
2 spring onions, trimmed and chopped
5 ml/1 tsp finely grated rind and juice of 1 lime
2.5 ml/½ tsp ground cumin
dash of Tabasco sauce
15 ml/1 tbsp reduced calorie mayonnaise
30 ml/2 tbsp chopped fresh coriander
salt and freshly ground black pepper
pinch of paprika and lime slices, to garnish

FOR THE CRUDITÉS
6 baby carrots
2 celery sticks
1 red-skinned eating apple
1 pear
15 ml/1 tbsp lemon or lime juice
6 baby sweetcorn

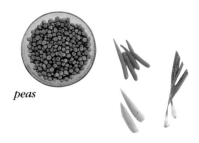

peas

vegetables

NUTRITIONAL NOTES
PER PORTION:

ENERGY 102Kcals/429KJ PROTEIN 4.83g
FAT 1.96g SATURATED FAT 0.22g
CARBOHYDRATE 17.1g
FIBRE 5.61g SUGAR 10g
SODIUM 54.8mg

1 Put the peas, garlic clove, spring onions, lime rind and juice, cumin, Tabasco sauce, mayonnaise and salt and freshly ground black pepper into a food processor or a blender for a few minutes and process until smooth.

2 Add the chopped coriander and process for a few more seconds. Spoon into a serving bowl, cover with clear film and chill in the refrigerator for 30 minutes, to let the flavours develop.

3 For the crudités, trim and peel the carrots. Halve the celery sticks lengthways and trim into sticks, the same length as the carrots. Quarter, core and thickly slice the apple and pear, then dip into the lemon or lime juice. Arrange with the baby sweetcorn on a platter.

4 Sprinkle the paprika over the guacamole and garnish with lime slices.

Minted Melon and Grapefruit Cocktail

Melon is always a popular starter. Here the flavour is complemented by the refreshing taste of citrus fruit and a simple dressing.

Serves 4

INGREDIENTS
1 small Galia melon, weighing about
    1 kg/2¼ lb
2 pink grapefruits
1 yellow grapefruit
5 ml/1 tsp Dijon mustard
5 ml/1 tsp raspberry or sherry vinegar
5 ml/1 tsp clear honey
15 ml/1 tbsp chopped fresh mint
sprigs of fresh mint, to garnish

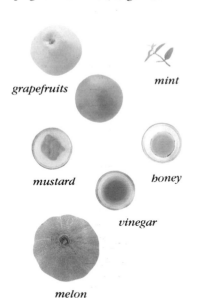

grapefruits   *mint*

mustard   *honey*

vinegar

melon

NUTRITIONAL NOTES

PER PORTION:

ENERGY 97 Kcals/409 KJ **PROTEIN** 2.22 g
FAT 0.63 g **SATURATED FAT** 0.
CARBOHYDRATE 22.45 g **FIBRE** 3.05 g
ADDED SUGAR 0.96 g **SALT** 0.24 g

1 Halve the melon and remove the seeds with a teaspoon. With a melon baller, carefully scoop the flesh into balls.

2 With a sharp knife, peel the grapefruit and remove all the white pith. Remove the segments by cutting between the membranes, holding the fruit over a small bowl to catch any juices.

3 Whisk the mustard, vinegar, honey, chopped mint and grapefruit juices together in a mixing bowl. Add the melon balls together with the grapefruit and mix well. Chill for 30 minutes.

4 Ladle into four dishes and serve garnished with a sprig of fresh mint.

Melon and Parma Ham Salad with Strawberry Salsa

Sections of cool fragrant melon wrapped with slices of air-dried ham make a delicious salad starter. If strawberries are in season, serve with a savoury-sweet strawberry salsa and watch it disappear.

Serves 6

Ingredients
1 large melon, cantaloupe, galia or charentais
175 g/6 oz Parma or Serrano ham, thinly sliced

Salsa
225 g/8 oz strawberries
5 ml/1 tsp caster (superfine) sugar
15 ml/1 tbsp sunflower oil
15 ml/1 tbsp orange juice
½ tsp finely grated orange zest
½ tsp finely grated fresh root ginger
salt and black pepper

1 Halve the melon and take the seeds out with a spoon. Cut the rind away with a paring knife, then slice the melon thickly. Chill until ready to serve.

2 To make the salsa, hull the strawberries and cut them into large dice. Place in a small mixing bowl with the sugar and crush lightly to release the juices. Add the oil, orange juice, zest and ginger. Season with salt and a generous twist of black pepper.

3 Arrange the melon on a serving plate, lay the ham over the top and serve with a bowl of salsa.

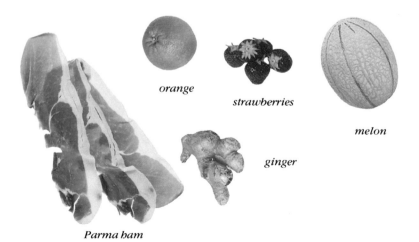

orange

strawberries

ginger

melon

Parma ham

Nutritional Notes
Per portion:

Energy 87 Kcals/47.3 KJ **Fat** 3.5 g
Saturated Fat 0.8 g

Mushroom and Bean Pâté

A light and tasty pâté, delicious served on wholemeal bread or toast for a starter or a suppertime snack.

Serves 12

INGREDIENTS
450 g/1 lb/6 cups
  mushrooms, sliced
1 onion, chopped
2 garlic cloves, crushed
1 red pepper, seeded and diced
30 ml/2 tbsp vegetable stock
30 ml/2 tbsp dry white wine
400 g/14 oz can red kidney beans,
  rinsed and drained
1 egg, beaten
50 g/2 oz/1 cup fresh
  wholemeal breadcrumbs
15 ml/1 tbsp chopped fresh thyme
15 ml/1 tbsp chopped
  fresh rosemary
salt and ground black pepper
lettuce and tomatoes, to garnish

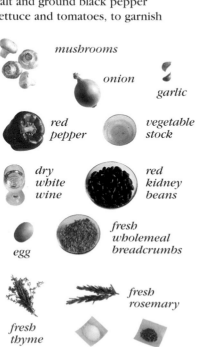

mushrooms
onion
garlic
red pepper
vegetable stock
dry white wine
red kidney beans
egg
fresh wholemeal breadcrumbs
fresh thyme
fresh rosemary
salt
black pepper

1 Preheat the oven to 180°C/350°F/Gas 4. Lightly grease and line a non-stick 900 g/2 lb loaf tin. Put the mushrooms, onion, garlic, red pepper, stock and wine in a saucepan. Cover and cook for 10 minutes, stirring occasionally.

2 Set aside to cool slightly, then purée the mixture with the kidney beans in a blender or food processor until smooth.

3 Transfer the mixture to a bowl, add the egg, breadcrumbs and herbs and mix thoroughly. Season to taste.

NUTRITIONAL NOTES
PER PORTION:

ENERGY 53Kcals/225KJ PROTEIN 3.42g
FAT 1.04g SATURATED FAT 0.26g
CARBOHYDRATE 7.65g FIBRE 2.33g
ADDED SUGAR 0.00g SODIUM 0.11g

4 Spoon into the prepared tin and level the surface. Bake for 45–60 minutes, until lightly set and browned on top. Place on a wire rack and allow the pâté to cool completely in the tin. Once cool, cover and refrigerate for several hours. Turn out of the tin and serve in slices. Garnish with lettuce and tomatoes.

Cannellini Bean Pureé with Grilled Radicchio

The slightly bitter flavours of the radicchio and chicory make a wonderful marriage with the creamy citrus bean purée.

Serves 4

INGREDIENTS

1 × 400 g/14 oz can cannellini beans
45 ml/3 tbsp low-fat fromage blanc
finely grated zest, rind and juice of 1
   large orange
15 ml/1 tbsp finely chopped fresh
   rosemary
4 heads of chicory
2 medium radicchio
15 ml/1 tbsp walnut oil

chicory

fromage blanc

cannellini beans

rosemary

raddichio

orange

1 Drain the beans, rinse, and drain again. Purée the beans in a blender or food processor with the fromage blanc, orange zest, orange juice and rosemary. Set aside.

2 Cut the chicory in half lengthwise.

3 Cut each radicchio into 8 wedges

4 Lay out the chicory and radicchio on a baking tray and brush with walnut oil. Grill for 2–3 minutes. Serve with the puree and scatter over the orange rind.

COOK'S TIP

Other suitable beans to use are haricot, mung or broad beans.

NUTRITIONAL NOTES
PER PORTION:

ENERGY 121 Kcals/508.3 KJ **FAT** 3.6 g
SATURATED FAT 0.4 g

Aubergine, Roast Garlic and Red Pepper Pâté

This is a simple pâté of smoky baked aubergine, sweet pink peppercorns and red peppers, with more than a hint of garlic!

Serves 4

INGREDIENTS
3 medium aubergines
2 red peppers
5 whole garlic cloves
7.5 ml/1½ tsp pink peppercorns in brine, drained and crushed
30 ml/2 tbsp chopped fresh coriander

aubergine

garlic

coriander

pink peppercorns

red pepper

1 Preheat the oven to 200°C/400°F/ Gas 6. Arrange the whole aubergines, peppers and garlic cloves on a baking sheet and place in the oven. After 10 minutes remove the garlic cloves and turn over the aubergines and peppers.

2 Peel the garlic cloves and place in the bowl of a blender.

3 After a further 20 minutes remove the blistered and charred peppers from the oven and place in a plastic bag. Leave to cool.

4 After a further 10 minutes remove the aubergines from the oven. Split in half and scoop the flesh into a sieve placed over a bowl. Press the flesh with a spoon to remove the bitter juices.

5 Add the mixture to the garlic in the blender and blend until smooth. Place in a large mixing bowl.

6 Peel and chop the red peppers and stir into the aubergine mixture. Mix in the peppercorns and fresh coriander and serve at once.

Crunchy Baked Mushrooms with Dill Dip

These crispy-coated bites are ideal as an informal starter or served with drinks.

NUTRITIONAL NOTES

Per portion:

ENERGY 173 Kcals/728 KJ **PROTEIN** 11.88 g
FAT 6.04 g **SATURATED FAT** 3.24 g
CARBOHYDRATE 19.23 g **FIBRE** 1.99 g
ADDED SUGAR 0 **SALT** 0.91 g

Serves 4–6

INGREDIENTS
115 g/4 oz/2 cups fresh fine white
   breadcrumbs
15 g/½ oz/1½ tbsp finely grated
   mature Cheddar cheese
5 ml/1 tsp paprika
225 g/8 oz button mushrooms
2 egg whites

FOR THE TOMATO AND DILL DIP
4 ripe tomatoes
115 g/4 oz/½ cup curd cheese
60 ml/4 tbsp natural low fat yogurt
1 garlic clove, crushed
30 ml/2 tbsp chopped fresh dill
salt and freshly ground black pepper
sprig of fresh dill, to garnish

paprika

mushrooms

dill

tomatoes

curd cheese

breadcrumbs

1 Pre-heat the oven to 190°C/375°F/ Gas 5. Mix together the breadcrumbs, cheese and paprika in a bowl.

2 Wipe the mushrooms clean and trim the stalks, if necessary. Lightly whisk the egg whites with a fork, until frothy.

3 Dip each mushroom into the egg whites, then into the breadcrumb mixture. Repeat until all the mushrooms are coated.

4 Put the mushrooms on a non-stick baking sheet. Bake in the pre-heated oven for 15 minutes, or until tender and the coating has turned golden and crunchy.

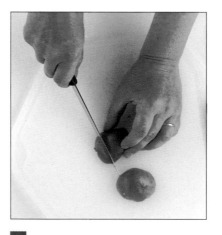

5 Meanwhile, to make the dip, plunge the tomatoes into a saucepan of boiling water for 1 minute, then into a saucepan of cold water. Slip off the skins. Halve, remove the seeds and cores and roughly chop the flesh.

6 Put the curd cheese, yogurt, garlic clove and dill into a mixing bowl and combine well. Season to taste. Stir in the chopped tomatoes. Spoon the mixture into a serving dish and garnish with a sprig of fresh dill. Serve the mushrooms hot, together with the dip.

Pasta Bonbons

Serves 4–6

INGREDIENTS
1 quantity of basic pasta dough
flour, for dusting
egg white, beaten
salt and pepper

FILLING
1 small onion, finely chopped
1 garlic clove, crushed
150 ml/¼ pint/⅔ cup chicken stock
225 g/8 oz minced turkey meat
2–3 fresh sage leaves, chopped
2 canned anchovy fillets, drained

SAUCE
150 ml/¼ pint/⅔ cup chicken stock
200 g/7 oz low-fat cream cheese
15 ml/1 tbsp lemon juice
5 ml/1 tsp caster sugar
2 tomatoes, skinned, seeded and
    finely diced
½ purple onion, finely chopped
6 small cornichons (pickled
    gherkins), sliced

1 To make the filling, put the onion, garlic and stock into a pan. Bring to the boil, cover and simmer for 5 minutes until tender. Uncover and boil for about 5 minutes or until the stock has reduced to 30 ml/2 tbsp.

2 Add the minced turkey, and stir over the heat until no longer pink in colour. Add the sage and anchovy fillets and season with salt and pepper. Cook uncovered for 5 minutes until all the liquid has been absorbed. Leave to cool.

3 Divide the pasta dough in half. Roll into thin sheets and cut into 9 × 6 cm/ 3½ × 2½ in rectangles. Lay on a lightly floured dish towel and repeat with the remaining dough.

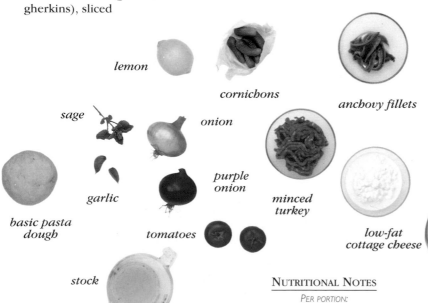

lemon

cornichons

anchovy fillets

sage

onion

garlic

purple onion

minced turkey

basic pasta dough

tomatoes

low-fat cottage cheese

stock

NUTRITIONAL NOTES

PER PORTION:

ENERGY 355Kcals/1492KJ **FAT** 6.4g
SATURATED FAT 1.4g **CHOLESTEROL** 150mg
CARBOHYDRATE 46g **FIBRE** 2.6g

4 Place a heaped teaspoon of the filling on the centre of each rectangle, brush around the meat with beaten egg white and roll up the pasta, pinching in the ends. Transfer to a floured dish towel and rest for 1 hour before cooking.

5 To make the sauce, put the stock, cream cheese, lemon juice and sugar into a pan. Heat gently and whisk until smooth. Add the diced tomatoes, onion and cornichons.

6 Cook the pasta in a large pan of boiling, salted water for 5 minutes. (Cook in batches to stop them sticking together). Remove with a slotted spoon, drain well and drop into the sauce. Repeat until all the bonbons are cooked. Simmer for 2–3 minutes. Serve in pasta bowls or soup plates and spoon over a little sauce.

Devilled Onions en Croûte

Fill crisp bread cups with tender button onions tossed in a mustardy glaze.

Serves 4–6

INGREDIENTS
12 thin slices of white bread
225 g/8 oz baby button onions or
  shallots
150 ml/¼ pint/⅔ cup vegetable stock
15 ml/1 tbsp dry white wine or dry
  sherry
2 turkey rashers, cut into thin strips
10 ml/2 tsp Worcestershire sauce
5 ml/1 tsp tomato purée
¼ tsp prepared English mustard
salt and freshly ground black pepper
sprigs of flat-leaf parsley, to garnish

button onions

stock

white bread

parsley

turkey rashers

NUTRITIONAL NOTES

PER PORTION:

ENERGY 178 Kcals/749 KJ **PROTEIN** 9.42 g
FAT 1.57 g **SATURATED FAT** 0.30 g
CARBOHYDRATE 33.26 g **FIBRE** 1.82 g
ADDED SUGAR 0 **SALT** 1.23 g

1 Pre-heat the oven to 200°C/400°F/ Gas 6. Stamp out the bread into rounds with a 7.5cm/3in fluted biscuit cutter and use to line a twelve-cup patty tin.

2 Cover each bread case with non-stick baking paper, and fill with baking beans or rice. Bake 'blind' for 5 minutes in the pre-heated oven. Remove the paper and beans and continue to bake for a further 5 minutes, until lightly browned and crisp.

3 Meanwhile, put the button onions in a bowl and cover with boiling water. Leave for 3 minutes, then drain and rinse under cold water. Trim off their top and root ends and slip them out of their skins.

4 Simmer the onions and stock in a covered saucepan for 5 minutes. Uncover and cook, stirring occasionally until the stock has reduced entirely. Add all the remaining ingredients, except the flat-leaf parsley. Cook for 2-3 minutes. Fill the toast cups with the devilled onions. Serve hot, garnished with sprigs of flat-leaf parsley.

Grilled Green Mussels with Cumin

Large green shelled mussels have a more distinctive flavour than the more common small black variety. Keep the empty shells to use as individual salt and pepper holders for fishy meals.

Serves 4

INGREDIENTS
45 ml/3 tbsp fresh parsley
45 ml/3 tbsp fresh coriander
1 garlic clove, crushed
pinch of ground cumin
20 g/½ oz/1 tbsp low-fat spread
25 g/1 oz/3 tbsp brown breadcrumbs
freshly ground black pepper
12 green mussels or 24 small mussels
    on the half-shell
chopped fresh parsley, to garnish

parsley

butter

garlic

bread

coriander

mussels

1 Chop the herbs finely.

2 Beat the garlic, herbs, cumin and butter together with a wooden spoon.

NUTRITIONAL NOTES
PER PORTION:

ENERGY 63 Kcals/263 KJ **FAT** 3.6 g
SATURATED FAT 0.8 g

3 Stir in the breadcrumbs and freshly ground black pepper.

4 Spoon a little of the mixture onto each mussel and grill for 2 minutes. Serve garnished with chopped fresh parsley.

Lemon and Ginger Spicy Beans

An extremely quick delicious meal, made with canned beans for speed. You probably won't need extra salt as canned beans tend to be already salted.

Serves 4

INGREDIENTS

5 cm/2 in piece fresh ginger root, peeled and roughly chopped
3 garlic cloves, roughly chopped
250 ml/8 fl oz/1 cup cold water
15 ml/1 tbsp sunflower oil
1 large onion, thinly sliced
1 fresh red chilli, seeded and finely chopped
¼ tsp cayenne pepper
10 ml/2 tsp ground cumin
5 ml/1 tsp ground coriander
½ tsp ground turmeric
30 ml/2 tbsp lemon juice
75 g/3 oz/⅓ cup chopped fresh coriander
1 × 400 g/14 oz can black-eyed beans, drained and rinsed
1 × 400 g/14 oz can aduki beans, drained and rinsed
1 × 400 g/14 oz can haricot beans, drained and rinsed
freshly ground black pepper

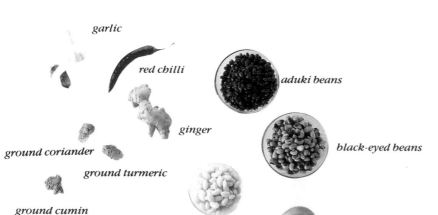

garlic · red chilli · aduki beans · ginger · black-eyed beans · ground coriander · ground turmeric · ground cumin · haricot beans · onion

1 Place the ginger, garlic and 60 ml/4 tbsp of the cold water in a blender and mix until smooth.

NUTRITIONAL NOTES
PER PORTION:

ENERGY 373 Kcals/1059 KJ **FAT** 4.4 g
SATURATED FAT 0.9 g

2 Heat the oil in a pan. Add the onion and chilli and cook gently for 5 minutes until softened.

3 Add the cayenne pepper, cumin, ground coriander and turmeric and stir-fry for 1 minute.

4 Stir in the ginger and garlic paste from the blender and cook for another minute.

5 Add the remaining water, lemon juice and fresh coriander, stir well and bring to the boil. Cover the pan tightly and cook for 5 minutes.

6 Add all the beans and cook for a further 5–10 minutes. Season with pepper and serve.

Red Pepper and Watercress Filo Parcels

Peppery watercress combines well with sweet red pepper in these crisp little parcels.

Makes 8

INGREDIENTS
3 red peppers
175 g/6 oz watercress
225 g/8 oz/1 cup ricotta cheese
50 g/2 oz/¼ cup blanched almonds,
   toasted and chopped
salt and freshly ground black pepper
8 sheets of filo pastry
30 ml/2 tbsp olive oil

ricotta

red pepper

watercress

almonds

filo pastry

NUTRITIONAL NOTES
PER PORTION:

ENERGY 151 Kcals/626 KJ **FAT** 10.2 g
SATURATED FAT 3 g

1 Preheat the oven to 190°C/375°F/ Gas 5. Place the peppers under a hot grill until blistered and charred. Place in a plastic bag. When cool enough to handle peel, seed and pat dry on kitchen paper.

2 Place the peppers and watercress in a food processor and pulse until coarsely chopped. Spoon into a bowl.

3 Mix in the ricotta and almonds, and season to taste.

4 Working with 1 sheet of filo pastry at a time, cut out 2 × 18 cm/7 in and 2 × 5 cm/2 in squares from each sheet. Brush 1 large square with a little olive oil and place a second large square at an angle of 90 degrees to form a star shape.

5 Place 1 of the small squares in the centre of the star shape, brush lightly with oil and top with a second small square.

6 Top with ⅛ of the red pepper mixture. Bring the edges together to form a purse shape and twist to seal. Place on a lightly greased baking sheet and cook for 25–30 minutes until golden.

Steamed Spiced Pork and Water Chestnut Wontons

Ginger and Chinese five-spice powder flavour this version of steamed open dumplings – a favourite snack in many teahouses.

Makes about 36

INGREDIENTS
2 large Chinese cabbage leaves, plus extra for lining the steamer
2 spring onions, finely chopped
1 cm/½ in piece fresh root ginger, finely chopped
50 g/2oz canned water chestnuts (drained weight), rinsed and finely chopped
225 g/8oz minced pork
2.5 ml/½ tsp Chinese five-spice powder
15 ml/1 tbsp cornflour
15 ml/1 tbsp light soy sauce
15 ml/1 tbsp Chinese rice wine
10 ml/2 tsp sesame oil
generous pinch of caster sugar
about 36 wonton wrappers, each 7.5 cm/3 in square
light soy sauce and hot chilli oil, for dipping

caster sugar

Chinese cabbage

spring onions

light soy sauce

sesame oil

cornflour

wonton wrappers

water chestnuts

pork

Chinese five-spice powder

Chinese rice wine

ginger

NUTRITIONAL NOTES
PER WONTON:

ENERGY 32 Kcals/142 KJ FAT 1.25 g
SATURATED FAT 0.7 g

VARIATION
These can also be deep fried, in which case fold the edges over the filling to enclose it completely. Press well to seal. Deep fry in batches in hot oil for about 2 minutes.

1 Place the Chinese cabbage leaves one on top of another. Cut them lengthways into quarters and then across into thin shreds.

2 Place the shredded Chinese cabbage leaves in a bowl. Add the spring onions, ginger, water chestnuts, pork, five-spice powder, cornflour, soy sauce, rice wine, sesame oil and sugar; mix well.

3 Set one wonton wrapper on a work surface. Place a heaped teaspoon of the filling in the centre of the wrapper, then lightly dampen the edges with water.

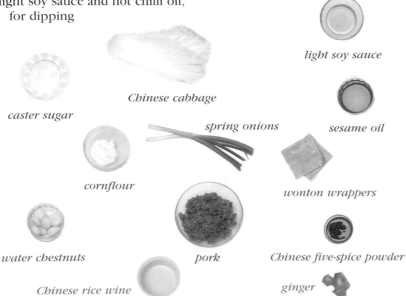

4 Lift the wrapper up around the filling, gathering to form a purse. Squeeze the wrapper firmly around the middle, then tap on the bottom to make a flat base. The top should be open. Place the wonton on a tray and cover with a damp dish towel.

5 Line the steamer with cabbage leaves and steam the dumplings for 12–15 minutes until tender. Remove each batch from the steamer as soon as they are cooked, cover with foil and keep warm. Serve hot with soy sauce and chilli oil for dipping.

Creamy Raspberry Dressing with Asparagus

Raspberry vinegar gives this quick low fat dressing a refreshing, tangy flavour – the perfect accompaniment to asparagus.

Serves 4

INGREDIENTS

675 g/1½ lb thin asparagus spears
30 ml/2 tbsp raspberry vinegar
2.5 ml/½ tsp salt
5 ml/1 tsp Dijon-style mustard
60 ml/4 tbsp half fat crème
 fraîche or natural low fat yogurt
ground white pepper
115 g/4 oz fresh raspberries

asparagus spears

raspberry vinegar

Dijon-style mustard

half-fat crème fraîche

fresh raspberries

NUTRITIONAL NOTES

PER PORTION:

ENERGY 60 Kcals/251 KJ **FAT** 1.3 g
SATURATED FAT 0.1 g **PROTEIN** 6.2 g
CARBOHYDRATE 6.0 g **FIBRE** 3.6 g

1 Fill a large wide frying pan, or wok, with water about 10 cm/4 in deep and bring to the boil.

2 Trim the tough ends of the asparagus spears. If desired, remove the "scales" using a vegetable peeler.

3 Tie the asparagus spears into two bundles. Lower the bundles into the boiling water and cook for 3–5 minutes, or until just tender.

4 Carefully remove the asparagus bundles from the boiling water using a slotted spoon and immerse them in cold water to stop the cooking. Drain and untie the bundles. Pat dry with kitchen paper. Chill the asparagus for at least 1 hour.

5 Mix together the vinegar and salt in a bowl and stir with a fork until dissolved. Stir in the mustard. Gradually stir in the crème fraîche or yogurt until blended. Add pepper to taste. To serve, place the asparagus on individual plates and drizzle the dressing across the middle of the spears. Garnish with the fresh raspberries and serve at once.

Thai Fish Cakes

Bursting with the flavours of chillies, lime and lemon grass, these little fish cakes make a wonderful starter.

Serves 4

INGREDIENTS
450 g/1 lb white fish fillets, such
   as cod or haddock
3 spring onions, sliced
30 ml/2 tbsp chopped fresh
   coriander
30 ml/2 tbsp Thai red curry paste
1 fresh green chilli, seeded and
   chopped
10 ml/2 tsp grated lime rind
15 ml/1 tbsp lime juice
30 ml/2 tbsp sesame oil
salt, to taste
crisp lettuce leaves, shredded
   spring onions, fresh red chilli
   slices, coriander sprigs and lime
   wedges, to serve

lettuce   *white fish fillets*

lime   *spring onions*

groundnut oil

coriander

red chilli

green chilli   *Thai red curry paste*

1 Cut the fish into chunks, then place in a blender or food processor.

2 Add the spring onions, coriander, red curry paste, green chilli, lime rind and juice to the fish. Season with salt. Process until finely minced.

NUTRITIONAL NOTES
PER PORTION:
ENERGY 154 Kcals/640 KJ **FAT** 7.2 g
SATURATED FAT 1.5 g

3 Using lightly floured hands, divide the mixture into 16 pieces and shape each one into a small cake about 4 cm/1½ in across. Place the fish cakes on a plate, cover with clear film and chill for about 2 hours until firm. Heat the wok over a high heat until hot. Add the oil and swirl it around.

4 Fry the fish cakes, a few at a time, for 6–8 minutes, turning them carefully until evenly browned. Drain each batch on kitchen paper and keep hot while cooking the remainder. Serve on a bed of crisp lettuce leaves with shredded spring onions, red chilli slices, coriander sprigs and lime wedges.

Prawn Salad with Curry Dressing

Curry spices add an unexpected twist to this salad. Warm flavours combine especially well with sweet prawns and grated apple.

Serves 6

INGREDIENTS
1 ripe tomato
½ iceberg lettuce, shredded
1 small onion
1 small bunch fresh coriander
15 ml/1 tbsp lemon juice
salt
450 g/1 lb cooked peeled prawns (shrimp)
1 apple, peeled

DRESSING

75 ml/5 tbsp low-fat mayonnaise
5 ml/1 tbsp mild curry paste
15 ml/1 tbsp tomato ketchup

TO DECORATE
8 whole prawns
8 lemon wedges
4 sprigs fresh coriander

2 Finely shred the lettuce, onion and coriander. Add the tomato, moisten with lemon juice and season with salt.

3 To make the dressing, combine the mayonnaise, curry paste and tomato ketchup in a small bowl. Add 30 ml/2 tbsp water to thin the dressing and season to taste with salt.

1 To peel the tomato, pierce the skin with a knife and immerse in boiling water for 20 seconds. Drain and cool under running water. Peel off the skin. Halve the tomato, push the seeds out with your thumb and discard them. Cut the flesh into large dice.

prawns

coriander

tomato

apple

lemon

onion

4 Combine the prawns (shrimp) with the dressing. Quarter and core the apple and grate into the mixture.

COOK'S TIP
Fresh coriander is inclined to wilt if kept out of water. Keep it in a jar of water in the refrigerator covered with a plastic bag and it will stay fresh for several days.

NUTRITIONAL NOTES
PER PORTION:

ENERGY 133 Kcals/556 KJ **FAT** 4.5 g
SATURATED FAT 0.2 g

5 Distribute the shredded lettuce mixture between 4 plates or bowls. Pile the prawn mixture in the centre of each and decorate with 2 whole prawns, 2 lemon wedges and a sprig of coriander.

Chicken Tikka

The red food colouring gives this dish its traditional bright colour. Serve with lemon wedges and a crisp mixed salad.

Serves 4

INGREDIENTS
1 × 1.75 kg/3½ lb chicken
mixed salad leaves, e.g. frisée and
    oakleaf lettuce or radicchio,
    to serve

FOR THE MARINADE
150 ml/¼ pint/⅔ cup plain low fat
    yogurt
5 ml/1 tsp ground paprika
10 ml/2 tsp grated fresh root ginger
1 garlic clove, crushed
10 ml/2 tsp garam masala
2.5 ml/½ tsp salt
red food colouring (optional)
juice of 1 lemon

lemon

chicken

salt

yogurt

paprika

ginger

garlic

garam masala

1 Joint the chicken and cut it into eight pieces, using a sharp knife.

2 Mix all the marinade ingredients in a large dish, add the chicken pieces to coat and chill for 4 hours or overnight to allow the flavours to penetrate the flesh.

NUTRITIONAL NOTES
PER PORTION:

ENERGY 131 Kcals/554 KJ **FAT** 4.5 g
SATURATED FAT 1.4 g
CHOLESTEROL 55.4 mg

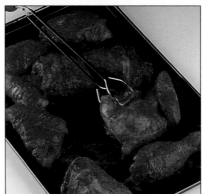

3 Preheat the oven to 200°C/400°F/ Gas 6. Remove the chicken pieces from the marinade and arrange them in a single layer in a large ovenproof dish. Bake for 30–40 minutes or until tender.

4 Baste with a little of the marinade while cooking. Arrange on a bed of salad leaves and serve hot or cold.

Sesame Seed Chicken Bites

Best served warm, these crunchy bites are delicious accompanied by a glass of chilled dry white wine.

Makes 20

INGREDIENTS
175 g/6 oz raw chicken breast
2 cloves garlic, crushed
2.5 cm/1 in piece root ginger, peeled
   and grated
1 × size 4 egg white
5 ml/1 tsp cornflour
25 g/1 oz/¼ cup shelled pistachios,
   roughly chopped
60 ml/4 tbsp sesame seeds
30 ml/2 tbsp grapeseed oil
salt and freshly ground black pepper

FOR THE SAUCE
45 ml/3 tbsp/¼ cup hoisin sauce
15 ml/1 tbsp sweet chilli sauce

TO GARNISH
root ginger, finely shredded
pistachios, roughly chopped
fresh dill sprigs

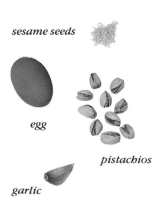

sesame seeds

egg

pistachios

garlic

ginger

1 Place the chicken, garlic, grated ginger, egg white and cornflour into the food processor and process them to a smooth paste.

2 Stir in the pistachios and season well with salt and pepper.

NUTRITIONAL NOTES
PER PORTION:
ENERGY 53 Kcals/223 KJ **FAT** 4.1 g
SATURATED FAT 0.6 g
CHOLESTEROL 3.8 mg

3 Roll into 20 balls and coat with sesame seeds. Heat the wok and add the oil. When the oil is hot, stir-fry the chicken bites in batches, turning regularly until golden. Drain on kitchen towels.

4 Make the sauce by mixing together the hoisin and chilli sauces in a bowl. Garnish the bites with shredded ginger, pistachios and dill, then serve hot, with a dish of sauce for dipping.

Grilled King Prawn Bhoona

The unusual and delicious flavour of this dish is achieved by grilling the prawns to give them a char-grilled taste and then adding them to fried onions and peppers.

Serves 4

INGREDIENTS
45ml/3 tbsp natural low fat yogurt
5ml/1 tsp paprika
5ml/1 tsp ginger pulp
12–14 frozen cooked king prawns, thawed and peeled
15ml/1 tbsp corn oil
3 medium onions, sliced
2.5ml/½ tsp fennel seeds, crushed
1 cinnamon bark
5ml/1 tsp garlic pulp
5ml/1 tsp chilli powder
1 medium yellow pepper, seeded and roughly chopped
1 medium red pepper, seeded and roughly chopped
salt
15ml/1 tbsp fresh coriander leaves, to garnish

fennel seeds *paprika*

chilli powder *ginger pulp*

garlic pulp

king prawns

cinnamon bark

yogurt

fresh coriander

onions

red pepper *yellow pepper*

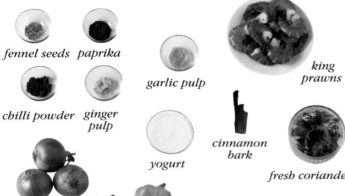

1 Blend together the yogurt, paprika, ginger, and salt to taste. Pour this mixture over the prawns and leave to marinate for 30–45 minutes.

2 Meanwhile, heat the oil in a non-stick wok or frying pan and fry the onions with the fennel seeds and the cinnamon bark.

3 Lower the heat and add the garlic and chilli powder.

4 Add the peppers and stir-fry gently for 3–5 minutes.

COOK'S TIP
Although frozen coriander is convenient and good to use in cooking, the fresh herb is more suitable for garnishes.

NUTRITIONAL NOTES
Per portion:
ENERGY 132 K Cals/552 K J **PROTEIN** 9.97g
FAT 3.94g **SATURATED FAT** 0.58g
CARBOHYDRATE 15.93g **FIBRE** 3.11g
ADDED SUGAR 0.02g
SALT 0.79g

5 Remove from the heat and transfer to a serving dish, discarding the cinnamon bark.

6 Preheat the grill and turn the heat to medium. Put the prawns in a grill pan or flameproof dish and place under the grill to darken their tops and achieve a char-grilled effect. Add the prawns to the onion mixture, garnish with the coriander and serve.

Raw Salmon Sushi

A quite complicated starter which needs to be made with very fresh fish. Try to buy green wasabi powder to mix with water and serve with the soy sauce and pickled ginger. It will give a very authentic taste.

Serves 4

INGREDIENTS
275 g/10 oz/1½ cups short grain rice
8 cm/3¼ in piece of konbu seaweed
15 ml/1 tbsp of sake or dry white wine
350 g/12 oz salmon fillet, skinned
1 cucumber, peeled
5 sheets of nori
10 ml/2 tsp sliced pickled (optional)
    ginger
1 small jar of salmon roe
40 ml/2½ tbsp rice vinegar
15 ml/1 tbsp caster sugar
salt and freshly ground black pepper
wasabi, for dipping
soy sauce, for dipping

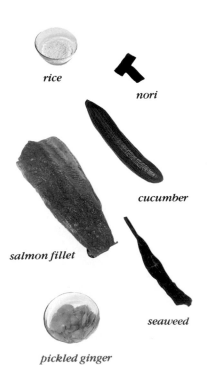

rice

nori

cucumber

salmon fillet

seaweed

pickled ginger

1 Wash the rice in cold running water until clear. Place in a large heavy-based saucepan with 350 ml/12 fl oz/1½ cups cold water, the konbu and the sake or dry white wine. Cover and bring to the boil. Remove the konbu and replace the lid. Turn the heat down and allow the rice to cook for a further 10–15 minutes. Using a wooden spoon, carefully mix the rice to fluff it up.

2 Transfer the rice to a shallow bowl. Leave to cool slightly. Cover with a damp dish towel to prevent the rice from drying.

3 Cut the salmon and cucumber into long strips. Lay the nori out flat on a dry dish towel.

4 Spoon a thin line of sushi rice across the width of the nori, leaving 5 cm/2 in of the nori clear. Then lay a line of the salmon, cucumber, pickled ginger, salmon roe and vinegar, sugar and seasoning across the top. Top with more sushi rice.

5 Fold over the end of the nori, then using the dish towel, roll tightly. Leave for 10 minutes, unwrap, then cut into 3 cm/1¼ in lengths. Repeat with the remaining ingredients. Serve with wasabi and soy sauce.

Meat
Dishes

Devilled Ham and Pineapple Salad

Serves 4

INGREDIENTS
225 g/8 oz wholewheat penne
150 ml/¼ pint/⅔ cup low-fat yogurt
15 ml/1 tbsp cider vinegar
5 ml/1 tsp wholegrain mustard
large pinch of caster sugar
30 ml/2 tbsp hot mango chutney
115 g/4 oz cooked lean ham, cubed
200 g/7 oz can pineapple chunks
2 sticks celery, chopped
½ green pepper, seeded and diced
15 ml/1 tbsp flaked toasted
    almonds, chopped roughly
salt and ground black pepper
crusty bread, to serve

celery

green pepper

wholewheat penne

hot mango chutney

pineapple chunks

low-fat yogurt

lean ham

flaked toasted almonds

1 Cook the pasta in a large pan of boiling, salted water until *al dente*. Drain and rinse thoroughly. Leave to cool.

2 To make the dressing, mix the yogurt, vinegar, mustard, sugar and mango chutney together. Season, add the pasta and toss lightly together.

3 Transfer the pasta to a serving dish. Scatter over the ham, pineapple, celery and pepper.

4 Sprinkle the top with toasted almonds. Serve with crusty bread.

NUTRITIONAL NOTES
PER PORTION:

ENERGY 303Kcals/1273KJ **FAT** 5.4g
SATURATED FAT 0.9g **CHOLESTEROL** 18.5mg
CARBOHYDRATE 51g **FIBRE** 6g

Stir-fried Pork with Lychees

Lychees have a very pretty pink skin which, when peeled, reveals a soft fleshy berry with a hard shiny stone. If you cannot buy fresh lychees, this dish can be made with drained canned lychees.

Serves 4

INGREDIENTS
450 g/1 lb lean pork, diced
30 ml/2 tbsp hoisin sauce
4 spring onions, sliced
175 g/6 oz lychees, peeled, stoned and
    cut into slivers
salt and freshly ground black pepper
fresh lychees and fresh parsley sprigs,
    to garnish

pork

hoisin sauce

spring onions

lychees

1 Cut the pork into bite-size pieces.

2 Pour the hoisin sauce over the pork and marinate for 30 minutes.

3 Heat the wok, then add the pork and stir-fry for 5 minutes until crisp and golden. Add the spring onions and stir-fry for a further 2 minutes.

4 Scatter the lychee slivers over the pork, and season well with salt and pepper. Garnish with fresh lychees and fresh parsley, and serve.

NUTRITIONAL NOTES
PER PORTION:
ENERGY 171 Kcals/721 KJ **FAT** 4.6 g
SATURATED FAT 1.6 g

Pork and Vegetable Stir-fry

A quick and easy stir-fry of pork and vegetables.

Serves 4

INGREDIENTS

225 g/8 oz can pineapple cubes
15 ml/1 tbsp cornflour
30 ml/2 tbsp light soy sauce
15 ml/1 tbsp each dry sherry,
  soft brown sugar and wine vinegar
5 ml/1 tsp five-spice powder
10 ml/2 tsp olive oil
1 red onion, sliced
1 garlic clove, crushed
1 fresh seeded red chilli, chopped
2.5 cm/1 in piece fresh root ginger
350 g/12 oz lean pork tenderloin,
  cut into thin strips
175 g/6 oz carrots
1 red pepper, seeded and sliced
175 g/6 oz mangetouts, halved
115 g/4 oz/½ cup beansprouts
200 g/7 oz can sweetcorn kernels
30 ml/2 tbsp chopped
  fresh coriander
15 ml/1 tbsp toasted sesame seeds,
  to garnish

pineapple cubes
light soy sauce
dry sherry
wine vinegar
five-spice powder
olive oil
red onion
garlic
red chilli
root ginger
red pepper
carrots
mangetouts
pork tenderloin
sweetcorn kernels
fresh coriander
beansprouts

1 Drain the pineapple, reserving the juice. In a small bowl, blend the cornflour with the pineapple juice. Add the soy sauce, sherry, sugar, vinegar and spice, stir to mix and set aside.

2 Heat the oil in a large non-stick frying pan or wok. Add the onion, garlic, chilli and ginger and stir-fry for 30 seconds. Add the pork and stir-fry for 2–3 minutes.

NUTRITIONAL NOTES

PER PORTION:

ENERGY 327Kcals/1380KJ PROTEIN 24.95g
FAT 7.90g SATURATED FAT 1.89g
CARBOHYDRATE 40.81g FIBRE 4.77g
ADDED SUGAR 5.38g SODIUM 0.73g

3 Cut the carrots into matchstick strips. Add to the wok with the red-pepper and stir-fry for 2–3 minutes. Add the mangetouts, beansprouts and the drained sweetcorn and stir-fry for 1–2 minutes.

4 Pour in the sauce mixture and the reserved pineapple and stir-fry until the sauce thickens. Reduce the heat and stir-fry for a further 1–2 minutes. Stir in the coriander and season to taste. Sprinkle with sesame seeds and serve immediately.

Sage and Orange Sauce with Pork Fillet

Sage is often partnered with pork – there seems to be a natural affinity – and the addition of orange to the sauce balances the flavour.

Serves 4

INGREDIENTS
2 pork fillets, about 350 g/
  12 oz each
10 ml/2 tsp unsalted butter
120 ml/4 fl oz/½ cup dry sherry
175 ml/6 fl oz/¾ cup chicken stock
2 garlic cloves, very finely chopped
grated rind and juice of
  1 unwaxed orange
3 or 4 sage leaves, finely chopped
10 ml/2 tsp cornflour
salt and pepper
orange wedges and sage leaves,
  to garnish

pork

butter

dry sherry

chicken stock

garlic cloves

orange

sage leaves

cornflour

NUTRITIONAL NOTES
PER PORTION:

ENERGY 330 Kcals/1384 KJ **FAT** 14.6 g
SATURATED FAT 5.8 g **PROTEIN** 36.8 g
CARBOHYDRATE 4.4 g **FIBRE** 0.1 g

1 Season the pork fillets lightly with salt and pepper. Melt the butter in a heavy flameproof casserole over a medium-high heat, then add the meat and cook for 5–6 minutes, turning to brown all sides evenly.

2 Add the sherry, boil for about 1 minute, then add the stock, garlic, orange rind and sage. Bring to the boil and reduce the heat to low, then cover and simmer for 20 minutes, turning once. The meat is cooked if the juices run clear when the meat is pierced with a knife or a meat thermometer inserted into the thickest part of the meat registers 66°C/150°F.

3 Transfer the pork to a warmed platter and cover to keep warm.

4 Bring the sauce to the boil. Blend the cornflour and orange juice and stir into the sauce, then boil gently over a medium heat for a few minutes, stirring frequently, until the sauce is slightly thickened. Strain into a gravy boat or serving jug.

5 Slice the pork diagonally and pour the meat juices into the sauce. Spoon a little sauce over the pork and garnish with orange wedges and sage leaves. Serve the remaining sauce separately.

Hot and Sour Pork

Chinese five-spice powder is made from a mixture of ground star anise, Szechuan pepper, cassia, cloves and fennel seed and has a flavour similar to liquorice. If you can't find any, use mixed spice instead.

NUTRITIONAL NOTES

PER PORTION:

ENERGY 196 K Cals / 823 KJ **PROTEIN** 19.78 g
FAT 7.29 g **SATURATED FAT** 2.37 g
CARBOHYDRATE 13.63 g **FIBRE** 1.16 g
ADDED SUGAR 0 **SALT** 0.77 g

Serves 4

INGREDIENTS
350 g/12 oz pork fillet
5 ml/1 tsp sunflower oil
2.5 cm/1 in piece root ginger, grated
1 red chilli, seeded and finely chopped
5 ml/1 tsp Chinese five-spice powder
15 ml/1 tbsp sherry vinegar
15 ml/1 tbsp soy sauce
225 g/8 oz can pineapple chunks in natural juice
175 ml/6 fl oz/¾ cup chicken stock
20 ml/4 tsp cornflour
1 small green pepper, seeded and sliced
115 g/4 oz baby sweetcorn, halved
salt and freshly ground black pepper
sprig of flat-leaf parsley, to garnish
boiled rice, to serve

pineapple chunks

pork fillet

chilli

cornflour

soy sauce

pepper

baby sweetcorn

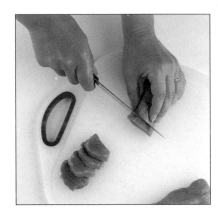

1 Pre-heat the oven to 160°C/325°F/ Gas 3. Trim away any visible fat from the pork and cut into 1 cm/½ in thick slices.

2 Brush the sunflower oil over the base of a flameproof casserole. Heat over a medium flame, then fry the meat for about 2 minutes on each side or until lightly browned.

3 Blend together the ginger, chilli, five-spice powder, vinegar and soy sauce.

4 Drain the pineapple chunks, reserving the juice. Make the stock up to 300 ml/½ pint/1 ¼ cups with the reserved juice, mix together with the spices and pour over the pork.

5 Slowly bring to the boil. Blend the cornflour with 15 ml/1 tbsp of cold water and gradually stir into the pork. Add the vegetables and season to taste.

6 Cover and cook in the oven for 30 minutes. Stir in the pineapple and cook for a further 5 minutes. Garnisn with flat-leaf parsley and serve with boiled rice.

Honey-roast Pork with Thyme and Rosemary

Herbs and honey add flavour and sweetness to tenderloin – the leanest cut of pork.

NUTRITIONAL NOTES

Per portion:

ENERGY 256 K Cals / 1078 KJ PROTEIN 25.01 g
FAT 8.92 g SATURATED FAT 2.92 g
CARBOHYDRATE 18.09 g FIBRE 1.10 g
ADDED SUGAR 10.57 g SALT 0.79 g

Serves 4

INGREDIENTS
450 g/1 lb pork tenderloin
30 ml/2 tbsp thick honey
30 ml/2 tbsp Dijon mustard
5 ml/1 tsp chopped fresh rosemary
2.5 ml/½ tsp chopped fresh thyme
¼ tsp whole tropical peppercorns
sprigs of fresh rosemary and thyme, to
 garnish
Potato Gratin and cauliflower,
 to serve

FOR THE RED ONION CONFIT
4 red onions
350 ml/12 fl oz/1½ cups
 vegetable stock
15 ml/1 tbsp red wine vinegar
15 ml/1 tbsp caster sugar
1 garlic clove, crushed
30 ml/2 tbsp ruby port
pinch of salt

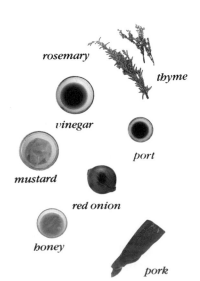

rosemary

thyme

vinegar

port

mustard

red onion

honey

pork

1 Pre-heat the oven to 180°C/350°F/ Gas 4. Trim off any visible fat from the pork. Put the honey, mustard, rosemary and thyme in a small bowl and mix them together well.

2 Crush the peppercorns using a pestle and mortar. Spread the honey mixture over the pork and sprinkle with the crushed peppercorns. Place in a non-stick roasting tin and cook in the pre-heated oven for 35-45 minutes.

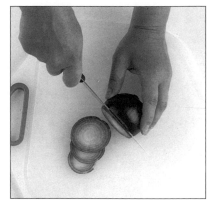

3 For the red onion confit, slice the onions into rings and put them into a heavy-based saucepan.

4 Add the stock, vinegar, sugar and garlic clove to the saucepan. Bring to the boil, then reduce the heat. Cover and simmer for 15 minutes.

5 Uncover and pour in the port and continue to simmer, stirring occasionally, until the onions are soft and the juices thick and syrupy. Season to taste with salt.

6 Cut the pork into slices and arrange on four warmed plates. Serve garnished with rosemary and thyme and accompanied with the red onion confit, Potato Gratin and cauliflower.

Tagliatelle with Milanese Sauce

Serves 4

INGREDIENTS
1 onion, finely chopped
1 stick celery, finely chopped
1 red pepper, seeded and diced
1–2 garlic cloves, crushed
150 ml/¼ pint/⅔ cup
   vegetable stock
400 g/14 oz can tomatoes
15 ml/1 tbsp concentrated
   tomato purée
10 ml/2 tsp caster sugar
5 ml/1 tsp mixed dried herbs
350 g/12 oz tagliatelle
115 g/4 oz button
   mushrooms, sliced
60 ml/4 tbsp white wine
115 g/4 oz lean cooked ham, diced
salt and ground black pepper
15 ml/1 tbsp chopped fresh parsley,
   to garnish

garlic

celery

tagliatelle

red pepper

onion

lean cooked ham

button mushrooms

parsley

tomato purée

vegetable stock

tomatoes

white wine

1 Put the chopped onion, celery, pepper and garlic into a non-stick pan. Add the stock, bring to the boil and cook for 5 minutes or until tender.

2 Add the tomatoes, tomato purée, sugar and herbs. Season with salt and pepper. Bring to the boil, simmer for 30 minutes until thick. Stir occasionally.

3 Cook the pasta in a large pan of boiling, salted water until *al dente*. Drain thoroughly.

4 Put the mushrooms into a pan with the white wine, cover and cook for 3–4 minutes until tender and all the wine has been absorbed.

5 Add the mushrooms and diced ham to the tomato sauce. Reheat gently.

6 Transfer the pasta to a warmed serving dish and spoon on the sauce. Garnish with parsley.

NUTRITIONAL NOTES

PER PORTION:

ENERGY 405Kcals/1700KJ **FAT** 3.5g
SATURATED FAT 0.8g **CHOLESTEROL** 17mg
CARBOHYDRATE 77g **FIBRE** 4.5g

Ham-filled Paprika Ravioli

Serves 4

INGREDIENTS

225 g/8 oz cooked smoked ham
60 ml/4 tbsp mango chutney
1 quantity of basic pasta dough,
    with 5 ml/1 tsp ground
    paprika added
egg white, beaten
flour, for dusting
1–2 garlic cloves, crushed
1 stick celery, sliced
50 g/2 oz sun-dried tomatoes
1 red chilli, seeded and chopped
150 ml/¼ pint/⅔ cup red wine
400 g/14 oz can chopped tomatoes
5 ml/1 tsp chopped fresh thyme,
    plus extra to garnish
10 ml/2 tsp caster sugar
salt and ground black pepper

garlic

celery   *red chilli*   *smoked ham*

thyme   *red wine*

sun-dried tomatoes   *chopped tomatoes*

mango chutney   *basic pasta dough*   *paprika*

1 Remove all traces of fat from the ham, place it with the mango chutney in a food processor or blender and mince the mixture finely.

2 Roll the pasta into thin sheets and lay one piece over a ravioli tray. Put a teaspoonful of the ham filling into each of the depressions.

3 Brush around the edges of each ravioli with egg white. Cover with another sheet of pasta and press the edges well together to seal.

4 Using a rolling-pin, roll over the top of the dough to cut and seal each pocket. Transfer to a floured dish towel and rest for 1 hour before cooking.

5 Put the garlic, celery, sun-dried tomatoes, chilli, wine, canned tomatoes and thyme into a pan. Cover and cook for 15–20 minutes. Season with salt, pepper and sugar.

6 Cook the ravioli in a large pan of boiling, salted water for 4–5 minutes. Drain thoroughly. Spoon a little of the sauce on to a serving plate and arrange the ravioli on top. Sprinkle with fresh thyme and serve at once.

NUTRITIONAL NOTES

PER PORTION:

ENERGY 380Kcals/1594KJ **FAT** 7.6g
SATURATED FAT 2.1g **CHOLESTEROL** 152mg
CARBOHYDRATE 52g **FIBRE** 2.4g

Bean and Ham Lasagne

Serve this tasty lasagne with a salad and bread.

Serves 6

INGREDIENTS

10 ml/2 tsp olive oil
350 g/12 oz/3 cups leeks, sliced
1 garlic clove, crushed
225g/8 oz/3 cups
  mushrooms, sliced
2 courgettes, sliced
350 g/12 oz baby broad beans
350 g/12 oz/2 cups lean smoked
  ham, diced
75 ml/5 tbsp chopped fresh parsley
30 ml/2 tbsp chopped fresh chives
50 g/2 oz/4 tbsp half-fat spread
50 g/2 oz/½ cup plain
  wholemeal flour
600 ml/1 pint/2½ cups
  skimmed milk
300 ml/½ pint/1¼ cups vegetable
  stock, cooled
175 g/6 oz/1½ cups low fat cheese
5 ml/1 tsp smooth mustard
225 g/8 oz no pre-cook
  wholewheat lasagne
25 g/1 oz/½ cup fresh
  wholemeal breadcrumbs
15 ml/1 tbsp grated Parmesan
salt and ground black pepper
fresh herb sprigs, to garnish

 garlic

 *olive
oil*

 leeks

 mushrooms

 courgettes

 *baby broad
beans*

 smoked ham

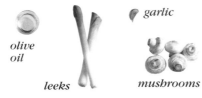 *fresh parsley*

*fresh
chives*

 *half-fat
spread*

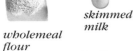 *wholemeal
flour*

 *skimmed
milk*

 *vegetable
stock*

 mustard

*low fat
cheese*

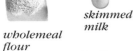 *wholewheat lasagne*

 *Parmesan
cheese*

*fresh
wholemeal
breadcrumbs*

salt

*black
pepper*

1 Preheat the oven to 180°C/350°F/ Gas 4. Heat the oil in a saucepan, add the leeks and garlic and cook for 3 minutes, stirring. Add the mushrooms and courgettes and cook for 5 minutes, stirring.

2 Remove the pan from the heat, and stir in the broad beans, ham and herbs. Set aside.

3 Make the cheese sauce. Put the half-fat spread, flour, milk and stock in a saucepan and heat gently, whisking continuously, until the sauce comes to the boil and thickens. Simmer gently for 3 minutes, stirring. Grate the cheese.

4 Remove the pan from the heat, add the mustard and grated cheese and stir until the cheese has melted and is well blended. Season to taste. Reserve 450 ml/¾ pint/1⅞ cups of cheese sauce and set aside. Mix the remaining sauce with the ham and vegetables.

5 Spoon half the ham mixture over the base of a shallow ovenproof dish or baking tin. Cover this with half the pasta. Repeat these layers with the remaining ham mixture and pasta, then pour the reserved cheese sauce over the pasta to cover it completely.

6 Mix together the breadcrumbs and Parmesan cheese and sprinkle over the lasagne. Bake for 45–60 minutes, until cooked and golden brown on top. Garnish with fresh herb sprigs and serve immediately.

NUTRITIONAL NOTES
PER PORTION:

ENERGY 448Kcals/1892KJ PROTEIN 38.45g
FAT 13.05g SATURATED FAT 5.07g
CARBOHYDRATE 46.16g FIBRE 10.86g
ADDED SUGAR 0.02g SODIUM 0.50g

Veal Escalopes with Artichokes

Artichokes are very hard to prepare fresh, so use canned artichoke hearts, instead – they have an excellent flavour and are simple to use.

Serves 4

INGREDIENTS
450 g/1 lb veal escalopes
1 shallot
115 g/4 oz smoked bacon,
    finely chopped
1 × 400 g/14 oz can of artichoke
    hearts in brine, drained and
    quartered
150 ml/¼ pint/⅔ cup veal stock
3 fresh rosemary sprigs
60 ml/4 tbsp double cream
salt and freshly ground black pepper
fresh rosemary sprigs, to garnish

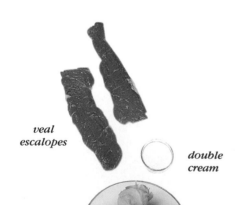

veal escalopes

double cream

artichoke hearts

I Cut the veal into thin slices.

2 Using a sharp knife, cut the shallot into thin slices.

NUTRITIONAL NOTES
PER PORTION:

ENERGY 33.2 Kcals/1183 KJ **FAT** 11.3 g
SATURATED FAT 5.9 g

3 Heat the wok, then add the bacon. Stir-fry for 2 minutes. When the fat is released, add the veal and shallot and stir-fry for 3–4 minutes.

4 Add the artichokes and stir-fry for 1 minute. Stir in the stock and rosemary and simmer for 2 minutes. Stir in the double cream, season with salt and pepper and serve garnished with sprigs of fresh rosemary.

Stir-fried Beef and Broccoli

This spicy beef may be served with noodles or on a bed of boiled rice for a speedy and low calorie Chinese meal.

Serves 4

INGREDIENTS

350 g/12 oz rump or lean prime casserole steak
15 ml/1 tbsp cornflour
5 ml/1 tsp sesame oil
350 g/12 oz broccoli, cut into small florets
4 spring onions, sliced on the diagonal
1 carrot, cut into matchstick strips
1 garlic clove, crushed
2.5 cm/1 in piece root ginger, cut into very fine strips
120 ml/4 fl oz/½ cup beef stock
30 ml/2 tbsp soy sauce
30 ml/2 tbsp dry sherry
10 ml/2 tsp soft light brown sugar
spring onion tassels, to garnish
noodles or rice, to serve

steak
ginger
broccoli
garlic
carrot
spring onions

NUTRITIONAL NOTES

Per portion:

ENERGY 195 K Cals/819 KJ **PROTEIN** 22.84 g
FAT 6.21 g **SATURATED FAT** 1.81 g
CARBOHYDRATE 10.35 g **FIBRE** 2.87 g
ADDED SUGAR 2.67 g **SALT** 1.36 g

1 Trim the beef and cut into thin slices across the grain. Cut each slice into thin strips. Toss in the cornflour to coat thoroughly.

2 Heat the sesame oil in a large non-stick frying pan or wok. Add the beef strips and stir-fry over a brisk heat for 3 minutes. Remove and set aside.

COOK'S TIP

To make spring onion tassels, trim the bulb base then cut the green shoot so that the onion is 7.5 cm/3 in long. Shred to within 2.5 cm/1 in of the base and put into iced water for 1 hour.

3 Add the broccoli, spring onions, carrot, garlic clove, ginger and stock to the frying pan or wok. Cover and simmer for 3 minutes. Uncover and cook, stirring until all the stock has reduced entirely.

4 Mix the soy sauce, sherry and brown sugar together. Add to the frying pan or wok with the beef. Cook for 2–3 minutes stirring continuously. Spoon into a warm serving dish and garnish with spring onion tassels. Serve on a bed of noodles or rice.

Sukiyaki-style Beef

This Japanese dish is a meal in itself; the recipe incorporates all the traditional elements – meat, vegetables, noodles and beancurd. If you want to do it all properly, eat the meal with chopsticks, and a spoon to collect the stock juices.

Serves 6

INGREDIENTS
450 g/1 lb thick rump steak
250 g/9 oz Japanese rice noodles
15 ml/1 tbsp shredded suet
200 g/7 oz hard beancurd, cut into
   cubes
8 shitake mushrooms, trimmed
2 medium leeks, sliced into 2.5 cm/
   1 in lengths
90 g/3½ oz baby spinach, to serve

FOR THE STOCK
15 ml/1 tbsp caster sugar
90 ml/6 tbsp rice wine
45 ml/3 tbsp dark soy sauce
125 ml/4 fl oz/½ cup water

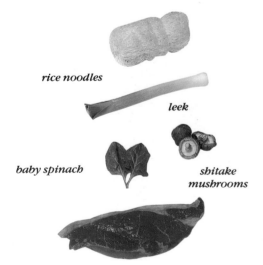

rice noodles

leek

baby spinach

shitake mushrooms

rump steak

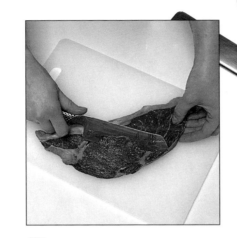

1 Cut the beef into thin slices.

2 Blanch the noodles in boiling water for 2 minutes. Strain well.

3 Mix together all the stock ingredients in a bowl.

4 Heat the wok, then add the suet. When the suet is melted, stir-fry the beef for 2–3 minutes until it is cooked, but still pink in colour.

5 Pour the stock over the beef.

NUTRITIONAL NOTES

PER PORTION:

ENERGY 406 Kcals/1700 KJ **FAT** 10.9 g
SATURATED FAT 2.6 g

6 Add the remaining ingredients and cook for 4 minutes, until the leeks are tender. Serve a selection of the different ingredients, with a few baby spinach leaves, to each person.

Oriental Beef

This sumptuously rich beef melts in the mouth, and is perfectly complemented by the cool, crunchy relish.

Serves 4

INGREDIENTS
450 g/1 lb rump steak

FOR THE MARINADE
15 ml/1 tbsp sunflower oil
2 cloves garlic, crushed
60 ml/4 tbsp dark soy sauce
30 ml/2 tbsp dry sherry
10 ml/2 tsp soft dark brown sugar

FOR THE RELISH
6 radishes
10 cm/4 in piece cucumber
1 piece stem ginger
4 whole radishes, to garnish

rump steak

brown sugar

soy sauce

garlic

radish

1 Cut the beef into thin strips. Place in a bowl.

2 To make the marinade, mix together the garlic, soy sauce, sherry and sugar in a bowl. Pour it over the beef and leave to marinate overnight.

NUTRITIONAL NOTES
PER PORTION:
ENERGY 110 Kcals/462 KJ **FAT** 4.9 g
SATURATED FAT 1.49 g

3 To make the relish, chop the radishes and cucumber into matchsticks and the ginger into small matchsticks. Mix well together in a bowl.

4 Heat the wok, then add the oil. When the oil is hot, add the meat and marinade and stir-fry for 3–4 minutes. Serve with the relish, and garnish with a whole radish on each plate.

Chilli Mince and Pipe Rigate

Serves 6

INGREDIENTS

450 g/1 lb extra lean minced beef
  or turkey
1 onion, finely chopped
2–3 garlic cloves, crushed
1–2 red chillies, seeded and
  finely chopped
400 g/14 oz can chopped tomatoes
45 ml/3 tbsp concentrated
  tomato purée
5 ml/1 tsp mixed dried herbs
450 ml/³/₄ pint1³/₄ cups water
450 g/1 lb pipe rigate
400 g/14 oz can red kidney
  beans, drained
salt and ground black pepper

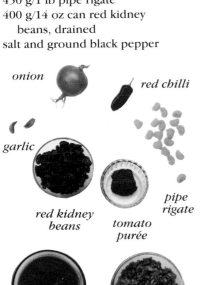

onion

red chilli

garlic

red kidney
beans

tomato
purée

pipe
rigate

chopped
tomatoes

minced beef

1 Cook the minced beef or turkey in a non-stick saucepan, breaking up any large pieces with a wooden spoon until browned all over.

2 Add the onion, garlic and chilli, cover with a lid and cook gently for 5 minutes.

NUTRITIONAL NOTES

PER PORTION:

ENERGY 425Kcals/1785KJ FAT 5.4g
SATURATED FAT 1.4g CHOLESTEROL 44mg
CARBOHYDRATE 70g FIBRE 6.1g

3 Add the tomatoes, tomato purée, herbs, water and seasoning. Bring to the boil and simmer for 1¹/₂ hours. Leave to cool slightly.

4 Cook the pasta in a large pan of boiling, salted water until *al dente*. Drain thoroughly. Skim off any fat from the surface of the mince. Add the red kidney beans and heat for 5–10 minutes. Pour over the cooked pasta, and serve.

Herbed Beef Salad

Serves 6

INGREDIENTS
450 g/1 lb beef fillet
450 g/1 lb fresh tagliatelle with sun-dried tomatoes and herbs
115 g/4 oz cherry tomatoes
¹/₂ cucumber

MARINADE
15 ml/1 tbsp soy sauce
15 ml/1 tbsp sherry
5 ml/1 tsp root ginger, grated
1 garlic clove, crushed

HERB DRESSING
30–45 ml/2–3 tbsp horseradish sauce
150 ml/¹/₄ pint/²/₃ cup low-fat yogurt
1 garlic clove, crushed
30–45 ml/2–3 tbsp chopped fresh herbs (chives, parsley, thyme)
salt and ground black pepper

cherry tomatoes

cucumber

fillet beef

root ginger

garlic

thyme

tagliatelle

low-fat yogurt

horseradish sauce

parsley

soy sauce

chives

1 Mix all the marinade ingredients together in a shallow dish, put the beef in and turn it over to coat it. Cover with clear film and leave for 30 minutes to allow the flavours to penetrate the meat.

2 Preheat the grill. Lift the fillet out of the marinade and pat it dry with kitchen paper. Place on a grill rack and grill for 8 minutes on each side, basting with the marinade during cooking.

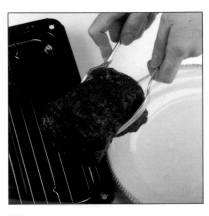

3 Transfer to a plate, cover with foil and leave to stand for 20 minutes.

4 Put all the dressing ingredients into a bowl and mix thoroughly together. Cook the pasta according to the directions on the packet, drain thoroughly, rinse under cold water and leave to dry.

5 Cut the cherry tomatoes in half. Cut the cucumber in half lengthways, scoop out the seeds with a teaspoon and slice thinly into crescents.

6 Put the pasta, cherry tomatoes, cucumber and dressing into a bowl and toss to coat. Slice the beef thinly and arrange on a plate with the pasta salad.

NUTRITIONAL NOTES
PER PORTION:

ENERGY 374Kcals/1572KJ **FAT** 5.7g
SATURATED FAT 1.7g **CHOLESTEROL** 46mg
CARBOHYDRATE 57g **FIBRE** 2.9g

Lasagne

Serves 6—8

1 large onion, chopped
2 garlic cloves, crushed
500 g/1¼ lb minced beef or
  turkey
450 g/1 lb passata
5 ml/1 tsp mixed dried herbs
225 g/8 oz frozen leaf spinach,
  defrosted
200 g/7 oz lasagne verdi
200 g/7 oz low-fat cottage cheese

SAUCE
25 g/1 oz low-fat margarine
25 g/1 oz plain flour
300 ml/½ pint/1¼ cups
  skimmed milk
1.5 ml/¼ tsp ground nutmeg
25 g/1 oz grated Parmesan cheese
salt and ground black pepper
mixed salad, to serve

minced turkey

spinach

garlic

nutmeg

Parmesan cheese

lasagne verdi

skimmed milk

plain flour

low-fat margarine

onion

low-fat cottage cheese

passata

1 Put the onion, garlic and minced meat into a non-stick saucepan. Brown quickly for 5 minutes, stirring with a wooden spoon to separate the pieces.

2 Add the passata, herbs and seasoning to the saucepan. Bring to the boil, cover and let simmer for about 30 minutes.

3 For the sauce: put all the sauce ingredients, except the Parmesan cheese, into a saucepan. Heat to thicken, whisking constantly until bubbling and smooth. Adjust the seasoning, add the cheese to the sauce and stir.

4 Preheat the oven to 190°C/375°F/Gas 5. Lay the spinach leaves out on kitchen paper and pat dry.

5 Layer the meat mixture, dried lasagne, cottage cheese and spinach in a 2 litre/3½ pint/8 cup ovenproof dish, starting and ending with a layer of meat.

6 Spoon the sauce over the top to cover and bake for 45-50 minutes or until bubbling. Serve with a mixed salad.

NUTRITIONAL NOTES
PER PORTION:

ENERGY 351Kcals/1472KJ **FAT** 6.0g
SATURATED FAT 1.7g **CHOLESTEROL** 52mg
CARBOHYDRATE 40g **FIBRE** 3g

Cannelloni

Serves 4

INGREDIENTS
2 garlic cloves, crushed
2 x 400 g/14 oz cans
    chopped tomatoes
10 ml/2 tsp soft brown sugar
15 ml/1 tbsp fresh basil
15 ml/1 tbsp fresh marjoram
450 g/1 lb frozen chopped spinach
large pinch ground nutmeg
115 g/4 oz cooked lean
    ham, minced
200 g/7 oz low-fat cottage cheese
12–14 cannelloni tubes
50 g/2 oz low-fat mozzarella
    cheese, diced
25 g/1 oz strong Cheddar
    cheese, grated
25 g/1 oz fresh white breadcrumbs
salt and ground black pepper
flat-leaf parsley, to garnish

1 To make the sauce put the garlic, canned tomatoes, sugar and herbs into a pan, bring to the boil and cook, uncovered, for 30 minutes, stirring occasionally, until fairly thick.

2 To make the filling put the spinach into a pan, cover and cook slowly until defrosted. Break up with a fork, then increase the heat to drive off any water. Season with salt, pepper and nutmeg. Turn the spinach into a bowl, cool slightly, then add the minced ham and cottage cheese.

3 Pipe the filling into each tube of uncooked cannelloni. It is easiest to hold them upright with one end flat on a chopping board, while piping from the other end.

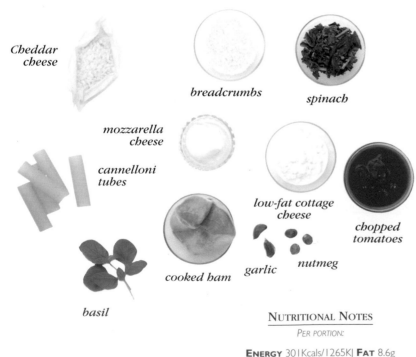

Cheddar cheese

breadcrumbs

spinach

mozzarella cheese

cannelloni tubes

low-fat cottage cheese

chopped tomatoes

cooked ham

garlic

nutmeg

basil

NUTRITIONAL NOTES

PER PORTION:

ENERGY 301Kcals/1265KJ **FAT** 8.6g
SATURATED FAT 3.6g **CHOLESTEROL** 34mg
CARBOHYDRATE 33g **FIBRE** 4.7g

4 Preheat the oven to 180°C/350°F/ Gas 4. Spoon half the tomato sauce into the bottom of a 20 cm/8 in square ovenproof dish. Lay two rows of filled cannelloni on top of the sauce.

5 Scatter over the diced mozzarella and cover with the rest of the sauce.

6 Sprinkle over the Cheddar cheese and breadcrumbs. Bake in a preheated oven for 30–40 minutes. Grill the top to brown, if necessary. Garnish with flat leaf parsley.

Ravioli (with Bolognese Sauce)

Serves 6

INGREDIENTS

225 g/8 oz low-fat cottage cheese
30 ml/2 tbsp grated Parmesan
    cheese, plus extra for serving
1 egg white, beaten, including extra
    for brushing
1.5 ml/¼ tsp ground nutmeg
1 quantity of basic pasta dough
flour, for dusting
1 medium onion, finely chopped
1 garlic clove, crushed
150 ml/¼ pint/⅔ cup beef stock
350 g/12 oz minced extra lean beef
120 ml/4 fl oz/½ cup red wine
30 ml/2 tbsp concentrated
    tomato purée
400 g/14 oz can chopped tomatoes
2.5 ml/½ tsp chopped
    fresh rosemary
1.5 ml/¼ tsp ground allspice
salt and ground black pepper

nutmeg

onion   *minced beef*   *stock*

tomato purée   *low-fat cottage cheese*   *red wine*

Parmesan cheese   *chopped tomatoes*

egg

rosemary

garlic

1 To make the filling mix the cottage cheese, grated Parmesan, egg white, seasoning and nutmeg together thoroughly.

2 Roll the pasta into thin sheets, place a small teaspoon of filling along the pasta in rows 5 cm/2 in apart.

3 Moisten between the filling with beaten egg white. Lay a second sheet of pasta lightly over the top and press between each pocket to remove any air and seal firmly.

4 Cut into rounds with a fluted ravioli or pastry cutter. Transfer to a floured cloth and rest for at least 30 minutes before cooking.

5 To make the Bolognese sauce cook the onion and garlic in the stock for 5 minutes or until all the stock has reduced. Add the beef and cook quickly to brown, breaking up the meat with a fork. Add the wine, tomato purée, chopped tomatoes, rosemary and allspice, bring to the boil and simmer for 1 hour. Adjust the seasoning to taste.

6 Cook the ravioli in a large pan of boiling, salted water for 4–5 minutes. (Cook in batches to stop them sticking together). Drain thoroughly. Serve topped with Bolognese sauce. Serve grated Parmesan cheese separately.

NUTRITIONAL NOTES

PER PORTION:

ENERGY 321Kcals/1347KJ **FAT** 8.8g
SATURATED FAT 3.1g **CHOLESTEROL** 158mg
CARBOHYDRATE 32g **FIBRE** 2g

Spaghetti alla Carbonara

Serves 4

INGREDIENTS

150 g/5 oz smoked turkey rashers
1 medium onion, chopped
1–2 garlic cloves, crushed
150 ml/¼ pint/⅔ cup chicken stock
150 ml/¼ pint/⅔ cup dry
    white wine
200 g/7 oz low-fat cream cheese
450 g/1 lb chilli and garlic-
    flavoured spaghetti
30 ml/2 tbsp chopped fresh parsley
salt and ground black pepper
shavings of Parmesan cheese,
    to serve

garlic

flavoured spaghetti

parsley

smoked turkey rashers   *low-fat cream cheese*

onion

white wine

stock

1 Cut the turkey rashers into 1 cm/½ in strips. Fry quickly in a non-stick pan for 2–3 minutes. Add the onion, garlic and stock to the pan. Bring to the boil, cover and simmer for 5 minutes until tender.

2 Add the wine and boil rapidly until reduced by half. Whisk in the cream cheese until smooth.

3 Meanwhile cook the spaghetti in a large pan of boiling, salted water for 10–12 minutes. Drain thoroughly.

4 Return to the pan with the sauce and parsley, toss well and serve immediately with shavings of Parmesan cheese.

NUTRITIONAL NOTES

PER PORTION:

ENERGY 500Kcals/2102KJ **FAT** 3.3g
SATURATED FAT 0.5g **CHOLESTEROL** 21mg
CARBOHYDRATE 89g **FIBRE** 4g

Spaghetti Bolognese

Serves 8

INGREDIENTS

1 medium onion, chopped
2–3 garlic cloves, crushed
300 ml/½ pint/1¼ cups beef or
  chicken stock
450 g/1 lb extra lean minced turkey
  or beef
2 x 400 g/14 oz cans
  chopped tomatoes
5 ml/1 tsp dried basil
5 ml/1 tsp dried oregano
60 ml/4 tbsp concentrated
  tomato purée
450 g/1 lb button mushrooms,
  quartered or sliced
150 ml/¼ pint/⅔ cup red wine
450 g/1 lb spaghetti
salt and ground black pepper

garlic

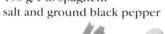

mushrooms

stock

spaghetti

onion

*minced
turkey*

red wine

*chopped
tomatoes*

*tomato
purée*

1 Put the chopped onion and garlic into a non-stick pan with half of the stock. Bring to the boil and cook for 5 minutes until the onions are tender and the stock has reduced completely.

2 Add the turkey or beef and cook for 5 minutes breaking the meat up with a fork. Add the tomatoes, herbs and tomato purée, bring to the boil, cover and simmer for about 1 hour.

NUTRITIONAL NOTES

PER PORTION:

ENERGY 321Kcals/1350KJ **FAT** 4.1g
SATURATED FAT 1.3g **CHOLESTEROL** 33mg
CARBOHYDRATE 49g **FIBRE** 3.7g

3 Meanwhile put the mushrooms into a non-stick pan with the wine, bring to the boil and cook for 5 minutes or until the wine has evaporated. Add the mushrooms to the meat.

4 Cook the pasta in a large pan of boiling, salted water for 8–10 minutes until tender. Drain thoroughly. Serve topped with meat sauce.

Spiced Lamb and Vegetable Couscous

A delicious stew of tender lamb and vegetables served with couscous.

Serves 6

INGREDIENTS
350 g/12 oz lean lamb fillet, cut
    into 2 cm/¾ in cubes
30 ml/2 tbsp wholemeal plain
    flour, seasoned
10 ml/2 tsp sunflower oil
1 onion, chopped
2 garlic cloves, crushed
1 red pepper, seeded and diced
5 ml/1 tsp ground coriander
5 ml/1 tsp ground cumin
5 ml/1 tsp ground allspice
2.5 ml/½ tsp hot chilli powder
300 ml/½ pint/1¼ cups lamb stock
400 g/14 oz can chopped tomatoes
225 g/8 oz carrots, sliced
175 g/6 oz parsnips, sliced
175 g/6 oz courgettes, sliced
175 g/6 oz closed cup
    mushrooms, quartered
225 g/8 oz frozen broad beans
115 g/4 oz/⅔ cup sultanas
450 g/1 lb quick-cook couscous
salt and ground black pepper
fresh coriander, to garnish

1 Toss the lamb in the flour. Heat the oil in a large saucepan and add the lamb, onion, garlic and pepper. Cook for 5 minutes, stirring frequently.

2 Add any remaining flour and the spices and cook for 1 minute, stirring.

lamb fillet

wholemeal plain flour

sunflower oil

onion

garlic

red pepper

ground coriander   **ground cumin**   **ground allspice**

hot chilli powder

lamb stock

chopped tomatoes

carrots

parsnips   *courgettes*   **closed cup mushrooms**

broad beans

sultanas

couscous

3 Gradually add the stock, stirring continuously, then add the tomatoes, carrots and parsnips and mix well.

4 Bring to the boil, stirring, then cover and simmer for 30 minutes, stirring occasionally.

NUTRITIONAL NOTES
PER PORTION:

ENERGY 439Kcals/1846KJ PROTEIN 23.29g
FAT 8.15g SATURATED FAT 2.57g
CARBOHYDRATE 72.98g FIBRE 7.34g
ADDED SUGAR 0.00g SODIUM 0.18g

COOK'S TIP

For a tasty alternative, serve the lamb and vegetable stew on a bed of cooked bulgur wheat or brown rice.

5 Add the courgettes, mushrooms, broad beans and sultanas. Cover, return to the boil and simmer for a further 20–30 minutes, until the lamb and vegetables are tender, stirring occasionally. Season to taste.

6 Meanwhile, soak the couscous and steam in a lined colander over a pan of boiling water for about 20 minutes, until cooked, or according to the packet instructions. Pile the cooked couscous on to a warmed serving platter or individual plates and top with the lamb and vegetable stew. Garnish with fresh coriander and serve immediately.

NUTRITIONAL NOTES
Per portion:

ENERGY 204 Kcals/850 KJ **FAT** 12.3 g
SATURATED FAT 5.2 g

Paper-thin Lamb with Spring Onions

Spring onions lend a delicious flavour to the lamb in this simple supper dish.

Serves 3–4

INGREDIENTS
450 g/1 lb lamb fillet
30 ml/2 tbsp Chinese rice wine
10 ml/2 tsp light soy sauce
2.5 ml/½ tsp roasted and ground
    Szechuan peppercorns
2.5 ml/½ tsp salt
2.5 m/½ tsp dark brown soft sugar
20 ml/4 tsp dark soy sauce
15 ml/1 tbsp sesame oil
30 ml/2 tbsp groundnut oil
2 garlic cloves, thinly sliced
2 bunches spring onions, cut
    into 7.5 cm/3 in lengths,
    then shredded
30 ml/2 tbsp chopped
    fresh coriander

spring onions

lamb

dark soy sauce

sesame oil

salt

Chinese rice wine

coriander

groundnut oil

garlic

1 Wrap the lamb and place in the freezer for about 1 hour until just frozen. Cut the meat across the grain into paper-thin slices. Put the lamb slices in a bowl, add 10 ml/2 tsp of the rice wine, the light soy sauce and ground Szechuan peppercorns. Mix well and leave to marinate for 15–30 minutes.

2 Make the sauce: in a bowl mix together the remaining rice wine, the salt, brown sugar, dark soy sauce and 10ml/2 tsp of the sesame oil. Set aside.

3 Heat a wok until hot, add the oil and swirl it around. Add the garlic and let it sizzle for a few seconds, then add the lamb. Stir-fry for about 1 minute until the lamb is no longer pink. Pour in the sauce and stir briefly.

4 Add the spring onions and coriander and stir-fry for 15–20 seconds until the spring onions just wilt. The finished dish should be slightly dry in appearance. Serve at once, sprinkled with the remaining sesame oil.

Balti Spring Lamb Chops

It is best to marinate the chops overnight as this makes them very tender and also helps them to absorb the maximum amount of flavour. Serve with a crisp salad.

Serves 4

INGREDIENTS
8 small lean spring lamb chops
1 large red chilli, seeded
30ml/2 tbsp chopped fresh
  coriander
15ml/1 tbsp chopped fresh mint
5ml/1 tsp salt
5ml/1 tsp soft brown sugar
5ml/1 tsp garam masala
5ml/1 tsp garlic pulp
5ml/1 tsp ginger pulp
175ml/6 fl oz/⅔ cup natural low
  fat yogurt
10ml/2 tsp corn oil

garlic pulp

garam masala

lamb chops

ginger pulp

mint

fresh coriander

salt

red chilli

yogurt

brown sugar

NUTRITIONAL NOTES
Per portion:
ENERGY 207 K Cals/864 K J PROTEIN 23.15g
FAT 10.29g SATURATED FAT 4.26g
CARBOHYDRATE 5.62g FIBRE 0.27g
ADDED SUGAR 1.01g
SALT 0.6g

1 Trim the lamb chops to remove any excess fat. Place them in a large bowl.

2 Finely chop the chilli, then mix with the coriander, mint, salt, brown sugar, garam masala, garlic pulp and ginger pulp.

COOK'S TIP
These chops can also be grilled. Remember to baste with oil.

3 Pour the yogurt into the herb mixture and, using a small whisk or a fork, mix thoroughly. Pour this mixture over the top of the chops and turn them with your fingers to make sure that they are completely covered. Leave to marinate overnight in the fridge.

4 Heat the oil in a large, non-stick wok or frying pan and add the chops. Lower the heat and allow to cook over a medium heat. Turn the chops over and continue frying until they are cooked right through – about 20 minutes – turning again if needed.

Mini Mince Koftas in Onion Sauce

This kofta curry is very popular in most Indian homes. It is also extremely easy to make. Serve with pilau rice.

Serves 4

INGREDIENTS
225g/8oz lean minced lamb
10ml/2 tsp poppy seeds
1 medium onion, chopped
5ml/1 tsp ginger pulp
5ml/1 tsp garlic pulp
5ml/1 tsp salt
5ml/1 tsp chilli powder
7.5ml/1½ tsp ground coriander
30ml/2 tbsp fresh coriander leaves
1 small egg

FOR THE SAUCE
85ml/3 fl oz/⅔ cup natural low
   fat yogurt
30ml/2 tbsp tomato purée
5ml/1 tsp chilli powder
5ml/1 tsp salt
5ml/1 tsp garlic pulp
5ml/1 tsp ginger pulp
5ml/1 tsp garam masala
10ml/2 tsp corn oil
1 cinnamon bark
425ml/⅔ pint/1⅔ cups water

ground coriander   *onion*   *lamb*

garlic pulp   *fresh coriander*   *poppy seeds*

ginger pulp   *salt*   *yogurt*

cinnamon bark   *garam masala*   *tomato purée*   *chilli powder*

1 Place the lamb in a food processor and mince for about 1 minute. Remove from the processor, put in a bowl, tip the poppy seeds on top and set aside.

2 Place the onion in the food processor, together with the ginger pulp, garlic pulp, salt, chilli powder, ground coriander and half the fresh coriander. Grind this mixture for about 30 seconds, then blend it into the minced lamb.

3 Whisk the egg and thoroughly mix it into the minced lamb. Leave to stand for about 1 hour.

4 For the sauce, whisk together the yogurt, tomato purée, chilli powder, salt, garlic pulp, ginger pulp and garam masala.

5 Heat the oil with the cinnamon bark in a non-stick wok or frying pan for about 1 minute, then pour in the sauce. Lower the heat and cook for about 1 minute. Remove the wok or frying pan from the heat and set aside.

NUTRITIONAL NOTES
Per portion:
ENERGY 155 K Cals/647 K J **PROTEIN** 14.74g
FAT 9.24g **SATURATED FAT** 2.79g
CARBOHYDRATE 7.56g **FIBRE** 1.16g
ADDED SUGAR 0
SALT 1.07g

COOK'S TIP
This curry is also absolutely delicious served with warm, freshly made chapatis.

6 Break off small balls of the mince mixture and make the koftas using your hands. When all the koftas are ready, return the sauce to the heat and add the water. Drop in the koftas one by one. Place the remaining fresh coriander on top, cover with a lid and cook for 7–10 minutes, stirring gently occasionally to turn the koftas around. Serve hot.

Balti Lamb with Peas and Potatoes

Fresh mint leaves are used in this dish, but if they are obtainable, use ready-minted frozen peas to bring an added freshness. Serve with rice.

Serves 4

INGREDIENTS

225g/8oz lean spring lamb
120ml/4 fl oz/½ cup natural low
    fat yogurt
1 cinnamon stick
2 green cardamom pods
3 black peppercorns
5ml/1 tsp garlic pulp
5ml/1 tsp ginger pulp
5ml/1 tsp chilli powder
5ml/1 tsp garam masala
5ml/1 tsp salt
30ml/2 tbsp roughly chopped
    fresh mint
15ml/3 tbsp corn oil
2 medium onions, sliced
300ml/½ pint/1¼ cups water
115g/4oz frozen peas
1 large potato, diced
1 firm tomato, skinned, seeded
    and diced

garlic pulp potato
        lamb
garam
masala onions salt
    cardamom cinnamon
    peppercorns stick
ginger
pulp
        mint
    peas
chilli powder tomato yogurt

1 Using a sharp knife, cut the lamb into strips, then place it in a bowl.

2 Add the yogurt, cinnamon, cardamoms, peppercorns, garlic, ginger, chilli powder, garam masala, salt and half the mint. Leave to marinate for about 2 hours.

3 Heat the oil in a non-stick wok or frying pan and fry the onions until golden brown. Stir in the lamb and the marinade and stir-fry for about 3 minutes.

4 Pour in the water, lower the heat and cook until the meat is cooked right through, about 15 minutes, depending on the age of the lamb. Meanwhile cook the potato in boiling water until just soft, but not mushy.

5 Add the peas and potato to the lamb and stir to mix gently.

NUTRITIONAL NOTES

Per portion:

ENERGY 231 K Cals/968 K J **PROTEIN** 17.54g
FAT 8.47g **SATURATED FAT** 2.79g
CARBOHYDRATE 22.72g **FIBRE** 3.73g
ADDED SUGAR 0
SALT 0.57g

COOK'S TIP

You can cook this dish in advance and keep it in the fridge. In fact, this will improve the flavour.

6 Finally, add the remaining mint and the tomato and cook for a further 5 minutes before serving.

Stir-fried Lamb with Baby Onions and Peppers

The baby onions are used whole in this recipe. Serve with rice or lentils.

NUTRITIONAL NOTES
Per portion:
ENERGY 155 K Cals/644 K J PROTEIN 12.75g
FAT 9.48g SATURATED FAT 2.82g
CARBOHYDRATE 5.74g FIBRE 1.49g
ADDED SUGAR 0
SALT 0.55g

Serves 4

INGREDIENTS
15ml/1 tbsp corn oil
8 baby onions
225g/8oz boned lean lamb, cut
    into strips
5ml/1 tsp ground cumin
5ml/1 tsp ground coriander
15ml/1 tbsp tomato purée
5ml/1 tsp chilli powder
5ml/1 tsp salt
15ml/1 tbsp lemon juice
2.5ml/½ tsp onion seeds
4 curry leaves
300ml/½ pint/1¼ cups water
1 small red pepper, seeded and
    roughly sliced
1 small green pepper, seeded and
    roughly sliced
15ml/1 tbsp chopped
    fresh coriander
15ml/1 tbsp chopped fresh mint

onions

green and red peppers   lamb

onion seeds

lemon juice

mint   curry leaves   fresh coriander

ground cumin   ground coriander   chilli powder

tomato purée   salt

1 Heat the oil in a non-stick wok or frying pan and stir-fry the whole baby onions for about 3 minutes. Using a slotted spoon, remove the onions from the wok and set aside to drain.

2 Mix together the lamb, cumin, ground coriander, tomato purée, chilli powder, salt and lemon juice in a bowl and set aside.

3 Reheat the oil and stir-fry the onion seeds and curry leaves for 2–3 minutes.

4 Add the lamb and spice mixture and stir-fry for about 5 minutes, then pour in the water, lower the heat and cook gently for about 10 minutes, until the lamb is cooked through.

5 Add the peppers and half the fresh coriander and mint. Stir-fry for a further 2 minutes.

6 Finally, add the baby onions and the remaining fresh coriander and chopped mint and serve.

COOK'S TIP
This dish benefits from being cooked a day in advance and kept in the fridge .

Balti Lamb with Cauliflower

Cauliflower and lamb go beautifully together. This curry is given a final tarka of cumin seeds and curry leaves, which enhances the flavour.

Serves 4

INGREDIENTS
10ml/2 tsp corn oil
2 medium onions, sliced
7.5ml/1½ tsp ginger pulp
5ml/1 tsp chilli powder
5ml/1 tsp garlic pulp
1.5ml/¼ tsp ground turmeric
2.5ml/½ tsp ground coriander
30ml/2 tbsp fresh fenugreek leaves
275g/10oz boned lean spring lamb,
   cut into strips
1 small cauliflower, cut into
   small florets
300ml/½ pint/1¼ cups water
30ml/2 tbsp fresh coriander leaves
½ red pepper, seeded and sliced
15ml/1 tbsp lemon juice

FOR THE TARKA
10ml/2 tsp corn oil
2.5ml/½ tsp white cumin seeds
4–6 curry leaves

ground coriander

cumin seeds

lemon juice

lamb

curry leaves

fenugreek

cauliflower

onions

chilli powder

garlic pulp

fresh coriander

red pepper

ground turmeric

ginger pulp

COOK'S TIP
If you wish, you may use a good-quality olive oil for the tarka.

1 Heat the oil in a non-stick wok or frying pan and fry the onions until golden brown. Lower the heat and add the ginger pulp, chilli powder, garlic pulp, turmeric and ground coriander, followed by the fenugreek.

2 Add the lamb strips to the wok and stir-fry until the lamb is completely coated with the spices. Add half the cauliflower florets and stir the mixture well.

3 Pour in the water, cover the wok, lower the heat and cook for 5–7 minutes until the cauliflower and lamb are almost cooked through.

4 Add the remaining cauliflower, half the fresh coriander, the red pepper and lemon juice and stir-fry for about 5 minutes, making sure that the sauce does not catch on the bottom of the wok.

NUTRITIONAL NOTES

Per portion:

ENERGY 202 K Cals/839 K J PROTEIN 18.42g
FAT 9.88g SATURATED FAT 3.24g
CARBOHYDRATE 10.86g FIBRE 2.88g
ADDED SUGAR 0
SALT 0.07g

5 Check that the lamb is completely cooked, then remove from the heat and set aside.

6 To make the tarka, heat the oil and fry the seeds and curry leaves for about 30 seconds. While it is still hot, pour the seasoned oil over the cauliflower and lamb and serve garnished with the remaining fresh coriander leaves.

Courgettes with Lamb

Lamb is cooked with yogurt and then the courgettes, which have already been grilled, are added to the mixture.

Serves 4

INGREDIENTS
15ml/1 tbsp corn oil
2 medium onions, chopped
225g/8oz lean lamb steaks, cut
   into strips
120ml/4 fl oz/½ cup natural low
   fat yogurt
5ml/1 tsp garam masala
5ml/1 tsp chilli powder
5ml/1 tsp garlic pulp
5ml/1 tsp ginger pulp
2.5ml/½ tsp ground coriander
2 medium courgettes, sliced
15ml/1 tbsp chopped fresh
   coriander, to garnish

onions
          lamb
    courgettes
garlic pulp   ginger pulp
     fresh coriander
chilli
powder
          ground
          coriander
garam masala
               yogurt

NUTRITIONAL NOTES
Per portion:
ENERGY 178 K Cals/742 K J **PROTEIN** 15.80g
FAT 8.36g **SATURATED FAT** 2.78g
CARBOHYDRATE 10.83g **FIBRE** 1.99g
ADDED SUGAR 0
SALT 0.08g

1 Heat the oil in a non-stick wok or frying pan and fry the onions until they are golden brown.

2 Add the lamb strips and stir-fry for 1 minute to seal the meat.

3 Put the yogurt, garam masala, chilli powder, garlic, ginger and ground coriander into a bowl. Whisk the mixture together.

4 Pour the yogurt mixture over the lamb and stir-fry for a further 2 minutes. Cover and cook over a medium to low heat for 12–15 minutes.

5 Put the courgettes in a flameproof dish and cook on a preheated grill for about 3 minutes, turning once.

6 Check that the lamb is cooked through and the sauce is quite thick, then add the courgettes and serve garnished with the fresh coriander.

Chicken & Poultry Dishes

Warm Chicken Salad with Shallots and Mangetouts

Succulent cooked chicken pieces are combined with vegetables in a light chilli dressing.

Serves 6

INGREDIENTS
50 g/2 oz mixed salad leaves
50 g/2 oz baby spinach leaves
50 g/2 oz watercress
30 ml/2 tbsp chilli sauce
30 ml/2 tbsp dry sherry
15 ml/1 tbsp light soy sauce
15 ml/1 tbsp tomato ketchup
10 ml/2 tsp olive oil
8 shallots, finely chopped
1 garlic clove, crushed
350 g/12 oz skinless, boneless
  chicken breast, cut into thin strips
1 red pepper, seeded and sliced
175 g/6 oz mangetouts, trimmed
400 g/14 oz can baby sweet corn,
  drained and halved
275 g/10 oz can brown rice
salt and ground black pepper
parsley sprig, to garnish

mixed salad leaves   *spinach*   *watercress*   *chilli sauce*   *dry sherry*

light soy sauce   *tomato ketchup*   *olive oil*   *shallots*   *garlic*

chicken breasts   *red pepper*   *mange-touts*   *baby sweetcorn*   *brown rice*

1 Arrange the mixed salad leaves, tearing up any large ones, and the spinach leaves on a serving dish. Add the watercress and toss to mix.

2 In a small bowl, mix together the chilli sauce, sherry, soy sauce and tomato ketchup and set aside.

3 Heat the oil in a large non-stick frying pan or wok. Add the shallots and garlic and stir-fry over a medium heat for 1 minute.

4 Add the chicken and stir-fry for 3–4 minutes.

NUTRITIONAL NOTES
PER PORTION:

ENERGY 188Kcals/795KJ PROTEIN 19.22g
FAT 2.81g SATURATED FAT 0.52g
CARBOHYDRATE 21.39g FIBRE 3.07g
ADDED SUGAR 0.71g SODIUM 1.07g

COOK'S TIP
Use other lean meat such as turkey breast, beef or pork in place of the chicken.

5 Add the pepper, mangetouts, sweetcorn and rice and stir-fry for 2–3 minutes.

6 Pour in the chilli sauce mixture and stir-fry for 2–3 minutes, until hot and bubbling. Season to taste. Spoon the chicken mixture over the salad leaves, toss together to mix and serve immediately, garnished with fresh parsley.

Grilled Chicken Salad with Lavender and Sweet Herbs

Lavender may seem like an odd salad ingredient, but its delightful scent has a natural affinity with sweet garlic, orange and other wild herbs. A serving of corn meal polenta makes this salad both filling and delicious.

Serves 4

INGREDIENTS
4 boneless chicken breasts
850 ml/1½ pints/3¾ cups light chicken stock
175 g/6 oz/1 cup fine polenta or corn meal
50 g/2 oz butter
450 g/1 lb young spinach
175 g/6 oz lamb's lettuce
8 sprigs fresh lavender
8 small tomatoes, halved
salt and black pepper

LAVENDER MARINADE
6 fresh lavender flowers
10 ml/2 tsp finely grated orange zest
2 cloves garlic, crushed
10 ml/2 tsp clear honey
salt
30 ml/2 tbsp olive oil, French or Italian
10 ml/2 tsp chopped fresh thyme
10 ml/2 tsp chopped fresh marjoram

lavender   *chicken breasts*

1 To make the marinade, strip the lavender flowers from the stems and combine with the orange zest, garlic, honey and salt. Add the olive oil and herbs. Slash the chicken deeply, spread the mixture over the chicken and leave to marinate in a cool place for at least 20 minutes.

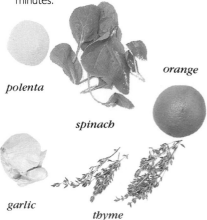

polenta

spinach

orange

garlic

thyme

2 To make the polenta, bring the chicken stock to the boil in a heavy saucepan. Add the corn meal in a steady stream, stirring all the time until thick: this will take 2–3 minutes. Turn the cooked polenta out on to a 2.5-cm/1-in-deep buttered tray and allow to cool.

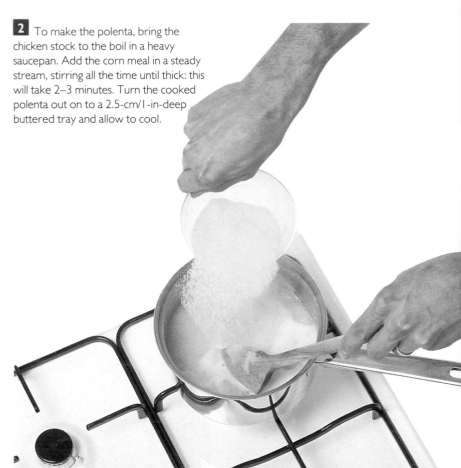

3 Heat the grill (broiler) to a moderate temperature. (If using a barbecue, let the embers settle to a steady glow.) Grill (broil) the chicken for about 15 minutes, turning once.

4 Cut the polenta into 2.5 cm/1 in cubes with a wet knife. Heat the butter in a large frying-pan (skillet) and fry the polenta until golden.

COOK'S TIP

Lavender marinade is a delicious flavouring for salt-water fish as well as chicken. Try it over grilled cod, haddock, halibut, sea bass and bream.

NUTRITIONAL NOTES
Per portion:

ENERGY 352 Kcals/1479 KJ **FAT** 9.4 g
SATURATED FAT 2.1 g
CHOLESTEROL 43.3 mg

5 Wash the salad leaves and spin dry, then divide between 4 large plates. Slice each chicken breast and lay over the salad. Place the polenta among the salad, decorate with sprigs of lavender and tomatoes, season and serve.

Lemon Chicken Stir-fry

It is essential to prepare all the ingredients before you begin so they are ready to cook. This dish is cooked in minutes.

Serves 4

INGREDIENTS
4 boned and skinned chicken breasts
15 ml/1 tbsp light soy sauce
75 ml/5 tbsp cornflour
1 bunch spring onions
1 lemon
1 garlic clove, crushed
15 ml/1 tbsp caster sugar
30 ml/2 tbsp sherry
150 ml/¼ pint/⅔ cup chicken stock
60 ml/4 tbsp olive oil
salt and freshly ground black pepper

NUTRITIONAL NOTES
PER PORTION:
ENERGY 298 Kcals/1249 KJ **FAT** 9.9 g
SATURATED FAT 2.13 g
CHOLESTEROL 53.8 mg

1 Divide the chicken breasts into two natural fillets. Place each between two sheets of clear film and flatten to a thickness of 5 mm/¼ in with a rolling pin.

2 Cut into 2.5 cm/1 in strips across the grain of the fillets. Put the chicken into a bowl with the soy sauce and toss to coat. Sprinkle over 60 ml/4 tbsp cornflour to coat each piece.

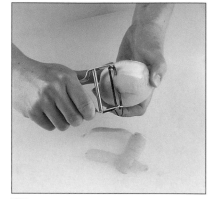

3 Trim the roots off the spring onions and cut diagonally into 1 cm/½ in pieces. With a swivel peeler, remove the lemon rind in thin strips and cut into fine shreds, or, if in a hurry, grate finely. Reserve the lemon juice. Have ready the garlic, sugar, sherry, stock, lemon juice and remaining cornflour blended to a paste with water.

caster sugar

garlic

olive oil   *spring onions*

lemon

soy sauce

cornflour

chicken breasts

4 Heat the oil in a wok or large frying pan and cook the chicken very quickly in small batches for 3–4 minutes until lightly coloured. Remove and keep warm while frying the rest of the chicken.

5 Add the spring onions and garlic to the pan and cook for 2 minutes.

6 Add the remaining ingredients and bring to the boil, stirring until thickened. Add more sherry or stock if necessary and stir until the chicken is evenly covered with sauce. Reheat for 2 more minutes. Serve immediately.

Chicken and Bean Bake

A delicious combination of chicken, fresh tarragon and mixed beans, topped with a layer of tender potatoes, ideal served with broccoli florets and baby carrots for a filling family meal.

Serves 6

INGREDIENTS
900 g/2 lb potatoes
50 g/2 oz/½ cup reduced-fat mature
  Cheddar cheese, finely grated
600 ml/1 pint/2½ cups skimmed
  milk, plus 30–45 ml/2–3 tbsp
  skimmed milk
30 ml/2 tbsp chopped fresh chives
2 leeks, washed and sliced
1 onion, sliced
30 ml/2 tbsp dry white wine
40 g/1½ oz/3 tbsp half-fat spread
40 g/1½ oz/⅓ cup plain
  wholemeal flour
300 ml/½ pint/1¼ cups chicken
  stock, cooled
350 g/12 oz cooked skinless
  chicken breast, diced
225 g/8 oz/3 cups brown cap
  mushrooms, sliced
300 g/11 oz can red kidney beans
400 g/14 oz can flageolet beans
400 g/14 oz can black-eyed beans
30–45 ml/2–3 tbsp chopped
  fresh tarragon
salt and ground black pepper

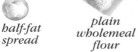

potatoes

reduced-fat mature Cheddar cheese

skimmed milk

fresh chives

leeks

onion

cooked chicken breasts

dry white wine

half-fat spread

plain wholemeal flour

chicken stock

flageolet beans

black-eyed beans

brown cap mushrooms

red kidney beans

fresh tarragon

1 Preheat the oven to 200°C/400°F/Gas 6. Cut the potatoes into chunks and cook in lightly salted, boiling water for 15–20 minutes, until tender. Drain thoroughly and mash. Add the cheese, 30–45 ml/2–3 tbsp milk and chives, season to taste and mix well. Keep warm and set aside.

2 Meanwhile, put the leeks and onion in a saucepan with the wine. Cover and cook gently for 10 minutes, until the vegetables are just tender, stirring occasionally.

3 In the meantime, put the half-fat spread, flour, remaining milk and stock in a saucepan. Heat gently, whisking continuously, until the sauce comes to the boil and thickens. Simmer gently for 3 minutes, stirring.

4 Remove the pan from the heat and add the leek mixture, chicken and mushrooms and mix well.

5 Add all the drained beans to the sauce and stir in with the tarragon and seasoning. Heat gently until the chicken mixture is piping hot, stirring.

COOK'S TIP

Sweet potatoes in place of
standard potatoes work just as
well in this recipe, and turkey or
lean ham can be used in place of
the chicken for a change.

6 Transfer it to an ovenproof dish
and spoon or pipe the potato mixture
over the top, to cover the chicken
mixture completely. Bake for about
30 minutes, until the potato topping
is crisp and golden brown. Serve
immediately.

NUTRITIONAL NOTES

Per portion:

ENERGY 445 Kcals/1871 KJ **FAT** 8.9 g
SATURATED FAT 1.9 g
CHOLESTEROL 50.4 mg

Chicken and Apricot Filo Pie

Filo is the low fat cook's best friend, as it contains little fat and needs only a light brushing of melted butter to create a crisp crust.

Serves 6

INGREDIENTS

75 g/3 oz/½ cup bulgur wheat
120 ml/4 fl oz/½ cup boiling water
30 ml/2 tbsp butter
1 onion, chopped
450 g/1 lb lean minced chicken
50 g/2 oz/¼ cup ready-to-eat dried
  apricots, finely chopped
25 g/1 oz/¼ cup blanched
  almonds, chopped
5 ml/1 tsp ground cinnamon
2.5 ml/½ tsp ground allspice
60 ml/4 tbsp low fat fromage frais
15 ml/1 tbsp snipped fresh chives
30 ml/2 tbsp chopped fresh parsley
10 large sheets of filo pastry
salt and ground black pepper
chives, to garnish

NUTRITIONAL NOTES
PER PORTION:

ENERGY 239 Kcals/1004 KJ **FAT** 6.3 g
SATURATED FAT 1.6 g
CHOLESTEROL 43.0 mg

bulgur wheat

onion

1 Preheat the oven to 200°C/400°F/ Gas 6. Put the bulgur wheat in a bowl and add the boiling water. Leave to soak for 5–10 minutes, until all the water is absorbed.

2 Heat 15 ml/1 tbsp of the butter in a non-stick pan, and gently fry the onion and chicken until pale golden.

3 Stir in the apricots, almonds and bulgur. Cook for 2 minutes more. Remove from the heat and stir in the cinnamon, allspice, fromage frais, fresh chives and parsley. Season to taste with salt and pepper.

4 Melt the remaining butter. Cut the filo pastry into 25 cm/10 in rounds. Cover the pastry rounds with a cloth.

ground allspice

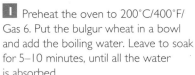
dried apricots

ground cinnamon

minced chicken

fromage frais

chives

filo pastry

5 Line a 23 cm/9 in loose-based flan tin with three of the pastry rounds, brushing each one lightly with butter as you layer them. Spoon in the chicken mixture, then cover with three more rounds, brushed with butter as before.

6 Crumple the remaining rounds and place them on top of the pie, then brush with melted butter. Bake for about 30 minutes, until golden brown and crisp. Serve the pie hot or cold, cut in wedges and garnished with chives.

Chicken with Cashews

This hot and spicy Indian dish has a deliciously thick and nutty sauce, and is best served with plenty of plain boiled rice.

Serves 6

INGREDIENTS
2 onions
30 ml/2 tbsp tomato purée
50 g/2 oz/½ cup cashew nuts
7.5 ml/1½ tsp garam masala
1 garlic clove, crushed
5 ml/1 tsp chilli powder
15 ml/1 tbsp lemon juice
1.5 ml/¼ tsp ground turmeric
5 ml/1 tsp salt
15 ml/1 tbsp low fat natural yogurt
15 ml/1 tbsp corn oil
15 ml/1 tbsp chopped fresh
  coriander, plus extra to garnish
15 ml/1 tbsp sultanas
450 g/1 lb boned and skinned
  chicken breasts, cubed
175 g/6 oz/1½ cups button
  mushrooms, halved
300 ml/½ pint/1¼ cups water

chilli powder

lemon juice

natural yogurt

button mushrooms

turmeric

onion

garlic

garam masala

corn oil

chicken

fresh coriander

cashew nuts

1 Cut the onions into quarters and place in a food processor or blender. Process for about 1 minute.

2 Add the tomato purée, cashews, garam masala, garlic, chilli powder, lemon juice, turmeric, salt and yogurt to the onions. Process for 1–1½ minutes more.

3 Heat the oil in a saucepan and fry the spice mixture over a medium heat for about 2 minutes, lowering the heat if necessary.

4 Add the coriander, sultanas and chicken and stir-fry for 1 minute more.

5 Add the mushrooms, pour in the water and bring to a simmer. Cover the pan and cook over a low heat for about 10 minutes.

6 After this time, check that the chicken is cooked through and the sauce is thick. Cook for a little longer if necessary. Garnish with chopped fresh coriander and serve.

NUTRITIONAL NOTES
PER PORTION:

ENERGY 187 Kcals/784 KJ **FAT** 9.8 g
SATURATED FAT 1.9 g
CHOLESTEROL 43.2 mg

sultanas

Chicken in Spicy Yogurt

Plan this dish well in advance; the extra-long marinating time is necessary to develop a really mellow spicy flavour.

NUTRITIONAL NOTES

PER PORTION:

ENERGY 158 Kcals/663 KJ **FAT** 5.1 g
SATURATED FAT 1.6 g
CHOLESTEROL 58 mg

Serves 6

INGREDIENTS
6 chicken pieces
juice of 1 lemon
5 ml/1 tsp salt

FOR THE MARINADE
5 ml/1 tsp coriander seeds
10 ml/2 tsp cumin seeds
6 cloves
2 bay leaves
1 onion, quartered
2 garlic cloves
5 cm/2 in piece root ginger, peeled and roughly chopped
2.5 ml/1/2 tsp chilli powder
5 ml/1 tsp turmeric
150 ml/1/4 pint/2/3 cup natural yogurt
lemon, lime or coriander, to garnish

lemon

yogurt

coriander seeds

root ginger

onion

bay leaves

garlic

chilli powder

turmeric

cloves

cumin seeds

1 Skin the chicken joints and make deep slashes in the fleshiest parts with a sharp knife. Sprinkle over the lemon and salt and rub in.

2 Spread the coriander and cumin seeds, cloves and bay leaves in the bottom of a large frying pan and dry-fry over a moderate heat until the bay leaves are crispy.

3 Cool the spices and grind coarsely with a pestle and mortar.

4 Finely mince the onion, garlic and ginger in a food processor or blender. Add the ground spices, chilli, turmeric and yogurt, then strain in the lemon juice from the chicken.

5 Arrange the chicken in a single layer in a roasting tin. Pour over the marinade, then cover and chill for 24–36 hours.

6 Occasionally turn the chicken pieces in the marinade. Preheat the oven to 200°C/400°F/Gas 6. Cook the chicken for 45 minutes. Serve hot or cold, garnished with fresh leaves and slices of lemon or lime.

Grilled Chicken with Pica de Gallo Salsa

This dish originates from Mexico. Its hot fruity flavours form the essence of Tex-Mex Cooking.

NUTRITIONAL NOTES
PER PORTION:

ENERGY 197 Kcals/826 KJ **FAT** 7.1 g
SATURATED FAT 1.7 g
CHOLESTEROL 53.8 mg

Serves 4

INGREDIENTS
4 chicken breasts
pinch of celery salt and cayenne
    pepper combined
30 ml/2 tbsp vegetable oil
corn chips, to serve

FOR THE SALSA
275 g/10 oz watermelon
175 g/6 oz canteloupe melon
1 small red onion
1–2 green chillies
30 ml/2 tbsp lime juice
60 ml/4 tbsp chopped fresh coriander
pinch of salt

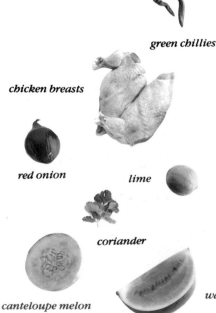

green chillies

chicken breasts

red onion

lime

coriander

canteloupe melon

watermelon

1 Preheat a moderate grill. Slash the chicken breasts deeply to speed up the cooking time.

2 Season the chicken with celery salt and cayenne, brush with oil and grill for about 15 minutes.

3 To make the salsa, remove the rind and as many seeds as you can from the melons. Finely dice the flesh and put it into a bowl.

4 Finely chop the onion, split the chillies (discarding the seeds which contain most of the heat) and chop. Take care not to touch sensitive skin areas when handling cut chillies. Mix with the melon.

5 Add the lime juice and chopped coriander, and season with a pinch of salt. Turn the salsa into a small bowl.

6 Arrange the grilled chicken on a plate and serve with the salsa and a handful of corn chips.

Chicken and Bean Risotto

Rice, beans, sweetcorn and broccoli add fibre to this healthy chicken dish.

Serves 4–6

INGREDIENTS
1 onion, chopped
2 garlic cloves, crushed
1 fresh red chilli, finely chopped
175 g/6 oz/2¼ cups
  mushrooms, sliced
2 celery sticks, chopped
225 g/8 oz/1 cup long grain
  brown rice
450 ml/¾ pint/1⅞ cups
  chicken stock
150 ml/¼ pint/⅔ cup white wine
225 g/8 oz cooked skinless chicken
  breast, diced
400 g/14 oz can red kidney beans
200 g/7 oz can sweetcorn kernels
115 g/4 oz/⅔ cup sultanas
175 g/6 oz small broccoli florets
30–45 ml/2–3 tbsp chopped fresh
  mixed herbs
salt and ground black pepper

onion

garlic

red chilli

celery

long grain brown rice

mushrooms

chicken stock

dry white wine

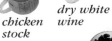
chicken breasts

red kidney beans

sweetcorn

sultanas

broccoli

fresh mixed herbs

1 Put the onion, garlic, chilli, mushrooms, celery, rice, stock and wine in a saucepan. Cover, bring to the boil and simmer for 25 minutes.

2 Stir in the chicken, kidney beans, sweetcorn and sultanas. Cook for a further 10 minutes, until almost all the liquid has been absorbed.

NUTRITIONAL NOTES
PER PORTION:

ENERGY 353 Kcals/1482 KJ **FAT** 4.2 g
SATURATED FAT 1.1 g
CHOLESTEROL 28.5 mg

3 Meanwhile, cook the broccoli in boiling water for 5 minutes, then drain thoroughly.

4 Stir in the broccoli and chopped herbs, season to taste and serve immediately.

COOK'S TIP
Use 5 ml/1 tsp hot chilli powder in place of the fresh chilli.

Chicken Fried Noodles

This delicious dish makes a filling meal. Take care when frying vermicelli as it has a tendency to spit when added to hot oil.

Serves 4

INGREDIENTS

125 ml/4 fl oz/½ cup vegetable oil
225 g/8 oz rice vermicelli
150 g/5 oz French beans, topped,
    tailed and halved lengthwise
1 onion, finely chopped
2 boneless, skinless chicken breasts,
    about 175 g/6 oz each, cut
    into strips
5 ml/1 tsp chilli powder
225 g/8 oz cooked prawns
45 ml/3 tbsp dark soy sauce
45 ml/3 tbsp white wine vinegar
10 ml/2 tsp caster sugar
fresh coriander sprigs, to garnish

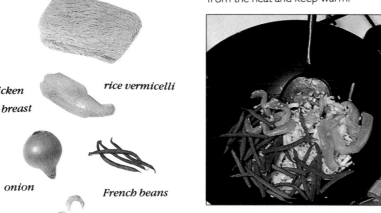

rice vermicelli

chicken breast

onion

French beans

prawns

NUTRITIONAL NOTES

PER PORTION:

ENERGY 487 Kcals/2045 KJ **FAT** 15 g
SATURATED FAT 2.6 g
CHOLESTEROL 83.2 mg

1 Heat the wok, then add 60 ml/4 tbsp of the oil. Break up the vermicelli into 7.5 cm/3 in lengths. When the oil is hot, fry the vermicelli in batches. Remove from the heat and keep warm.

2 Heat the remaining oil in the wok, then add the French beans, onion and chicken and stir-fry for 3 minutes until the chicken is cooked.

3 Sprinkle in the chilli powder. Stir in the prawns, soy sauce, vinegar and sugar, and stir-fry for 2 minutes.

4 Serve the chicken, prawns and vegetables on the vermicelli, garnished with sprigs of fresh coriander.

Balti Chicken in Orange and Black Pepper Sauce

Use virtually fat-free fromage frais to give this sauce a rich, creamy flavour.

Serves 4

INGREDIENTS
225g/8oz fromage frais
50ml/2 fl oz/¼ cup natural low
 fat yogurt
120ml/4 fl oz/½ cup orange juice
7.5ml/1½ tsp ginger pulp
5ml/1 tsp garlic pulp
5ml/1 tsp freshly ground
 black pepper
5ml/1 tsp salt
5ml/1 tsp ground coriander
1 baby chicken, about 675g/1½lb,
 skinned and cut into 8 pieces
15ml/1 tbsp corn oil
1 bay leaf
1 large onion, chopped
15ml/1 tbsp fresh mint leaves
1 green chilli, seeded and chopped

orange
juice

ginger
pulp   chicken

    onion

 mint

  green   garlic   fromage
  chilli   pulp   frais
           bay leaf

NUTRITIONAL NOTES
Per portion:
ENERGY 199 K Cals/836 K J **PROTEIN** 26.07g
FAT 5.11g **SATURATED FAT** 1.06g
CARBOHYDRATE 13.20g **FIBRE** 1.02g
ADDED SUGAR 1.20g **SALT** 0.6g

1 In a bowl, whisk together the fromage frais, yogurt, orange juice, ginger, garlic, pepper, salt and coriander.

2 Pour this over the chicken and set aside for 3–4 hours.

COOK'S TIP
If you prefer the taste of curry leaves, you can use them instead of the bay leaf, but you need to double the quantity.

3 Heat the oil with the bay leaf in a non-stick wok or frying pan and fry the onion until soft.

4 Pour in the chicken mixture and stir-fry for 3–5 minutes over a medium heat. Lower the heat, cover with a lid and cook for 7–10 minutes, adding a little water if the sauce is too thick. Finally add the fresh mint and chilli and serve.

Balti Chicken in a Thick Creamy Coconut Sauce

If you like the flavour of coconut, you will really love this curry.

Serves 4

INGREDIENTS

15ml/1 tbsp ground almonds
15ml/1 tbsp desiccated coconut
85ml/3 fl oz/⅔ cup coconut milk
175g/6oz/⅔ cup fromage frais
7.5ml/1½ tsp ground coriander
5ml/1 tsp chilli powder
5ml/1 tsp garlic pulp
7.5ml/1½ tsp ginger pulp
5ml/1 tsp salt
15ml/1 tbsp corn oil
225g/8oz skinned chicken, cubed
3 green cardamom pods
1 bay leaf
1 dried red chilli, crushed
30ml/2 tbsp chopped
   fresh coriander

almonds
chilli powder
fresh coriander
chicken
garlic pulp
bay leaf
cardamom
red chilli
salt
coconut
fromage frais
coconut milk
ginger pulp
ground coriander

NUTRITIONAL NOTES

Per portion:

ENERGY 166 K Cals/696 K J   **PROTEIN** 18.58g
FAT 8.30g   **SATURATED FAT** 2.84g
CARBOHYDRATE 5.52g   **FIBRE** 0.95g
ADDED SUGAR 0.86g
SALT 0.57g

1   Using a heavy-based saucepan, dry-roast the ground almonds and desiccated coconut until they turn a shade darker. Transfer to a mixing bowl.

2   Add the coconut milk, fromage frais, ground coriander, chilli powder, garlic, ginger and salt to a mixing bowl.

COOK'S TIP

Cut the chicken into small, equal-size cubes for quick and even cooking.

3   Heat the oil in a non-stick wok or frying pan and add the chicken cubes, cardamoms and bay leaf. Stir-fry for about 2 minutes to seal the chicken.

4   Pour in the coconut milk mixture and blend everything together. Lower the heat, add the chilli and fresh coriander, cover and cook for 10–12 minutes, stirring occasionally. Uncover, then stir and cook for a further 2 minutes before serving.

Country Chicken Casserole

Succulent chicken joints in a vegetable sauce are
excellent served with brown rice or pasta.

NUTRITIONAL NOTES
PER PORTION:

ENERGY 377 Kcals/1585 KJ **FAT** 11.7 g
SATURATED FAT 2.9 g
CHOLESTEROL 76.1 mg

Serves 4

INGREDIENTS
2 chicken breasts, skinned
2 chicken legs, skinned
30 ml/2 tbsp plain wholemeal flour
15 ml/1 tbsp sunflower oil
300 ml/½ pint/1¼ cups chicken stock
300 ml/½ pint/1¼ cups white wine
30 ml/2 tbsp passata
15 ml/1 tbsp tomato purée
4 rashers lean smoked back bacon
1 large onion, sliced
1 garlic clove, crushed
1 green pepper, seeded and sliced
225 g/8 oz/3 cups button
  mushrooms
225 g/8 oz carrots, sliced
1 bouquet garni
225 g/8 oz frozen Brussels sprouts
175 g/6 oz/1½ cups frozen
  petit pois
salt and ground black pepper
chopped fresh parsley, to garnish

*chicken breasts
and legs*

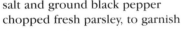

*plain
wholemeal
flour*

*sunflower
oil*

*chicken
stock*

*dry
white
wine*

passata

*tomato
purée*

*smoked back
bacon*

onion

garlic

*green
pepper*

*button
mushrooms*

carrots

*bouquet
garni*

*Brussels
sprouts*

petit pois

1 Preheat the oven to 180°C/350°F/
Gas 4. Coat the chicken joints with
seasoned flour.

2 Heat the oil in a large flameproof
casserole, add the chicken and cook
until browned all over. Remove the
chicken using a slotted spoon and
keep warm.

3 Add any remaining flour to the pan
and cook for 1 minute. Gradually stir
in the stock and wine, then add the
passata and tomato purée.

4 Bring to the boil, stirring continuously, then add the chicken, bacon, onion,
garlic, pepper, mushrooms, carrots and bouquet garni and stir. Cover and bake for
1½ hours, stirring once or twice.

COOK'S TIP
Use fresh Brussels sprouts and peas if available, and use red wine in place of white for a change.

5 Stir in the Brussels sprouts and petit pois, re-cover and bake for a further 30 minutes.

6 Remove and discard the bouquet garni. Add seasoning to the casserole, garnish with chopped fresh parsley and serve immediately.

Tagine of Chicken

Based on a traditional Moroccan dish. The chicken and couscous can be cooked the day before and reheated for serving.

Serves 8

INGREDIENTS
8 chicken legs (thighs and drumsticks)
30 ml/2 tbsp olive oil
1 medium onion, finely chopped
2 garlic cloves, crushed
5 ml/1 tsp ground turmeric
2.5 ml/½ tsp ground ginger
2.5 ml/½ tsp ground cinnamon
450 ml/¾ pint/1⅞ cups chicken
    stock
150 g/5 oz/1¼ cups stoned green
    olives
1 lemon, sliced
salt and freshly ground black pepper
fresh coriander sprigs, to garnish

FOR THE VEGETABLE COUSCOUS
600 ml/1 pint/2½ cups chicken stock
450 g/1 lb couscous
4 courgettes, thickly sliced
2 carrots, thickly sliced
2 small turnips, peeled and cubed
45 ml/3 tbsp olive oil
1 × 450 g/15 oz can chick peas,
    drained

1 Preheat the oven to 180°C/350°F/ Gas 4. Cut the chicken legs into two through the joint.

2 Heat the oil in a large flameproof casserole and working in batches, brown the chicken on both sides. Remove and keep warm.

3 Add the onion and crushed garlic to the flameproof casserole and cook gently until tender. Add the spices and cook for 1 minute. Pour over the stock, bring to the boil, and return the chicken. Cover and bake for 45 minutes until tender.

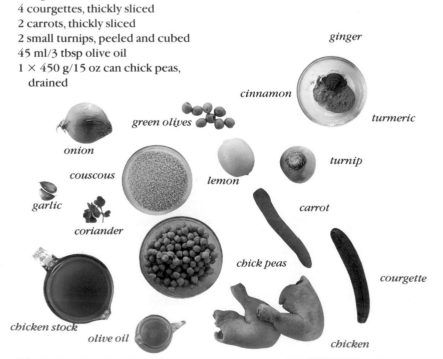

ginger
cinnamon
turmeric
green olives
onion
turnip
couscous
lemon
garlic
carrot
coriander
chick peas
courgette
chicken stock
olive oil
chicken

4 Transfer the chicken to a bowl, cover and keep warm. Remove any fat from the cooking liquid and boil to reduce by one-third. Meanwhile, blanch the olives and lemon slices in a pan of boiling water for 2 minutes until the lemon skin is tender. Drain and add to the cooking liquid, adjusting the seasoning to taste.

5 To cook the couscous, bring the stock to the boil in a large pan and sprinkle in the couscous slowly, stirring all the time. Remove from the heat, cover and leave to stand for 5 minutes.

COOK'S TIP

The couscous can be reheated with 30 ml/2 tbsp olive oil in a steamer over a pan of boiling water, stirring occasionally. If you cook the chicken in advance, undercook the chicken by 15 minutes and reheat in the oven for 20–30 minutes.

NUTRITIONAL NOTES

Per portion:

ENERGY 350 Kcals/1470 KJ **FAT** 10.8 g
SATURATED FAT 2.3 g
CHOLESTEROL 65.7 mg

6 Meanwhile, cook the vegetables, drain and put them into a large bowl. Add the couscous and oil and season. Stir the grains to fluff them up, add the chick peas and finally the chopped coriander. Spoon onto a large serving plate, cover with the chicken pieces, and spoon over the liquid. Garnish with fresh coriander sprigs.

Oat-crusted Chicken with Sage

Oats make a good coating for savoury foods and sealing in the natural juices means that you do not need to add extra fat.

Serves 4

INGREDIENTS

45 ml/3 tbsp skimmed milk
10 ml/2 tsp mustard powder
40 g/1½ oz/½ cup rolled oats
45 ml/3 tbsp chopped sage leaves
8 skinned chicken thighs or drumsticks
120 ml/4 fl oz/½ cup low fat fromage frais
5 ml/1 tsp wholegrain mustard
salt and ground black pepper
fresh sage leaves, to garnish

skimmed milk

mustard powder

rolled oats

sage leaves

fromage frais

chicken thighs

wholegrain mustard

1 Preheat the oven to 200°C/400°F/Gas 6. Mix the milk and mustard powder in a cup. Mix the oats with 30 ml/2 tbsp of the sage in a shallow dish. Add salt and pepper to taste. Brush the chicken with the mustard and milk mixture and press into the oats to coat evenly.

2 Place the chicken on a baking sheet and bake for about 40 minutes, or until the juices run clear, not pink, when pierced through the thickest part.

3 Meanwhile, mix the low fat fromage frais, mustard and remaining sage. Season to taste. Garnish the chicken with fresh sage and serve hot or cold, with the sauce.

COOK'S TIP

If fresh sage is not available, choose another fresh herb such as thyme or parsley, instead of using a dried alternative.

NUTRITIONAL NOTES

PER PORTION:

ENERGY 214 Kcals/898 KJ **FAT** 6.6 g
SATURATED FAT 1.8 g
CHOLESTEROL 64.6 mg

Tuscan Chicken

This simple peasant casserole has all the flavours of traditional Italian ingredients.

Serves 4

INGREDIENTS
5 ml/1 tsp olive oil
8 skinned chicken thighs
1 onion, thinly sliced
2 red peppers, seeded and sliced
1 garlic clove, crushed
300 ml/½ pint/1¼ cups passata
150 ml/¼ pint/⅔ cup dry white wine
1 large fresh oregano sprig, or
  5 ml/1 tsp dried oregano
400 g/14 oz can cannellini
  beans, drained
45 ml/3 tbsp fresh white
  breadcrumbs
salt and ground black pepper

chicken thighs

olive oil

red pepper

sprig oregano

cannellini beans

onion

fresh breadcrumbs

garlic

dry white wine

1 Heat the oil in a non-stick frying pan and fry the chicken until golden brown. Remove with a slotted spoon and keep hot. Add the onion and peppers to the pan and sauté gently until softened, but not brown. Stir in the garlic.

2 Add the chicken, passata, white wine and oregano. Season well, then bring to the boil with the lid on.

NUTRITIONAL NOTES
PER PORTION:

ENERGY 248 Kcals/1045 KJ **FAT** 7.5 g
SATURATED FAT 2.1 g
CHOLESTEROL 73 mg

3 Lower the heat and simmer gently, without a lid, for 30–35 minutes or until the chicken is tender and cooked through. Stir occasionally.

4 Stir in the cannellini beans and simmer for 5 minutes more to heat through. Sprinkle evenly with the breadcrumbs and flash under a hot grill until golden brown.

Piquant Chicken with Spaghetti

Serves 4

INGREDIENTS

1 onion, finely chopped
1 carrot, diced
1 garlic clove, crushed
300 ml/½ pint/1¼ cups vegetable
    stock or water
4 small chicken breasts, boned
    and skinned
bouquet garni (bay leaf, parsley
    stalks and thyme)
115 g/4 oz button mushrooms,
    sliced thinly
5 ml/1 tsp wine vinegar or
    lemon juice
350 g/12 oz spaghetti
½ cucumber, peeled and cut
    into fingers
2 firm ripe tomatoes, skinned,
    seeded and chopped
30 ml/2 tbsp low-fat crème fraîche
15 ml/1 tbsp chopped fresh parsley
15 ml/1 tbsp snipped chives
salt and ground black pepper

carrot

chicken breasts *tomatoes*

cucumber
chives

spaghetti

thyme *parsley*

button *vegetable stock* *onion*
mushrooms

bay leaf

1 Put the onion, carrot, garlic, stock or water into a saucepan with the chicken breasts and bouquet garni. Bring to the boil, cover and simmer gently for 15–20 minutes or until tender. Transfer the chicken to a plate and cover with foil.

2 Remove the chicken and strain the liquid. Discard the vegetables and return the liquid to the pan. Add the sliced mushrooms, wine vinegar or lemon juice and simmer for 2–3 minutes until tender.

3 Cook the spaghetti in a large pan of boiling, salted water until *al dente*. Drain thoroughly.

4 Blanch the cucumber in boiling water for 10 seconds. Drain and rinse under cold water.

5 Cut the chicken breasts into bite-size pieces. Boil the stock to reduce by half, then add the chicken, tomatoes, crème fraîche, cucumber and herbs. Season with salt and pepper to taste.

6 Transfer the spaghetti to a warmed serving dish and spoon over the piquant chicken. Serve at once.

NUTRITIONAL NOTES

PER PORTION:

ENERGY 472Kcals/1981KJ **FAT** 7.6g
SATURATED FAT 2.5g **CHOLESTEROL** 65mg
CARBOHYDRATE 72g **FIBRE** 4.8g

Tortellini

Serves 6–8 as a starter or 4–6 as a main course

INGREDIENTS
115 g/4oz smoked, lean ham
115 g/4 oz chicken breast, boned
   and skinned
900 ml/1½ pint/3¾ cups chicken or
   vegetable stock
coriander stalks
30 ml/2 tbsp grated Parmesan
   cheese, plus extra for serving
1 egg, beaten, plus egg white
   for brushing
30 ml/2 tbsp chopped
   fresh coriander
1 quantity of basic pasta dough
flour, for dusting
salt and ground black pepper
coriander leaves, to garnish

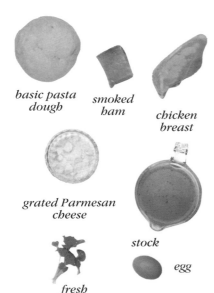

basic pasta dough   *smoked ham*   *chicken breast*

grated Parmesan cheese

stock

egg

fresh coriander

1 Cut the ham and chicken into large chunks and put them into a saucepan with 150 ml/¼ pint/⅔ cup of the chicken or vegetable stock and some coriander stalks. Bring to the boil, cover and simmer for 20 minutes until tender. Cool slightly in the stock.

2 Drain the ham and chicken and mince finely (reserve the stock). Put into a bowl with the Parmesan cheese, beaten egg, chopped coriander and season with salt and pepper.

3 Roll the pasta into thin sheets, cut into 4 cm/1½ in squares. Put 2.5 ml/½ tsp of filling on each. Brush edges with egg white and fold each square into a triangle; press out any air and seal firmly.

4 Curl each triangle around the tip of a forefinger and press the two ends together firmly.

5 Lay on a lightly floured tea towel to rest for 30 minutes before cooking.

NUTRITIONAL NOTES
PER PORTION:

ENERGY 335Kcal/1405KJ **FAT** 9.7g
SATURATED FAT 3.6g **CHOLESTEROL** 193mg
CARBOHYDRATE 39g **FIBRE** 1.6g

6 Strain the reserved stock and add to the remainder. Put into a pan and bring to the boil. Lower the heat to a gentle boil and add the tortellini. Cook for 5 minutes. Then turn off the heat, cover the pan and stand for 20–30 minutes. Serve in soup plates with some of the stock, garnish with coriander leaves. Serve grated Parmesan separately.

Stir-fried Duck with Blueberries

Serve this conveniently quick dinner party dish with sprigs of fresh mint, which will give a wonderful fresh aroma as you bring the meal to the table.

Serves 6

INGREDIENTS
2 duck breasts, about 175 g/6 oz each
30 ml/2 tbsp sunflower oil
15 ml/1 tbsp red wine vinegar
5 ml/1 tsp sugar
5 ml/1 tsp red wine
5 ml/1 tsp *crème de cassis*
115 g/4 oz fresh blueberries
15 ml/1 tbsp fresh mint, chopped
salt and freshly ground black pepper
fresh mint sprigs, to garnish

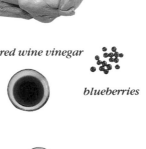

duck

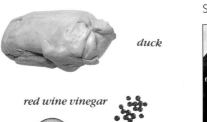

red wine vinegar

blueberries

red wine

mint

1 Cut the duck breasts into neat slices. Season well with salt and pepper.

2 Heat the wok, then add the oil. When the oil is hot, stir-fry the duck for 3 minutes.

NUTRITIONAL NOTES
PER PORTION:

ENERGY 186 Kcals/776 KJ **FAT** 11.2 g
SATURATED FAT 2.4 g

3 Add the red wine vinegar, sugar, red wine and *crème de cassis*. Bubble for 3 minutes, to reduce to a thick syrup.

4 Stir in the blueberries, sprinkle over the mint and serve garnished with sprigs of fresh mint.

Duck and Ginger Chop Suey

Chicken can also be used in this recipe, but duck gives a richer contrast of flavours.

Serves 4

INGREDIENTS
2 duck breasts, about 175 g/6 oz each
45 ml/3 tbsp sunflower oil
1 × size 4 egg, lightly beaten
1 clove garlic
175 g/6 oz beansprouts
2 slices root ginger, cut into matchsticks
10 ml/2 tsp oyster sauce
2 spring onions, cut into matchsticks
salt and freshly ground pepper

FOR THE MARINADE
15 ml/1 tbsp clear honey
10 ml/2 tsp rice wine
10 ml/2 tsp light soy sauce
10 ml/2 tsp dark soy sauce

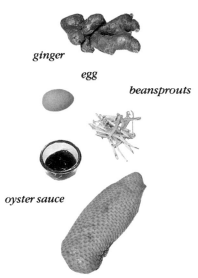

ginger

egg

beansprouts

oyster sauce

duck breast

NUTRITIONAL NOTES
PER PORTION:
ENERGY 186 Kcals/782 KJ **FAT** 7.5 g
SATURATED FAT 0.2 g

1 Remove the fat from the duck, cut the breasts into thin strips and place in a bowl. Mix the marinade ingredients together, pour over the duck, cover, chill and marinate overnight.

2 Next day, make the egg omelette. Heat a small frying pan and add 15 ml/ 1 tbsp of the oil. When the oil is hot, pour in the egg and swirl around to make an omelette. Once cooked, leave it to cool and cut into strips. Drain the duck and discard the marinade.

3 Bruise the garlic with the flat blade of a knife. Heat the wok, then add 10 ml/ 2 tsp oil. When the oil is hot, add the garlic and fry for 30 seconds, pressing it to release the flavour. Discard. Add the beansprouts with seasoning and stir-fry for 30 seconds. Transfer to a heated dish, draining off any liquid.

4 Heat the wok and add the remaining oil. When the oil is hot, stir-fry the duck for 3 minutes until cooked. Add the ginger and oyster sauce and stir-fry for a further 2 minutes. Add the beansprouts, egg strips and spring onions, stir-fry briefly and serve.

Duck Breast Salad

Serves 6

INGREDIENTS

2 duck breasts, boned
5 ml/1 tsp coriander seeds, crushed
350 g/12 oz rigatoni
150 ml/¼ pint/⅔ cup fresh
 orange juice
15 ml/1 tbsp lemon juice
10 ml/2 tsp runny honey
1 shallot, finely chopped
1 garlic clove, crushed
1 stick celery, chopped
75 g/3 oz dried cherries
45 ml/3 tbsp port
15 ml/1 tbsp chopped fresh mint,
 plus extra for garnish
30 ml/2 tbsp chopped fresh
 coriander, plus extra for garnish
1 eating apple, diced
2 oranges, segmented
salt and ground black pepper

rigatoni

port

coriander

coriander
seeds

duck breasts

orange

mint

apple

dried
cherries

shallot

garlic

celery

1 Remove the skin and fat from the duck breasts and season with salt and pepper. Rub with crushed coriander seeds. Preheat the grill, then grill for 7–10 minutes depending on size. Wrap in foil and leave for 20 minutes.

2 Cook the pasta in a large pan of boiling, salted water until *al dente*. Drain thoroughly and rinse under cold running water. Leave to cool.

3 To make the dressing, put the orange juice, lemon juice, honey, shallot, garlic, celery, cherries, port, mint and fresh coriander into a bowl, whisk together and leave to marinate for 30 minutes.

4 Slice the duck very thinly. (It should be pink in the centre.)

5 Put the pasta into a bowl, add the dressing, diced apple and segments of orange. Toss well to coat the pasta. Transfer the salad to a serving plate with the duck slices and garnish with the extra coriander and mint.

NUTRITIONAL NOTES

PER PORTION:

ENERGY 348Kcals/1460KJ **FAT** 3.8g
SATURATED FAT 0.9g **CHOLESTEROL** 55mg
CARBOHYDRATE 64g **FIBRE** 1.3g

Turkey and Tomato Hot-pot

Turkey is not just for festive occasions. Here, it's turned into tasty meatballs and simmered with rice in a tomato sauce.

Serves 4

INGREDIENTS
25 g/1 oz white bread, crusts removed
30 ml/2 tbsp skimmed milk
1 garlic clove, crushed
2.5 ml/½ tsp caraway seeds
225 g/8 oz minced turkey
1 egg white
350 ml/12 fl oz/1½ cups chicken stock
400 g/14 oz can plum tomatoes
15 ml/1 tbsp tomato purée
90 g/3½ oz/½ cup easy-cook rice
salt and freshly ground black pepper
15 ml/1 tbsp chopped fresh basil, to garnish
carrot and courgette ribbons, to serve

basil

minced turkey

rice

bread

tomato purée

plum tomatoes

caraway seeds

garlic

COOK'S TIP

To make carrot and courgette ribbons, cut the vegetables lengthways into thin strips using a vegetable peeler, and blanch or steam until cooked through.

1 Cut the bread into small cubes and put into a mixing bowl. Sprinkle over the milk and leave to soak for 5 minutes.

2 Add the garlic clove, caraway seeds, turkey, salt and freshly ground black pepper to the bread. Mix together well.

3 Whisk the egg white until stiff, then fold, half at a time, into the turkey mixture. Chill for 10 minutes in the refrigerator.

4 Put the stock, tomatoes and tomato purée into a large, heavy-based saucepan and bring to the boil.

5 Add the rice, stir and cook briskly for about 5 minutes. Turn the heat down to a gentle simmer.

6 Meanwhile, shape the turkey mixture into 16 small balls. Carefully drop them into the tomato stock and simmer for a further 8-10 minutes, or until the turkey balls and rice are cooked. Garnish with chopped basil, and serve with carrot and courgette ribbons.

Turkey Tonnato

This low fat version of the Italian dish 'vitello tonnato' is garnished with fine strips of red pepper instead of the traditional anchovy fillets.

NUTRITIONAL NOTES

Per portion:

ENERGY 235 Kcals / 988 KJ PROTEIN 35.47 g
FAT 7.09 g SATURATED FAT 1.33 g
CARBOHYDRATE 7.80 g FIBRE 1.37 g
ADDED SUGAR 1.04 g SALT 0.87 g

Serves 4

INGREDIENTS

450 g/1 lb turkey fillets
1 small onion, sliced
1 bay leaf
4 black peppercorns
350 ml/12 fl oz/1½ cups
  chicken stock
200 g/7 oz can tuna in brine, drained
75 ml/5 tbsp reduced calorie
  mayonnaise
30 ml/2 tbsp lemon juice
2 red peppers, seeded and
  thinly sliced
about 25 capers, drained
pinch of salt
mixed salad and tomatoes, to serve

tuna

lemon

onion

bay leaf

capers

mayonnaise

pepper

turkey fillet

stock

1 Put the turkey fillets in a single layer in a large, heavy-based saucepan. Add the onion, bay leaf, peppercorns and stock. Bring to the boil and reduce the heat. Cover and simmer for 12 minutes, or until tender.

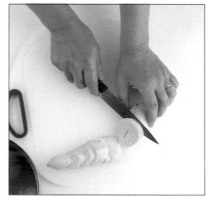

2 Turn off the heat and leave the turkey to cool in the stock, then remove with a slotted spoon. Slice thickly and arrange on a serving plate.

3 Boil the stock until reduced to about 75 ml/5 tbsp. Strain and leave to cool.

4 Put the tuna, mayonnaise, lemon juice, 45 ml/3 tbsp of the reduced stock and salt into a blender or food processor and purée until smooth.

5 Stir in enough of the remaining stock to reduce the sauce to the thickness of double cream. Spoon over the turkey.

6 Arrange the strips of red pepper in a lattice pattern over the turkey. Put a caper in the centre of each square. Chill in the refrigerator for 1 hour and serve with a fresh mixed salad and tomatoes.

Penne with Spinach

Serves 4

INGREDIENTS
225 g/8 oz fresh spinach
1 garlic clove, crushed
1 shallot or small onion,
    finely chopped
1/2 small red pepper, seeded and
    finely chopped
1 small red chilli, seeded
    and chopped
150 ml/1/4 pint/2/3 cup stock
350 g/12 oz penne
150 g/5 oz smoked turkey rashers
45 ml/3 tbsp low-fat crème fraîche
30 ml/2 tbsp grated
    Parmesan cheese
shavings of Parmesan cheese,
    to garnish

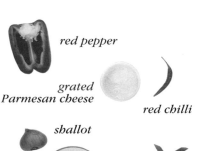

red pepper

*grated
Parmesan cheese*

red chilli

shallot

*smoked turkey
rashers*

penne

stock

*low-fat crème
fraîche*

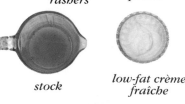

garlic

spinach

2 Put the garlic, shallot or small onion, pepper and chilli into a large frying pan. Add the stock, cover and cook for about 5 minutes until tender. Add the prepared spinach and cook quickly for a further 2–3 minutes until it has wilted.

1 Wash the spinach and remove the hard central stalks. Shred finely.

3 Cook the pasta in a large pan of boiling, salted water until *al dente*. Drain thoroughly.

4 Grill the smoked turkey rashers, cool a little, and chop finely.

5 Stir the crème fraîche and grated Parmesan into the pasta with the spinach, and toss carefully together.

6 Transfer to serving plates and sprinkle with chopped turkey and shavings of Parmesan cheese.

NUTRITIONAL NOTES
PER PORTION:

ENERGY 422Kcals/1772KJ **FAT** 6.8g
SATURATED FAT 3.2g **CHOLESTEROL** 38mg
CARBOHYDRATE 71g **FIBRE** 4.4g

Turkey and Pasta Bake

Serves 4

INGREDIENTS
275 g/10 oz minced turkey
150 g/5 oz smoked turkey
    rashers, chopped
1–2 garlic cloves, crushed
1 onion, finely chopped
2 carrots, diced
30 ml/2 tbsp concentrated
    tomato purée
300 ml/¹/₂ pint/1¹/₄ cups
    chicken stock
225 g/8 oz rigatoni
30 ml/2 tbsp grated
    Parmesan cheese
salt and ground black pepper

turkey rashers *carrots* *onion*

garlic *rigatoni*

tomato purée *Parmesan cheese*

minced turkey *stock*

1 Brown the minced turkey in a non-stick saucepan, breaking up any large pieces with a wooden spoon, until well browned all over.

2 Add the chopped turkey rashers, garlic, onion, carrots, purée, stock and seasoning. Bring to the boil, cover and simmer for 1 hour until tender.

3 Preheat the oven to 180°C/350°F/Gas 4. Cook the pasta in a large pan of boiling, salted water until *al dente*. Drain thoroughly and mix with the turkey sauce.

4 Transfer to a shallow ovenproof dish and sprinkle with grated Parmesan cheese. Bake in the preheated oven for 20–30 minutes until lightly browned.

NUTRITIONAL NOTES

PER PORTION:

ENERGY 391Kcals/1641KJ **FAT** 4.9g
SATURATED FAT 2.2g **CHOLESTEROL** 60mg
CARBOHYDRATE 55g **FIBRE** 3.5g

Macaroni Cheese

Serves 4

INGREDIENTS

1 medium onion, chopped
150 ml/¹/₄ pint/²/₃ cup vegetable or
   chicken stock
25 g/1 oz low-fat margarine
40 g/1¹/₂ oz plain flour
300 ml/¹/₂ pint/¹/₄ cup skimmed milk
50 g/2 oz reduced-fat Cheddar
   cheese, grated
5 ml/1 tsp mustard
225 g/8 oz quick-cook macaroni
4 smoked turkey rashers, cut in half
2–3 firm tomatoes, sliced
a few fresh basil leaves
15 ml/1 tbsp grated Parmesan
   cheese
salt and ground black pepper

tomatoes

onion

smoked turkey rashers

basil

Parmesan cheese

low-fat margarine

macaroni

flour

stock

skimmed milk

Cheddar cheese

1 Put the onion and stock into a nonstick frying pan. Bring to the boil, stirring occasionally and cook for 5–6 minutes or until the stock has reduced entirely and the onions are transparent.

2 Put the margarine, flour, milk, and seasoning into a saucepan and whisk together over the heat until thickened and smooth. Draw aside and add the cheese, mustard and onions.

NUTRITIONAL NOTES
Per portion:

ENERGY 152Kcals/637KJ **FAT** 2.8g
SATURATED FAT 0.7g **CHOLESTEROL** 12mg
CARBOHYDRATE 23g **FIBRE** 1.1g

3 Cook the macaroni in a large pan of boiling, salted water for 6 minutes or according to the instructions on the packet. Drain thoroughly and stir into the sauce. Transfer the macaroni to a shallow ovenproof dish.

4 Arrange the turkey rashers and tomatoes so that they overlap on top of the macaroni cheese. Tuck the basil leaves over the tomatoes. Lightly sprinkle with Parmesan cheese and grill to lightly brown the top.

Rolled Stuffed Cannelloni

Serves 4

INGREDIENTS
12 sheets lasagne
fresh basil leaves, to garnish

FILLING
2–3 garlic cloves, crushed
1 small onion, finely chopped
150 ml/¼ pint/⅔ cup white wine
450 g/1 lb minced turkey
15 ml/1 tbsp dried basil
15 ml/1 tbsp dried thyme
40 g/1½ oz fresh white
    breadcrumbs
salt and ground black pepper

SAUCE
25 g/1 oz low-fat margarine
25 g/1 oz plain flour
300 ml/½ pint/1¼ cups
    skimmed milk
4 sun-dried tomatoes, chopped
15 ml/1 tbsp mixed chopped fresh
    herbs (basil, parsley, marjoram)
30 ml/2 tbsp grated Parmesan cheese

skimmed milk

sliced white bread

lasagne

sun-dried tomatoes

minced turkey

garlic

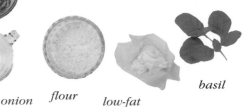

parsley

grated Parmesan cheese

white wine

onion

flour

low-fat margarine

basil

1 Put the garlic, onion and half the wine into a pan. Cover and cook for about 5 minutes until tender. Increase the heat, add the turkey and break up with a wooden spoon. Cook quickly until all the liquid has evaporated and the turkey begins to brown slightly.

2 Lower the heat, add the remaining wine, seasoning and dried herbs. Cover and cook for 20 minutes. Draw off the heat and stir in the breadcrumbs. Leave to cool.

3 Cook the lasagne sheets in a large pan of boiling, salted water until *al dente*. Cook in batches to prevent them sticking together. Drain thoroughly and rinse in cold water. Pat dry on a clean dish towel.

4 Lay the lasagne on a chopping board. Spoon the turkey mixture along one short edge and roll it up to encase the filling. Cut the tubes in half.

5 Preheat the oven to 200°C/400°F/Gas 6. Put the margarine, flour and skimmed milk into a pan, heat and whisk until smooth. Add the chopped tomatoes, fresh herbs and seasoning.

6 Spoon a thin layer of the sauce into a shallow ovenproof dish and arrange a layer of cannelloni on top. Spoon over a layer of sauce and cover with more cannelloni and sauce. Sprinkle with grated Parmesan and bake for 10–15 minutes until lightly browned. Serve at once, garnished with fresh basil leaves.

NUTRITIONAL NOTES
PER PORTION:

ENERGY 336Kcals/1411KJ **FAT** 7.4g
SATURATED FAT 2.7g **CHOLESTEROL** 65mg
CARBOHYDRATE 26g **FIBRE** 1.4g

Fish &
Seafood Dishes

Herby Fishcakes with Lemon and Chive Sauce

The wonderful flavour of fresh herbs makes these fishcakes the catch of the day.

Serves 4

INGREDIENTS
350 g/12 oz potatoes, peeled
75 ml/5 tbsp skimmed milk
350 g/12 oz haddock or hoki fillets, skinned
15 ml/1 tbsp lemon juice
15 ml/1 tbsp creamed horseradish sauce
30 ml/2 tbsp chopped fresh parsley
flour, for dusting
115 g/4 oz/2 cups fresh wholemeal breadcrumbs
salt and freshly ground black pepper
sprig of flat-leaf parsley, to garnish
mange tout and a sliced tomato and onion salad, to serve

FOR THE LEMON AND CHIVE SAUCE
thinly pared rind and juice of ½ small lemon
120 ml/4 fl oz/½ cup dry white wine
2 thin slices fresh root ginger
10 ml/2 tsp cornflour
30 ml/2 tbsp snipped fresh chives

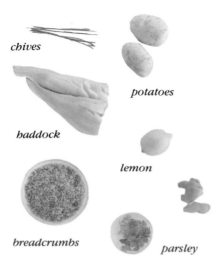

chives

potatoes

haddock

lemon

breadcrumbs

ginger

parsley

1 Cook the potatoes in a large saucepan of boiling water for 15-20 minutes. Drain and mash with the milk and season to taste.

2 Purée the fish together with the lemon juice and horseradish sauce in a blender or food processor. Mix together with the potatoes and parsley.

3 With floured hands, shape the mixture into eight fishcakes and coat with the breadcrumbs. Chill in the refrigerator for 30 minutes.

4 Cook the fishcakes under a pre-heated moderate grill for 5 minutes on each side, until browned.

5 To make the sauce, cut the lemon rind into julienne strips and put into a large saucepan together with the lemon juice, wine and ginger and season to taste.

NUTRITIONAL NOTES

Per portion:

ENERGY 266Kcals/1130KJ PROTEIN 27g
FAT 2.1g SATURATED FAT 0.4g
CARBOHYDRATE 32g
FIBRE 3.43g SUGAR 3.36g
SODIUM 289.7mg

6 Simmer uncovered for 6 minutes. Blend the cornflour with 15 ml/1 tbsp of cold water. Add to the saucepan and simmer until clear. Stir in the chives immediately before serving. Serve the sauce hot with the fishcakes, garnished with sprigs of flat-leaf parsley and accompanied with mange tout and a sliced tomato and onion salad.

Salmon and Broccoli Pilaff

This quick and easy pilaff is an ideal choice for a tasty suppertime meal.

Serves 4

INGREDIENTS
1 red onion, chopped
1 garlic clove, crushed
4 sticks celery, chopped
1 yellow pepper, seeded and diced
225 g/8 oz/1 cup brown basmati rice
600 ml/1 pint/2½ cups fish stock
300 ml/½ pint/1¼ cups white wine
400 g/14 oz can pink salmon,
  drained and flaked
400 g/14 oz can red kidney
  beans, rinsed and drained
350 g/12 oz small broccoli florets
45 ml/3 tbsp chopped fresh parsley
15-30 ml/1-2 tbsp light soy sauce
salt and ground black pepper
25 g/1 oz toasted flaked almonds,
  to garnish

red onion

garlic

celery

yellow pepper

brown basmati rice

fish stock

dry white wine

pink salmon

red kidney beans

broccoli

fresh parsley

1 Put the onion, garlic, celery, pepper, rice, stock and wine in a saucepan and bring to the boil, stirring. Simmer uncovered for 25–30 minutes, until almost all the liquid has been absorbed, stirring occasionally.

2 Stir the salmon and kidney beans into the rice mixture. Cook gently for a further 5–10 minutes until the pilaff is piping hot.

3 Meanwhile, cook the broccoli florets in boiling water for about 5 minutes, until tender. Drain thoroughly and keep warm.

4 Fold the broccoli into the pilaff, then stir in the parsley and soy sauce, and season to taste. Garnish with flaked almonds and serve immediately.

NUTRITIONAL NOTES
PER PORTION:

ENERGY 550Kcals/2319KJ PROTEIN 33.38g
FAT 11.98g SATURATED FAT 2.00g
CARBOHYDRATE 69.55g FIBRE 9.51g
ADDED SUGAR 0.34g SODIUM 1.39g

Plaice Provençal

Re-create the taste of the Mediterranean with this easy-to-make fish casserole.

Serves 4

INGREDIENTS
4 large plaice fillets
2 small red onions
120 ml/4 fl oz/½ cup vegetable stock
60 ml/4 tbsp dry red wine
1 garlic clove, crushed
2 courgettes, sliced
1 yellow pepper, seeded and sliced
400 g/14 oz can chopped tomatoes
15 ml/1 tbsp chopped fresh thyme
salt and freshly ground black pepper
potato gratin, to serve

plaice

thyme

courgettes

red onion   *pepper*

NUTRITIONAL NOTES

PER PORTION:

ENERGY 167Kcals/710KJ PROTEIN 27.5g
FAT 2.55g SATURATED FAT 0.39g
CARBOHYDRATE 6.60g
FIBRE 1.6g SUGAR 6.3g
SODIUM 222mg

1 Pre-heat the oven to 180°C/350°F/ Gas 4. Skin the plaice with a sharp knife by laying it skin-side down. Holding the tail end, push the knife between the skin and flesh in a sawing movement. Hold the knife at a slight angle with the blade towards the skin.

2 Cut each onion into eight wedges. Put into a heavy-based saucepan with the stock. Cover and simmer for 5 minutes. Uncover and continue to cook, stirring occasionally, until the stock has reduced entirely. Add the wine and garlic clove to the pan and continue to cook until the onions are soft.

3 Add the courgettes, yellow pepper, tomatoes and thyme and season to taste. Simmer for 3 minutes. Spoon the sauce into a large casserole.

4 Fold each fillet in half and place on top of the sauce. Cover and cook in the pre-heated oven for 15-20 minutes until the fish is opaque and cooked. Serve with potato gratin.

Spicy Seafood and Okra Stew

This spicy combination of seafood and vegetables is good served with herbed brown rice.

Serves 4–6

INGREDIENTS

10 ml/2 tsp olive oil
1 onion, chopped
1 garlic clove, crushed
2 sticks celery, chopped
1 red pepper, seeded and diced
5 ml/1 tsp each ground coriander, ground cumin and ground ginger
2.5 ml/½ tsp hot chilli powder
2.5 ml/½ tsp garam masala
30 ml/2 tbsp plain wholemeal flour
300 ml/½ pint/1¼ cups each fish stock and dry white wine
225 g/8 oz can chopped tomatoes
225 g/8 oz okra, trimmed and sliced
225 g/8 oz/3 cups mushrooms, sliced
450 g/1 lb frozen cooked, shelled seafood, defrosted
175 g/6 oz/1 cup frozen sweetcorn kernels
225 g/8 oz/1 cup long grain brown rice
30–45 ml/2–3 tbsp chopped fresh mixed herbs
salt and ground black pepper
fresh parsley sprigs, to garnish

1 Heat the oil in a large saucepan. Add the onion, garlic, celery and pepper and cook for 5 minutes, stirring occasionally.

2 Add the spices and cook for 1 minute, stirring, then add the flour and cook for a further 1 minute, stirring.

3 Gradually stir in the stock and wine and add the tomatoes, okra and mushrooms. Bring to the boil, stirring continuously, then cover and simmer for 20 minutes, stirring occasionally.

4 Stir in the seafood and sweetcorn and cook for a further 10–15 minutes, until piping hot.

olive oil • *onion* • *garlic* • *celery* • *red pepper* • *ground coriander*

ground cumin • *ground ginger* • *hot chilli powder* • *garam masala* • *plain wholemeal flour*

fish stock • *dry white wine* • *chopped tomatoes* • *okra* • *mushrooms*

seafood • *sweetcorn* • *long grain brown rice* • *fresh mixed herbs*

NUTRITIONAL NOTES

PER PORTION:

ENERGY 541Kcals/2284KJ PROTEIN 34.96g
FAT 7.18g SATURATED FAT 1.42g
CARBOHYDRATE 76.05g FIBRE 7.25g
ADDED SUGAR 0.01g SODIUM 1.35g

COOK'S TIP
Use fresh cooked seafood in place of the frozen if it is available.

5 Meanwhile, cook the rice in a large saucepan of lightly salted, boiling water for about 35 minutes, until tender.

6 Rinse the rice in fresh boiling water and drain thoroughly, then toss together with the mixed herbs. Season the stew and serve on a bed of herby rice. Garnish with fresh parsley sprigs.

Marinated Monkfish and Mussel Skewers

You can cook these fish kebabs on the barbecue – when the weather allows!

Serves 4

INGREDIENTS
450 g/1 lb monkfish, skinned and
    boned
5 ml/1 tsp olive oil
30 ml/2 tbsp lemon juice
5 ml/1 tsp paprika
1 garlic clove, crushed
4 turkey rashers
8 cooked mussels
8 raw prawns
15 ml/1 tbsp chopped fresh dill
salt and freshly ground black pepper
lemon wedges, to garnish
salad leaves and long-grain and wild
    rice, to serve

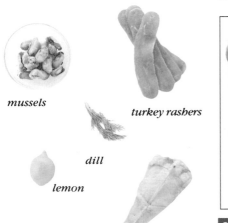

mussels

turkey rashers

dill

lemon

monkfish

NUTRITIONAL NOTES

PER PORTION:

ENERGY 159Kcals/674KJ PROTEIN 33.5g
FAT 2.52g SATURATED FAT 0.42g
CARBOHYDRATE 0.82g
FIBRE 0.13g SUGAR 0.16g
SODIUM 75mg

1 Cut the monkfish into 2.5 cm/1 in cubes and place in a shallow glass dish. Mix together the oil, lemon juice, paprika, and garlic clove and season with pepper.

2 Pour the marinade over the fish and toss to coat evenly. Cover and leave in a cool place for 30 minutes.

COOK'S TIP

Monkfish is ideal for kebabs, but can be expensive. Cod or hake are good alternatives.

3 Cut the turkey rashers in half and wrap each strip around a mussel. Thread onto skewers alternating with the fish cubes and raw prawns.

4 Cook the kebabs under a hot grill for 7-8 minutes, turning once and basting with the marinade. Sprinkle with chopped dill and salt. Garnish with lemon wedges and serve with salad and rice.

Lemon Sole baked in a Paper Case

Make sure that these paper parcels are well sealed, so that none of the delicious juices can escape.

Serves 4

INGREDIENTS
4 lemon sole fillets, each weighing
    about 150 g/5 oz
½ small cucumber, sliced
4 lemon slices
60 ml/4 tbsp dry white wine
sprigs of fresh dill, to garnish
new potatoes and braised celery,
    to serve

FOR THE YOGURT HOLLANDAISE
150 ml/¼ pint natural low fat yogurt
5 ml/1 tsp lemon juice
2 egg yolks
5 ml/1 tsp Dijon mustard
salt and freshly ground black pepper

sole

dill

egg

cucumber

lemon

mustard

NUTRITIONAL NOTES
PER PORTION:

ENERGY 186Kcals/793KJ PROTEIN 29.5g
FAT 5.4g SATURATED FAT 1.25g
CARBOHYDRATE 3.16g
FIBRE 0.05g SUGAR 3.12g
SODIUM 216mg

1 Pre-heat the oven to 180°C/350°F/ Gas 4. Cut out four heart shapes from non-stick baking paper, each about 20 × 15 cm/8 × 6 in.

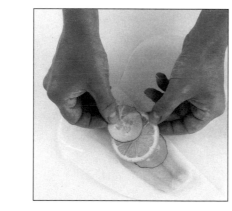

2 Place a sole fillet on one side of each heart. Arrange the cucumber and lemon slices on top of each fillet. Sprinkle with the wine and close the parcels by turning the edges of the paper and twisting to secure. Put on a baking tray and cook in the pre-heated oven for 15 minutes.

3 For the hollandaise, beat together the yogurt, lemon juice and egg yolks in a double boiler or bowl placed over a saucepan. Cook over simmering water, stirring for 15 minutes, or until thickened. (The sauce will become thinner after 10 minutes, but will thicken again.)

4 Remove from the heat and stir in the mustard. Season to taste with salt and freshly ground black pepper. Open the fish parcels, garnish with a sprig of dill and serve accompanied with the sauce, new potatoes and braised celery.

Steamed Chilli Mussels

Make sure all the mussels open when the dish is cooked as any closed ones would be dead before cooking. Add more red chillies if you really enjoy spicy food.

Serves 6

INGREDIENTS
2 fresh red chillies
6 ripe tomatoes
30 ml/2 tbsp peanut oil
2 garlic cloves, crushed
2 shallots, finely chopped
1.1 kg/2½ lb fresh mussels
30 ml/2 tbsp white wine
30ml/2 tbsp chopped fresh parsley, to garnish
French bread, to serve

mussels

red chilli

tomato

shallot

parsley

garlic

1 Roughly chop and deseed the chillies. Roughly chop the tomatoes.

2 Heat the oil in a large, heavy-based saucepan and gently sauté the garlic and shallots until soft.

NUTRITIONAL NOTES
PER PORTION:

ENERGY 106 Kcals/445.5 KJ **FAT** 5.2 g
SATURATED FAT 0.8 g

3 Stir in the tomatoes and chilli and simmer for 10 minutes.

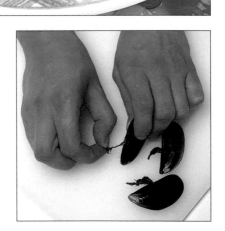

4 Clean the mussels. Add the mussels and white wine to the pan, cover and cook until all the mussel shells are open – this should take about 5 minutes. Scatter over the chopped parsley. Serve in a large bowl with chunks of fresh French bread.

Quick Tomato Sauce with Fish Balls

This quick sauce is ideal to serve with fish balls and makes a good choice for children. If you like, add a dash of chilli sauce.

Serves 4

INGREDIENTS

450 g/1 lb hoki or other white fish
   fillets, skinned
60 ml/4 tbsp fresh wholemeal
   breadcrumbs
30 ml/2 tbsp snipped chives or
   spring onions
400 g/14 oz can chopped tomatoes
50 g/2 oz/¾ cup button
   mushrooms, sliced
salt and pepper

white fish fillets

fresh wholemeal breadcrumbs

spring onions

chopped tomatoes

button mushrooms

1 Cut the fish fillets into fairly large chunks and place in a food processor. Add the wholemeal breadcrumbs and chives or spring onions. Season to taste with salt and pepper and process until the fish is finely chopped but still has some texture left.

2 Divide the fish mixture into about 16 even-size pieces, then mould them into balls with your hands.

3 Place the tomatoes and mushrooms in a wide saucepan and cook over a medium heat until boiling. Add the fish balls, cover and simmer for about 10 minutes, until cooked. Serve hot.

COOK'S TIP

Hoki is a good choice for this dish but if it's not available, use cod, haddock or whiting instead.

NUTRITIONAL NOTES
PER PORTION:

ENERGY 137 Kcals/573 KJ **FAT** 1.4 g
SATURATED FAT 0.2 g **PROTEIN** 22.3 g
CARBOHYDRATE 9.4 g **FIBRE** 1.8 g

Salmon, Courgette and Sweetcorn Frittata

A delicious and exciting change from an omelette, serve this filling frittata with a mixed tomato and pepper salad and warm wholemeal bread rolls.

NUTRITIONAL NOTES

PER PORTION:

ENERGY 336Kcals/1415KJ PROTEIN 25.85g
FAT 12.20g SATURATED FAT 3.57g
CARBOHYDRATE 32.83g FIBRE 4.34g
ADDED SUGAR 0.00g SODIUM 0.49g

COOK'S TIP

Use canned tuna or crab in place of the salmon and mushrooms instead of the courgettes.

Serves 4–6

INGREDIENTS
10 ml/2 tsp olive oil
1 onion, chopped
175 g/6 oz/1⅓ cups courgettes, thinly sliced
225 g/8 oz boiled potatoes (with skins left on), diced
3 eggs, plus 2 egg whites
30 ml/2 tbsp skimmed milk
200 g/7 oz can pink salmon in brine, drained and flaked
200 g/7 oz can sweetcorn kernels, drained
10 ml/2 tsp dried mixed herbs
50 g/2 oz/½ cup reduced-fat mature Cheddar cheese, finely grated
salt and ground black pepper
chopped fresh mixed herbs and basil leaves, to garnish

olive oil

onion

courgettes

potatoes

eggs

skimmed milk

pink salmon

sweetcorn

dried mixed herbs

Cheddar cheese

salt

black pepper

1 Heat the oil in a large non-stick frying pan. Add the onion and courgettes and cook for 5 minutes, stirring occasionally.

2 Add the potatoes and cook for 5 minutes, stirring occasionally.

3 Beat the eggs, egg whites and milk together, add the salmon, sweetcorn, herbs and seasoning and pour the mixture evenly over the vegetables.

4 Cook over a medium heat until the eggs are beginning to set and the frittata is golden brown underneath.

5 Preheat the grill. Sprinkle the cheese over and place the frittata under a medium heat until the cheese has melted and the top is golden brown.

6 Sprinkle with chopped fresh herbs, garnish with basil leaves and serve immediately cut into wedges.

Red Mullet in Banana Leaves

Watch out for the bones in red mullet as there tend to be a lot of them. Greaseproof paper packages are as effective as the banana leaves for keeping in the flavour.

Serves 4

INGREDIENTS
8 small red mullet, about 175 g/6 oz
    each
4 sprigs fresh rosemary
banana leaves or greaseproof paper
30 ml/2 tbsp olive oil
salt and freshly ground black pepper

rosemary

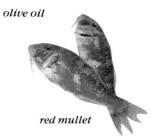

banana leaves

olive oil

red mullet

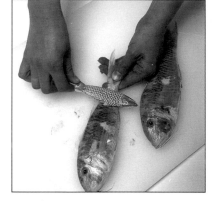

1 Pre-heat the oven to 220°C/425°F/ Gas 7. Wash, scale and gut the fish.

2 Lay the fresh rosemary inside the cavity of each fish.

3 Cut a piece of banana leaf or greaseproof paper large enough to wrap up each fish.

4 Drizzle each one with a little olive oil.

5 Season each fish well.

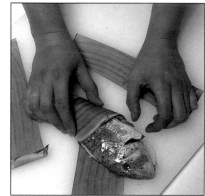

6 Wrap each fish tightly with the seam of the parcel on the underside. Bake for about 12 minutes in the pre-heated oven and unwrap to serve.

NUTRITIONAL NOTES

PER PORTION:

ENERGY 338 Kcals/1419 KJ **FAT** 15.6 g
SATURATED FAT 3.6 g

Sorrel Sauce with Salmon Steaks

The sharp flavour of the sorrel sauce balances the richness of the fish. If sorrel is not available, use finely chopped watercress instead.

Serves 2

INGREDIENTS
2 salmon steaks (about 250 g/
  9 oz each)
5 ml/1 tsp olive oil
15 g/½ oz/1 tbsp butter
2 shallots, finely chopped
45 ml/3 tbsp half fat crème fraîche
100 g/3½ oz fresh sorrel leaves,
  washed and patted dry
salt and pepper
fresh sage, to garnish

salmon

olive oil

shallots

butter

half fat crème fraîche

sorrel leaves

sage

1 Season the salmon steaks with salt and pepper. Brush a non-stick frying pan with the oil.

2 In a small saucepan, melt the butter over a medium heat. Add the shallots and fry for 2–3 minutes, stirring frequently, until just softened.

3 Add the crème fraîche and the sorrel to the shallots and cook until the sorrel is completely wilted, stirring constantly.

4 Meanwhile, place the frying pan over a medium heat until hot.

5 Add the salmon steaks and cook for about 5 minutes, turning once, until the flesh is opaque next to the bone. If you're not sure, pierce with the tip of a sharp knife; the juices should run clear.

COOK'S TIP
If preferred, cook the salmon steaks in a microwave oven for about 4–5 minutes, tightly covered, or according to the manufacturer's guidelines.

6 Arrange the salmon steaks on two warmed plates, garnish with sage and serve with the sorrel sauce.

NUTRITIONAL NOTES
PER PORTION:

ENERGY 86 Kcals/362 KJ **FAT** 6.8 g
SATURATED FAT 3.9 g **PROTEIN** 3.7 g
CARBOHYDRATE 2.8 g **FIBRE** 1.0 g

Fillets of Hake Baked with Thyme and Garlic

Quick cooking is the essence of this dish. Use the freshest garlic available and half the amount of dried thyme if fresh is not available.

Serves 4

INGREDIENTS

4 × 120g/4 oz hake fillets
1 shallot, finely chopped
2 garlic cloves, thinly sliced
4 sprigs fresh thyme, plus extra to garnish
grated rind and juice of 1 lemon, plus extra juice for drizzling
30 ml/2 tbsp extra virgin olive oil
salt and freshly ground black pepper

garlic

lemon

shallot

hake fillet

thyme

1 Pre-heat the oven to 180°C/350°F/ Gas 4. Lay the hake fillets into the base of a large roasting tin. Scatter the shallot, garlic cloves and thyme on top.

2 Season well with salt and pepper.

3 Drizzle over the lemon juice and oil. Bake for about 15 minutes in the pre-heated oven. Serve scattered with finely grated lemon rind and garnished with thyme sprigs.

VARIATION

If hake is not available you can use cod or haddock fillets for this recipe. You can also use a mixture of fresh herbs rather than just thyme.

NUTRITIONAL NOTES

PER PORTION:

ENERGY 169 Kcals/705 KJ **FAT** 8.3 g
SATURATED FAT 1.2 g

Cod and Spinach Parcels

The best way to serve this dish is to slice each parcel into about four and reveal the meaty large flakes of white fish. Drizzle the sauce over the slices.

Serves 4

INGREDIENTS
4 × 175 g/6 oz pieces of thick cod
   fillet, skinned
225 g/8 oz large spinach leaves
2.5 g/½ tsp freshly ground nutmeg
45 ml/3 tbsp white wine
salt and freshly ground black pepper

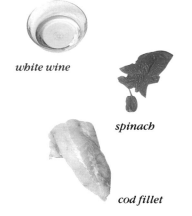

white wine

spinach

cod fillet

1 Pre-heat the oven to 180°C/350°F/ Gas 4. Season the fish well with salt and freshly ground black pepper.

2 Blanch the spinach leaves in boiling water for a minute and refresh under cold water.

NUTRITIONAL NOTES
PER PORTION:

ENERGY 162 Kcals/679 KJ **FAT** 1.7 g
SATURATED FAT 0.2 g

3 Pat the spinach leaves dry on absorbent kitchen paper.

4 Wrap the spinach around each fish fillet. Sprinkle with nutmeg. Place in a roasting tin, pour over the wine and poach for 15 minutes. Slice and serve hot.

Thick Cod Fillet with Fresh Mixed-herb Crust

Mixed fresh herbs make this a delicious crust. Season well and serve with large lemon wedges.

Serves 4

INGREDIENTS
25 g/1 oz/2 tbsp butter
15 ml/1 tbsp fresh chervil
15 ml/1 tbsp fresh parsley
15 ml/1 tbsp fresh chives
175 g/6 oz/3 cups wholemeal
  breadcrumbs
4 × 225 g/8 oz thickly cut cod fillets,
  skinned
15 ml/1 tbsp olive oil
lemon wedges, to garnish
salt and freshly ground black pepper

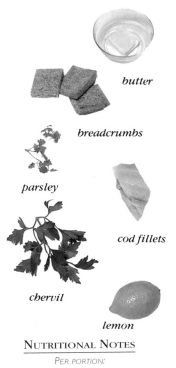

butter

breadcrumbs

parsley

cod fillets

chervil

lemon

NUTRITIONAL NOTES
PER PORTION:

ENERGY 348 Kcals/1464 KJ **FAT** 10.6 g
SATURATED FAT 2 g

1 Pre-heat the oven to 200°C/400°F/ Gas 6. Melt the butter and chop the herbs finely.

2 Mix the butter with the breadcrumbs, herbs and seasoning.

3 Press a quarter of the mixture on top of each fillet. Place on a baking sheet and drizzle over the olive oil. Bake in the pre-heated oven for 15 minutes until the fish flesh is firm and the top turns golden. Serve garnished with lemon wedges.

Mexican Barbecue Sauce

This spicy, tomato and mustard sauce is delicious served with char-grilled salmon fillets – cook them either on a barbecue or under a hot grill.

NUTRITIONAL NOTES

PER PORTION:

ENERGY 125 Kcals/525 KJ **FAT** 3.5 g
SATURATED FAT 1.4 g **PROTEIN** 2.8 g
CARBOHYDRATE 21.9 g **FIBRE** 1.6 g

Serves 4

INGREDIENTS
1 small red onion
1 garlic clove
6 plum tomatoes
10 ml/2 tsp butter
45 ml/3 tbsp tomato ketchup
30 ml/2 tbsp Dijon mustard
30 ml/2 tbsp dark brown sugar
15 ml/1 tbsp runny honey
5 ml/1 tsp ground cayenne pepper
15 ml/1 tbsp ancho chilli powder
15 ml/1 tbsp ground paprika
15 ml/1 tbsp Worcestershire sauce
4 x 175 g/6 oz salmon fillets

1 Finely chop the red onion and finely dice the garlic.

2 Dice the tomatoes.

3 Melt the butter in a large, heavy-based saucepan and gently cook the onion and garlic until translucent.

cayenne pepper

Dijon mustard

dark brown sugar

plum tomato

salmon fillet

red onion

tomato ketchup

4 Add the tomatoes and simmer for 15 minutes.

5 Add the remaining ingredients except the salmon and simmer for a further 20 minutes. Process the mixture in a food processor fitted with a metal blade and leave to cool.

6 Brush the salmon with the sauce and chill for at least 2 hours. Barbecue or grill for about 2–3 minutes either side, brushing on the sauce when necessary.

Millionaire's Lobster Salad

When money is no object and you're in a decadent mood, this salad will satisfy your every whim. It is ideally served with a cool Chardonnay, Chablis or Pouilly-Fuissé wine.

Serves 4

INGREDIENTS
1 medium lobster, live or cooked
1 bay leaf
1 sprig thyme
700 g/1½ lb new potatoes, scrubbed
2 ripe tomatoes
4 oranges
½ frisée lettuce
175 g/6 oz lamb's lettuce
30 ml/2 tbsp extra-virgin olive oil
200 g/7 oz can young artichokes in
    brine, quartered
salt
1 small bunch tarragon, chervil or
    flat-leaf parsley, to garnish

DRESSING
30 ml/2 tbsp frozen concentrated
    orange juice, thawed
75 g/3 oz low-fat spread, diced
salt and cayenne pepper

COOK'S TIP

The rich delicate flavour of this salad depends on using the freshest lobsters. If North Atlantic lobsters (pictured here) are not available, use spiny rock lobsters or crawfish.

new potatoes

lamb's lettuce   *lobster*

orange

tarragon

frisée lettuce

tomato

1 If the lobster needs cooking, add to a large pan of salted water with the bay leaf and thyme. Bring to the boil and simmer for 15 minutes. Cool under running water. Twist off the legs and claws, and separate the tail piece from the body section. Break the claws open with a hammer and remove the meat intact. Cut the tail piece open from the underside with a pair of kitchen shears. Slice the meat and set aside.

2 Bring the potatoes to the boil in salted water and simmer for 20 minutes. Drain, cover and keep warm. Cover the tomatoes with boiling water and leave for 20 seconds to loosen their skins. Cool under running water and slip off the skins. Halve the tomatoes, discard the seeds, then cut the flesh into large dice.

4 To make the dressing, measure the thawed orange juice into a glass bowl and set it over a saucepan containing 2.5 cm/ 1 in of simmering water. Heat the juice for 1 minute, remove from the heat, then whisk in the butter a little at a time until the dressing reaches a coating consistency. Season to taste with salt and a pinch of cayenne pepper, cover and keep warm.

3 To segment the oranges, remove the peel from the top, bottom and sides with a serrated knife. With a small paring knife, loosen the orange segments by cutting between the flesh and the membranes, holding the fruit over a small bowl.

5 Wash the salad leaves and spin dry. Dress with olive oil, then divide between 4 large serving plates. Moisten the potatoes, artichokes and orange segments with olive oil and distribute among the leaves. Lay the sliced lobster over the salad, spoon on the warm butter dressing, add the diced tomato and decorate with fresh herbs. Serve at room temperature.

NUTRITIONAL NOTES
PER PORTION:
ENERGY 371 Kcals/1564 KJ **FAT** 14.2 g
SATURATED FAT 3.3 g

Grilled Salmon and Spring Vegetable Salad

Spring is the time to enjoy sweet young vegetables. Cook them briefly, cool to room temperature, dress and serve with a piece of lightly grilled salmon topped with sorrel and quail's eggs.

Serves 4

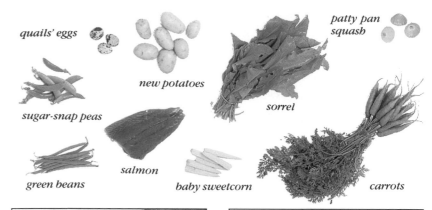

quails' eggs

new potatoes

patty pan squash

sorrel

sugar-snap peas

green beans

salmon

baby sweetcorn

carrots

INGREDIENTS

350 g/12 oz small new potatoes, scrubbed or scraped

4 quails' eggs

125 g/4 oz young carrots, peeled

125 g/4 oz baby sweetcorn

125 g/4 oz sugar-snap peas, topped and tailed

125 g/4 oz fine green beans, topped and tailed

125 g/4 oz young courgettes (zucchini)

125 g/4 oz patty pan squash (optional)

4 salmon fillets, each weighing 100 g/3½ oz, skinned

125 ml/4 fl oz fat-free French Dressing

125 g/4 oz sorrel or young spinach, stems removed

NUTRITIONAL NOTES

Per portion:

ENERGY 335 Kcals/125.5 KJ **FAT** 14 g
SATURATED FAT 2.6 g

1 Bring the potatoes to the boil in salted water and cook for 15–20 minutes. Drain, cover and keep warm.

2 Cover the quails' eggs with boiling water and cook for 8 minutes. Refresh under cold water, shell and cut in half.

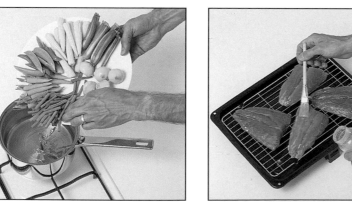

3 Bring a saucepan of salted water to the boil, add all the vegetables and cook for 2–3 minutes. Drain well. Place the hot vegetables and potatoes in a salad bowl, moisten with French Dressing and allow to cool.

4 Brush the salmon fillets with French Dressing and grill (broil) for 6 minutes, turning once.

5 Place the sorrel in a stainless-steel or enamel saucepan with 60 ml/4 tbsp French Dressing, cover and soften over a gentle heat for 2 minutes. Strain in a small sieve and cool to room temperature. Moisten the vegetables with the remaining dressing.

6 Divide the potatoes and vegetables between 4 large plates, then position a piece of salmon to one side of each plate. Finally place a spoonful of sorrel on each piece of salmon and top with a halved quail's egg. Season and serve at room temperature.

Vietnamese Stuffed Squid

The smaller the squid the sweeter the dish will taste.
Be very careful not to overcook the flesh as it becomes
tough very quickly.

NUTRITIONAL NOTES
Per portion:
ENERGY 339 Kcals/1425 KJ **FAT** 11.4 g
SATURATED FAT 3 g

Serves 4

INGREDIENTS
6 small squid, cleaned
50 g/2 oz cellophane noodles
30 ml/2 tbsp sesame oil
2 spring onions, finely chopped
8 shitake mushrooms, halved if large
250 g/9 oz minced pork
1 garlic clove, chopped
30 ml/2 tbsp Thai fish sauce
5 ml/1 tsp caster sugar
15 ml/1 tbsp finely chopped fresh
    coriander
5 ml/1 tsp lemon juice
salt and freshly ground pepper

noodles

garlic

fresh coriander

minced pork

squid

spring onion

shitake mushrooms

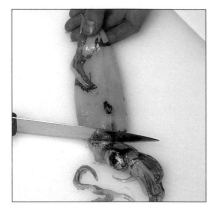

1 Pre-heat the oven to 200°C/400°F/
Gas 6. Clean the squid and remove any
excess membrane and tentacles.

2 Put the noodles into a saucepan of
boiling water. Remove the pan from the
heat and soak the noodles for 20 minutes.

3 Heat 15 ml/1 tbsp of the oil in a wok
and stir-fry the spring onions,
mushrooms, pork and garlic for 4 minutes
until the meat is golden.

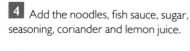

4 Add the noodles, fish sauce, sugar,
seasoning, coriander and lemon juice.

5 Stuff the squid two-thirds full with the
mixture and secure with cocktail or satay
sticks. Drizzle over the remaining oil,
prick the squid twice and bake in the
pre-heated oven for 10 minutes. Serve
hot.

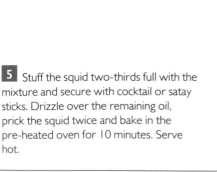

Roast Monkfish with Garlic and Fennel

Monkfish was sometimes used as a substitute for lobster meat because it is very similar in texture. It is now appreciated in its own right and is delicious quickly roasted.

Serves 4

INGREDIENTS
500g/1¼ lb monkfish tail
8 garlic cloves
15 ml/1 tbsp olive oil
2 bulbs fennel, sliced
juice of 1 lemon
1 bay leaf
salt and freshly ground black pepper

NUTRITIONAL NOTES
PER PORTION:
ENERGY 117 Kcals/493 KJ **FAT** 3.3 g
SATURATED FAT 0.5 g

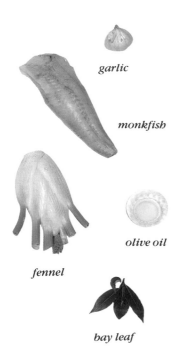

garlic

monkfish

fennel

olive oil

bay leaf

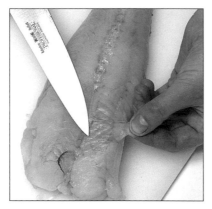

1 Pre-heat the oven to 220°C/425°F/ Gas 7. With a filleting knife, cut away the thin membrane covering the outside of the fish.

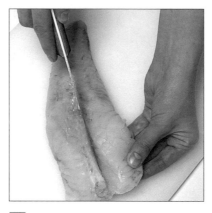

2 Cut along one side of the central bone to remove the fillet. Repeat on the other side.

3 Tie the fillets together with string.

4 Peel and slice the garlic cloves and cut incisions into the fish flesh. Place the garlic slices into the incisions.

5 Heat the oil in a large, heavy-based saucepan and seal the fish on all sides.

6 Place the fish in a roasting dish together with the fennel, lemon juice, seasoning and bay leaf. Roast in the pre-heated oven for about 20 minutes and serve immediately.

Sea Bass en Papillote

A dramatic presentation to delight your guests. Bring the unopened parcels to the table and let them unfold their own fish to release the delicious aroma.

Serves 4

INGREDIENTS
4 small sea bass, gutted
25 g/1 oz butter
450 g/1 lb spinach
3 shallots, finely chopped
60 ml/4 tbsp white wine
4 bay leaves
salt and freshly ground black pepper

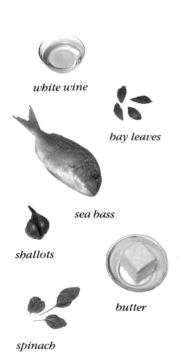

white wine

bay leaves

sea bass

shallots

butter

spinach

NUTRITIONAL NOTES
PER PORTION:
ENERGY 264 Kcals/1103 KJ **FAT** 10.4 g
SATURATED FAT 4.2 g

1 Pre-heat the oven to 180°C/350°F/Gas 4. Season both the inside and outside of the fish. Melt 50 g/2 oz/4 tbsp of the butter in a large, heavy-based saucepan and add the spinach. Cook gently until the spinach has broken down into a smooth purée. Set aside to cool.

2 Melt another 50 g/2 oz/4 tbsp of the butter in a clean pan and add the shallots. Gently sauté for 5 minutes until soft. Add to the spinach and leave to cool.

3 Stuff the insides of the fish with the spinach filling.

4 For each fish, fold a large sheet of greaseproof paper in half and cut around the fish laid on one half, to make a heart shape when unfolded. It should be at least 5 cm/2 in larger than the fish. Melt the remaining butter and brush a little onto the paper. Set the fish on one side of the paper.

5 Add a little wine and a bay leaf to each package.

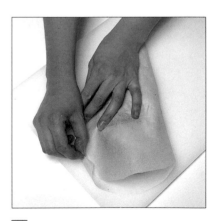

6 Fold the other side of the paper over the fish and make small pleats to seal the two edges, starting at the curve of the heart. Brush the outsides with butter. Transfer the packages to a baking sheet and bake for 20–25 minutes until the packages are brown. Serve with new potatoes and glazed carrots.

Penne with Salmon and Dill

Serves 6

INGREDIENTS

350 g/12 oz fresh salmon
    fillet, skinned
115 g/4 oz sliced smoked salmon
1–2 shallots, finely chopped
115 g/4 oz button mushrooms,
    quartered
150 ml/^{1}/$_4$ pint/^{2}/$_3$ cup light red or
    rosé wine
150 ml/^{1}/$_4$ pint/^{2}/$_3$ cup fish stock
150 ml/^{1}/$_4$ pint/^{2}/$_3$ cup low-fat
    crème fraîche
30 ml/2 tbsp chopped fresh dill
350 g/12 oz penne
salt and ground black pepper
sprigs of dill, to garnish

1 Cut the fresh salmon into 2.5 cm/ 1 in cubes. Cut the smoked salmon into 1 cm/^{1}/$_2$ in strips.

2 Put the shallots and mushrooms into a non-stick pan with the red or rosé wine. Bring to the boil and cook for about 5 minutes or until the wine has reduced almost completely.

3 Add the fish stock and crème fraîche and stir until smooth. Then add the fresh salmon, cover the pan and cook gently for 2–3 minutes.

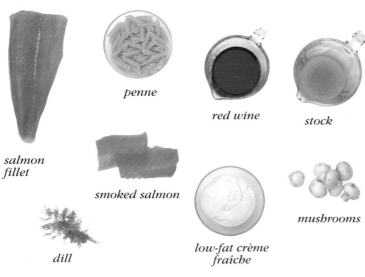

salmon fillet

penne

red wine

stock

smoked salmon

low-fat crème fraîche

mushrooms

dill

NUTRITIONAL NOTES

PER PORTION:

ENERGY 394Kcals/1656KJ **FAT** 12.8g
SATURATED FAT 4.6g **CHOLESTEROL** 64mg
CARBOHYDRATE 45g **FIBRE** 2g

4 Remove from the heat and stir in the chopped dill and seasoning.

5 Meanwhile cook the pasta in a large pan of boiling, salted water according to the instructions on the packet. Drain thoroughly and transfer to a warm serving dish. Add the smoked salmon to the sauce and pour over the pasta. Toss lightly to mix. Serve at once, garnished with sprigs of dill.

Seafood Pasta Shells with Spinach Sauce

You'll need very large pasta shells, measuring about 4 cm/1½ in long for this dish; don't try stuffing smaller shells – they're much too fiddly!

NUTRITIONAL NOTES
PER PORTION:

ENERGY 363Kcals/1539KJ PROTEIN 34.94g
FAT 6.08g SATURATED FAT 2.09g
CARBOHYDRATE 45g
FIBRE 3.98g SUGAR 9.16g
SODIUM 622mg

Serves 4

INGREDIENTS
15 g/½ oz/1 tbsp low fat spread
8 spring onions, finely sliced
6 tomatoes
32 large dried pasta shells
225 g/8 oz/1 cup low fat soft cheese
90 ml/6 tbsp skimmed milk
pinch of freshly grated nutmeg
225 g/8 oz prawns
175 g/6 oz can white crabmeat,
  drained and flaked
115 g/4 oz frozen chopped spinach,
  thawed and drained
salt and freshly ground black pepper

spring onions

prawns

pasta shells

crabmeat

spinach

tomatoes

1 Pre-heat the oven to 150°C/300°F/ Gas 2. Melt the low fat spread in a small saucepan and gently cook the spring onions for 3-4 minutes, or until softened.

2 Plunge the tomatoes into a saucepan of boiling water for 1 minute, then into a saucepan of cold water. Slip off the skins. Halve the tomatoes, remove the seeds and cores and roughly chop the flesh.

3 Cook the pasta shells in lightly salted boiling water for about 10 minutes, or until *al dente*. Drain well.

4 Put the low fat soft cheese and skimmed milk into a saucepan and heat gently, stirring until blended. Season with salt, freshly ground black pepper and a pinch of nutmeg. Measure 30 ml/2 tbsp of the sauce into a bowl.

5 Add the spring onions, tomatoes, prawns, and crabmeat to the bowl. Mix well. Spoon the filling into the shells and place in a single layer in a shallow ovenproof dish. Cover with foil and cook in the pre-heated oven for 10 minutes.

6 Stir the spinach into the remaining sauce. Bring to the boil and simmer gently for 1 minute, stirring all the time. Drizzle over the pasta shells and serve hot.

Smoked Haddock in Parsley Sauce

Serves 4

INGREDIENTS
450 g/1 lb smoked haddock fillet
1 small leek or onion, sliced thickly
300 ml/½ pint/1¼ cups
    skimmed milk
a bouquet garni (bay leaf, thyme
    and parsley stalks)
25 g/1 oz low-fat margarine
25 g/1 oz plain flour
30 ml/2 tbsp chopped fresh parsley
225 g/8 oz pasta shells
salt and ground black pepper
15 g/½ oz toasted flaked almonds,
    to serve

leek
haddock fillet
salt
parsley
bay leaves
pepper
pasta shells
skimmed milk
plain flour
low-fat margarine

1 Remove all the skin and any bones from the haddock. Put into a pan with the leek or onion, milk and bouquet garni. Bring to the boil, cover and simmer gently for about 8–10 minutes until the fish flakes easily.

2 Strain, reserving the milk for making the sauce, and discard the bouquet garni.

NUTRITIONAL NOTES
PER PORTION:

ENERGY 405Kcals/1700KJ **FAT** 6.9g
SATURATED FAT 1.0g **CHOLESTEROL** 42mg
CARBOHYDRATE 58g **FIBRE** 3.7g

3 Put the margarine, flour and reserved milk into a pan. Bring to the boil and whisk until smooth. Season and add the fish and leek or onion.

4 Cook the pasta in a large pan of boiling water until *al dente*. Drain thoroughly and stir into the sauce with the chopped parsley. Serve immediately, scattered with almonds.

Fusilli with Smoked Trout

Serves 4–6

INGREDIENTS

2 carrots, cut in julienne sticks
1 leek, cut in julienne sticks
2 sticks celery, cut in julienne sticks
150 ml/¼ pint/⅔ cup
  vegetable stock
225 g/8 oz fresh trout fillets, skinned
  and cut into strips
200 g/7 oz low-fat cream cheese
150 ml/¼ pint/⅔ cup medium sweet
  white wine or fish stock
15 ml/1 tbsp chopped fresh dill
  or fennel
225 g/8 oz long curly fusilli
salt and ground black pepper
dill sprigs, to garnish

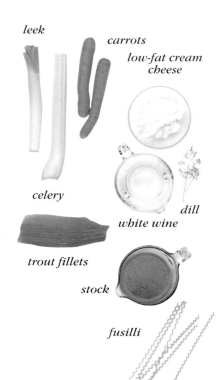

leek
carrots
low-fat cream
cheese
celery
dill
white wine
trout fillets
stock
fusilli

1 Put the carrots, leek and celery into a pan with the vegetable stock. Bring to the boil and cook quickly for 4–5 minutes until tender and most of the stock has evaporated. Remove from the heat and add the smoked trout.

2 To make the sauce, put the cream cheese and wine or fish stock into a saucepan, heat and whisk until smooth. Season with salt and pepper. Add the chopped dill or fennel.

3 Cook the fusilli in a large pan of boiling, salted water until *al dente*. Drain thoroughly.

4 Return the fusilli to the pan with the sauce, toss lightly and transfer to a serving bowl. Top with the cooked vegetables and trout. Serve immediately, garnished with dill sprigs.

NUTRITIONAL NOTES
PER PORTION:

ENERGY 339Kcals/1422KJ **FAT** 4.7g
SATURATED FAT 0.8g **CHOLESTEROL** 57mg
CARBOHYDRATE 49g **FIBRE** 4.1g

Saffron Pappardelle

Serves 4

INGREDIENTS

large pinch of saffron strands
4 sun-dried tomatoes, chopped
5 ml/1 tsp fresh thyme
12 large prawns in their shells
225 g/8 oz baby squid
225 g/8 oz monkfish fillet
2–3 garlic cloves, crushed
2 small onions, quartered
1 small bulb fennel, trimmed
    and sliced
150 ml/¼ pint/⅔ cup white wine
225 g/8 oz pappardelle
salt and ground black pepper
30 ml/2 tbsp chopped fresh parsley,
    to garnish

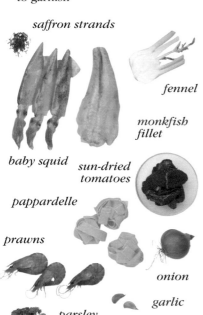

saffron strands

fennel

*monkfish
fillet*

baby squid *sun-dried
tomatoes*

pappardelle

prawns

onion

garlic

parsley

*white
wine*

thyme

1 Put the saffron, sun-dried tomatoes and thyme into a bowl with 60 ml/4 tbsp hot water. Leave to soak for 30 minutes.

2 Wash the prawns and carefully remove the shells, leaving the heads and tails intact. Pull the head from the body of each squid and remove the quill. Cut the tentacles from the head and rinse under cold water. Pull off the outer skin and cut into 5 mm/¼ in rings. Cut the monkfish into 2.5 cm/1 in cubes.

3 Put the garlic, onions and fennel into a pan with the wine. Cover and simmer for 5 minutes until tender.

4 Add the monkfish, saffron, tomatoes and thyme in their liquid. Cover and cook for 3 minutes. Then add the prawns and squid. Cover and cook gently for 1–2 minutes (do not overcook or the squid will become tough).

5 Meanwhile cook the pasta in a large pan of boiling, salted water until *al dente*. Drain thoroughly.

6 Divide the pasta among four serving dishes and top with the fish and shellfish sauce. Sprinkle with parsley and serve at once.

NUTRITIONAL NOTES

PER PORTION:

ENERGY 381Kcals/1602KJ **FAT** 3.5g
SATURATED FAT 0.6g **CHOLESTEROL** 34mg
CARBOHYDRATE 52g **FIBRE** 3.2g

Sweet and Sour Prawns with Chinese Egg Noodles

Serves 4–6

INGREDIENTS

15 g/¹/₂ oz dried porcini mushrooms
300 ml/¹/₂ pint/1¹/₄ cups hot water
bunch of spring onions, cut into
    thick diagonal slices
2.5 cm/1 in piece of root ginger,
    peeled and grated
1 red pepper, seeded and diced
225 g/8 oz can water
    chestnuts, sliced
45 ml/3 tbsp light soy sauce
30 ml/2 tbsp sherry
350 g/12 oz large peeled prawns
225 g/8 oz Chinese egg noodles

root
ginger

red pepper

prawns

spring
onions

water
chestnuts

egg noodles

soy
sauce

porcini
mushrooms

1 Put the dried porcini mushrooms into a bowl with the hot water and soak for 15 minutes.

2 Put the spring onions, ginger and diced red pepper into a pan with the mushrooms and their liquid. Bring to the boil, cover and cook for about 5 minutes until tender.

NUTRITIONAL NOTES

PER PORTION:

ENERGY 391Kcals/1640KJ **FAT** 7.1g
SATURATED FAT 0.3g **CHOLESTEROL** 88mg
CARBOHYDRATE 54g **FIBRE** 2.8g

3 Add the water chestnuts, soy sauce, sherry and prawns. Cover and cook gently for 2 minutes.

4 Cook the egg noodles according to the instructions on the packet. Drain thoroughly and transfer to a warmed serving dish. Spoon the hot prawns on top. Serve at once.

Pasta with Scallops in Warm Green Tartare Sauce

Serves 4

INGREDIENTS

120 ml/4 fl oz/¹/₂ cup low-fat
   crème fraîche
10 ml/2 tsp wholegrain mustard
2 garlic cloves, crushed
30–45 ml/2–3 tbsp fresh lime juice
60 ml/4 tbsp chopped fresh parsley
30 ml/2 tbsp snipped chives
350 g/12 oz black tagliatelle
12 large scallops
60 ml/4 tbsp white wine
150 ml/¹/₄ pint/²/₃ cup fish stock
salt and ground black pepper
lime wedges and parsley sprigs,
   to garnish

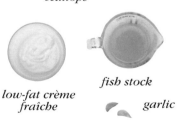

chives

lime

parsley

black tagliatelle

scallops

white wine

low-fat crème fraîche

fish stock

garlic

1 To make the tartare sauce, mix the crème fraîche, mustard, garlic, lime juice, herbs and seasoning together in a bowl.

2 Cook the pasta in a large pan of boiling, salted water until *al dente*. Drain thoroughly.

3 Slice the scallops in half, horizontally. Keep any coral whole. Put the white wine and fish stock into a saucepan. Heat to simmering point. Add the scallops and cook very gently for 3–4 minutes (no longer or they will become tough).

4 Remove the scallops. Boil the wine and stock to reduce by half and add the green sauce to the pan. Heat gently to warm, replace the scallops and cook for 1 minute. Spoon over the pasta and garnish with lime wedges and parsley.

Cod with a Spicy Mushroom Sauce

The cod is grilled before it is added to the sauce to prevent it from breaking up during cooking.

Serves 4

INGREDIENTS
4 cod fillets
15ml/1 tbsp lemon juice
15ml/1 tbsp olive oil
1 medium onion, chopped
1 bay leaf
4 black peppercorns, crushed
115g/4oz mushrooms
175ml/6fl oz/⅔ cup natural low
  fat yogurt
5ml/1 tsp ginger pulp
5ml/1 tsp garlic pulp
2.5ml/½ tsp garam masala
2.5ml/½ tsp chilli powder
5ml/1 tsp salt
15ml/1 tbsp fresh coriander leaves,
  to garnish
lightly cooked green beans, to serve

ginger pulp onion
lemon juice cod fillets
  mushrooms
chilli powder bay leaf
garam masala garlic pulp fresh coriander yogurt

NUTRITIONAL NOTES
Per portion:
ENERGY 170 K Cals/715 K J **PROTEIN** 25.80g
FAT 4.32g **SATURATED FAT** 0.79g
CARBOHYDRATE 7.67g **FIBRE** 1.00g
ADDED SUGAR 0 **SALT** 0.61g

1 Remove the skin and any bones from the cod fillets. Sprinkle with lemon juice, then grill under a preheated grill for about 5 minutes on each side. Remove from the heat and set aside.

2 Heat the oil in a non-stick wok or frying pan and fry the onion with the bay leaf and peppercorns for 2–3 minutes. Lower the heat, then add the mushrooms and stir-fry for 4–5 minutes.

3 In a bowl mix together the yogurt, ginger and garlic, garam masala, chilli powder and salt. Pour this over the onions and stir-fry for 3 minutes.

4 Add the cod to the sauce and cook for a further 2 minutes. Serve garnished with the coriander and accompanied by lightly cooked green beans.

Stir-fried Vegetables with Monkfish

Monkfish is a rather expensive fish, but ideal to use in stir-fry recipes as it is quite tough and does not break easily.

Serves 4

INGREDIENTS
30ml/2 tbsp corn oil
2 medium onions, sliced
5ml/1 tsp garlic pulp
5ml/1 tsp ground cumin
5ml/1 tsp ground coriander
5ml/1 tsp chilli powder
175g/6 oz monkfish, cut into cubes
30ml/2 tbsp fresh fenugreek leaves
2 tomatoes, seeded and sliced
1 courgette, sliced
15ml/1 tbsp lime juice
salt

onions

courgette *monkfish*

tomatoes *fenugreek* *lime juice*

chilli powder *ground cumin*

ground coriander *garlic pulp*

NUTRITIONAL NOTES
Per portion:
ENERGY 86 K Cals/360 KJ **PROTEIN** 9.18g
FAT 2.38g **SATURATED FAT** 0.35g
CARBOHYDRATE 8.30g **FIBRE** 1.87g
ADDED SUGAR 0.02g
SALT 0.27g

1 Heat the oil in a non-stick wok or frying pan and fry the onions over a low heat until soft.

2 Meanwhile mix together the garlic, cumin, coriander and chilli powder. Add this spice mixture to the onions and stir for about 1 minute.

COOK'S TIP
Try to use monkfish for this recipe, but if it is not available, either cod or prawns make a suitable substitute.

3 Add the fish and continue to stir-fry for 3–5 minutes until the fish is well cooked through.

4 Add the fenugreek, tomatoes and courgette, followed by salt to taste, and stir-fry for a further 2 minutes. Sprinkle with lime juice before serving.

Prawn and Vegetable Balti

A simple and delicious accompaniment to many other Balti dishes.

Serves 4

INGREDIENTS

175g/6 oz frozen cooked,
    peeled prawns
30ml/2 tbsp corn oil
1.5ml/¼ tsp onion seeds
4–6 curry leaves
115g/4oz frozen peas
115g/4oz frozen sweetcorn
1 large courgette, sliced
1 medium red pepper, seeded and
    roughly diced
5ml/1 tsp crushed coriander seeds
5ml/1 tsp crushed dried red chillies
15ml/1 tbsp lemon juice
salt
15ml/1 tbsp fresh coriander leaves,
    to garnish

prawns   peas   sweetcorn

curry leaves
red pepper

courgette

fresh coriander

onion seeds

dried red chillies   coriander seeds

lemon juice

NUTRITIONAL NOTES
Per portion:
ENERGY 134 K Cals/566 K J **PROTEIN** 13.94g
FAT 3.04g **SATURATED FAT** 0.51g
CARBOHYDRATE 14.03g **FIBRE** 2.96g
ADDED SUGAR 0
SALT 1.03g

COOK'S TIP
The best way to crush whole seeds is to use an electric spice grinder or a small marble pestle and mortar.

1 Thaw the prawns and drain them of any excess liquid.

2 Heat the oil with the onion seeds and curry leaves in a non-stick wok or frying pan.

3 Add the prawns to the wok and stir-fry until the liquid has evaporated.

4 Next add the peas, sweetcorn, courgette and red pepper. Continue to stir for 3–5 minutes.

5 Finally, add the coriander seeds, chillies, salt to taste and lemon juice.

6 Serve immediately, garnished with fresh coriander leaves.

Vegetarian Dishes

Sweet Potato Roulade

Sweet potato works particularly well as the base for this roulade. Serve in thin slices for a truly impressive dinner party dish.

Serves 6

INGREDIENTS

225 g/8 oz/1 cup low-fat soft cheese such as Quark
75 ml/5 tbsp low-fat yogurt
6–8 spring onions, finely sliced
30 ml/2 tbsp chopped brazil nuts, roasted
450 g/1 lb sweet potatoes, peeled and cubed
12 allspice berries, crushed
4 eggs, separated
50 g/2 oz/¼ cup Edam cheese, finely grated
salt and freshly ground black pepper
15 ml/1 tbsp sesame seeds

soft cheese

sesame seeds

sweet potato

yogurt

Edam

brazil nuts

spring onions

egg

peppercorns

1 Preheat the oven to 200°C/400°F/ Gas 6. Grease and line a 33 × 25 cm/ 13 × 10 in Swiss roll tin with non-stick baking paper, snipping the corners with scissors to fit.

2 In a small bowl, mix together the soft cheese, yogurt, spring onions and brazil nuts. Set aside.

3 Boil or steam the sweet potato until tender. Drain well. Place in a food processor with the allspice and blend until smooth. Spoon into a bowl and stir in the egg yolks and Edam. Season to taste.

4 Whisk the egg whites until stiff but not dry. Fold ⅓ of the egg whites into the sweet potatoes to lighten the mixture before gently folding in the rest.

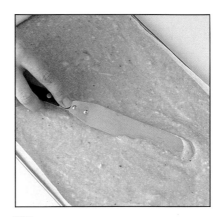

5 Pour into the prepared tin, tipping it to get the mixture right into the corners. Smooth gently with a palette knife and cook in the oven for 10–15 minutes.

COOK'S TIP

Choose the orange-fleshed variety of sweet potato for the most striking colour.

NUTRITIONAL NOTES

PER PORTION:

ENERGY 240 Kcals/1005 KJ **FAT** 11.8 g
SATURATED FAT 3.8 g

6 Meanwhile, lay a large sheet of greaseproof paper on a clean tea-towel and sprinkle with the sesame seeds. When the roulade is cooked, tip it onto the paper, trim the edges and roll it up. Leave to cool. When cool carefully unroll, spread with the filling and roll up again. Cut into slices to serve.

Pumpkin and Pistachio Risotto

This elegant combination of creamy golden rice and orange pumpkin can be as pale or bright as you like by adding different quantities of saffron.

Serves 4

INGREDIENTS

1.1 litres/2 pints/5 cups vegetable stock or water
generous pinch of saffron threads
30 ml/2 tbsp olive oil
1 medium onion, chopped
2 garlic cloves, crushed
450 g/1 lb arborio rice
900 g/2 lb pumpkin, peeled, seeded and cut into 2 cm/¾ in cubes
200 ml/7 fl oz/¾ cup dry white wine
15 g/½ oz Parmesan cheese, finely grated
50 g/2 oz/½ cup pistachios
45 ml/3 tbsp chopped fresh marjoram or oregano, plus extra leaves, to garnish
salt, freshly grated nutmeg and ground black pepper

saffron

pumpkin

white wine

onion

garlic

marjoram

Parmesan

arborio rice

pistachios

1 Bring the stock or water to the boil and reduce to a low simmer. Ladle a little stock into a small bowl. Add the saffron threads and leave to infuse.

4 Gradually add the stock or water, a ladleful at a time, allowing the rice to absorb the liquid before adding more and stirring all the time. After 20–30 minutes the rice should be golden yellow and creamy, and *al dente* when tested.

2 Heat the oil in a large saucepan. Add the onion and garlic and cook gently for about 5 minutes until softened. Add the rice and pumpkin and cook for a few more minutes until the rice looks transparent.

3 Pour in the wine and allow it to bubble hard. When it is absorbed add ¼ of the stock and the infused saffron and liquid. Stir constantly until all the liquid is absorbed.

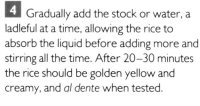

NUTRITIONAL NOTES

PER PORTION:

ENERGY 427 Kcals/1802.5 KJ **FAT** 11.7 g
SATURATED FAT 2.4 g

5 Stir in the Parmesan cheese, cover the pan and leave to stand for 5 minutes.

6 To finish, stir in the pistachios and marjoram or oregano. Season to taste with a little salt, nutmeg and pepper, and scatter over a few extra marjoram or oregano leaves.

COOK'S TIP
Italian arborio rice must be used to make an authentic risotto. Choose unpolished white arborio as it contains more starch.

Wild Rice Rösti with Carrot and Orange Purée

Rösti is a traditional dish from Switzerland. This variation has the extra nuttiness of wild rice and a bright simple sauce as a fresh accompaniment.

Serves 6

INGREDIENTS
50 g/2 oz/½ cup wild rice
900 g/2 lb large potatoes
45 ml/3 tbsp walnut oil
5 ml/1 tsp yellow mustard seeds
1 onion, coarsely grated and drained
   in a sieve
30 ml/2 tbsp fresh thyme leaves
salt and freshly ground black pepper

FOR THE PURÉE
350 g/12 oz carrots, peeled and
   roughly chopped
rind and juice of 1 large orange

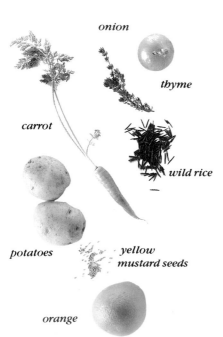

onion

thyme

carrot

wild rice

potatoes

yellow
mustard seeds

orange

1 For the purée, place the carrots in a pan, cover with cold water and add 2 pieces of orange rind. Bring to the boil and cook for 10 minutes or until tender. Drain well and discard the rind.

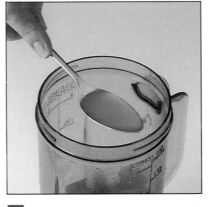

2 Purée the mixture in a blender with 60 ml/4 tbsp of the orange juice. Return to the pan to reheat.

3 Place the wild rice in a clean pan and cover with water. Bring to the boil and cook for 30–40 minutes, until the rice is just starting to split, but still crunchy. Drain the rice.

4 Scrub the potatoes, place in a large pan and cover with cold water. Bring to the boil and cook for 10–15 minutes until just tender. Drain well and leave to cool slightly. When the potatoes are cool, peel and coarsely grate them into a large bowl. Add the cooked rice.

5 Heat 30 ml/2 tbsp of the walnut oil in a non-stick frying pan and add the mustard seeds. When they start to pop, add the onion and cook gently for 5 minutes until softened. Add to the bowl of potato and rice, together with the thyme, and mix thoroughly. Season to taste with salt and pepper.

6 Heat the remaining oil in the frying pan and add the potato mixture. Press down well and cook for 10 minutes or until golden brown. Cover the pan with a plate and flip over, then slide the rösti back into the pan for another 10 minutes to cook the other side. Serve with the reheated carrot and orange purée.

Sweet Vegetable Couscous

A wonderful combination of sweet vegetables and spices, this makes a substantial winter dish.

Serves 4–6

INGREDIENTS

1 generous pinch of saffron threads
45 ml/3 tbsp boiling water
15 ml/1 tbsp olive oil
1 red onion, sliced
2 garlic cloves crushed
1–2 fresh red chillies, seeded and
 finely chopped
2.5 ml/½ tsp ground ginger
2.5 ml/½ tsp ground cinnamon
1 × 400 g/14 oz can chopped
 tomatoes
300 ml/½ pint/1¼ cups vegetable
 stock or water
4 medium carrots, peeled and cut into
 5 mm/¼ in slices
2 medium turnips, peeled and cut into
 2 cm/¾ in cubes
450 g/1 lb sweet potatoes, peeled and
 cut into 2 cm/¾ in cubes
75 g/3 oz/⅓ cup raisins
2 medium courgettes, cut into 5 mm/
 ¼ in slices
1 × 400 g/14 oz can chick-peas,
 drained and rinsed
45 ml/3 tbsp chopped fresh parsley
45 ml/3 tbsp chopped fresh coriander
450 g/1 lb quick-cook couscous

1 Leave the saffron to infuse in the boiling water.

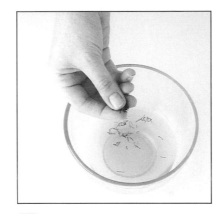

2 Heat the oil in a large saucepan. Add the onion, garlic and chillies and cook gently for 5 minutes.

3 Add the ground ginger and cinnamon and cook for a further 1–2 minutes.

4 Add the tomatoes, stock or water, infused saffron and liquid, carrots, turnips, sweet potatoes and raisins, cover and simmer for 25 minutes.

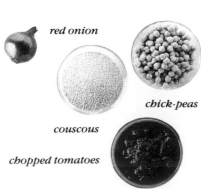

red onion

chick-peas

couscous

chopped tomatoes

carrot

courgette

red chilli

garlic

turnip

raisins

sweet potato

5 Add the courgettes, chick-peas, parsley and coriander and cook for another 10 minutes.

6 Meanwhile prepare the couscous following the packet instructions and serve with the vegetables.

NUTRITIONAL NOTES

PER PORTION:

ENERGY 402 Kcals/1693 KJ **FAT** 5.2 g
SATURATED FAT 1.2 g

Vegetarian Cassoulet

Every town in south-west France has its own version of this popular classic. Warm French bread is all that is needed to complete this hearty vegetable version.

Serves 4–6

INGREDIENTS
400 g/14 oz/2 cups dried
   haricot beans
1 bay leaf
2 onions
3 whole cloves
2 garlic cloves, crushed
5 ml/1 tsp olive oil
2 leeks, thickly sliced
12 baby carrots
115 g/4 oz button mushrooms
400 g/14 oz can chopped tomatoes
15 ml/1 tbsp tomato purée
5 ml/1 tsp paprika
15 ml/1 tbsp chopped fresh thyme
30 ml/2 tbsp chopped fresh parsley
115 g/4 oz/2 cups fresh white
   breadcrumbs
salt and freshly ground black pepper

chopped tomatoes   *bay leaf*

breadcrumbs   *leek*

carrots   *mushrooms*

COOK'S TIP
If you're short of time use canned haricot beans – you'll need two 400 g/ 14 oz cans. Drain, reserving the bean juices and make up to 400 ml/14 fl oz/1⅔ cups with vegetable stock.

1 Soak the beans overnight in plenty of cold water. Drain and rinse under cold running water. Put them in a saucepan together with 1.75 litres/3 pints/7½ cups of cold water and the bay leaf. Bring to the boil and cook rapidly for 10 minutes.

2 Peel one of the onions and spike with cloves. Add to the beans and reduce the heat. Cover and simmer gently for 1 hour, until the beans are almost tender. Drain, reserving the stock but discarding the bay leaf and onion.

3 Chop the remaining onion and put it into a large flameproof casserole together with the garlic cloves and olive oil. Cook gently for 5 minutes, or until softened.

4 Pre-heat the oven to 160°C/325°F/ Gas 3. Add the leeks, carrots, mushrooms, chopped tomatoes, tomato purée, paprika, thyme and 400 ml/ 14 fl oz/1⅔ cups of the reserved stock to the casserole.

5 Bring to the boil, cover and simmer gently for 10 minutes. Stir in the cooked beans and parsley. Season to taste.

NUTRITIONAL NOTES

PER PORTION:

ENERGY 305.5Kcals/1296KJ PROTEIN 18.8g
FAT 3.33g SATURATED FAT 0.58g
CARBOHYDRATE 53.3g
FIBRE 16.33g SUGAR 12.16g
SODIUM 208.66mg

6 Sprinkle with the breadcrumbs and bake uncovered in the pre-heated oven for 35 minutes, or until the topping is golden brown and crisp.

Chilli Bean Bake

The contrasting textures of saucy beans, vegetables and crunchy cornbread topping make this a memorable meal.

Serves 4

INGREDIENTS
225 g/8 oz/1⅓ cups red kidney beans
1 bay leaf
1 large onion, finely chopped
1 garlic clove, crushed
2 celery sticks, sliced
5 ml/1 tsp ground cumin
5 ml/1 tsp chilli powder
400 g/14 oz can chopped tomatoes
15 ml/1 tbsp tomato purée
5 ml/1 tsp dried mixed herbs
15 ml/1 tbsp lemon juice
1 yellow pepper, seeded and diced
salt and freshly ground black pepper
mixed salad, to serve

FOR THE CORNBREAD TOPPING
175 g/6 oz/1½ cups corn meal
15 ml/1 tbsp wholemeal flour
5 ml/1 tsp baking powder
1 egg, beaten
175 ml/6 fl oz/¾ cup skimmed milk

kidney beans

celery

tomato purée

pepper

NUTRITIONAL NOTES
PER PORTION:

ENERGY 396.75Kcals/1676KJ PROTEIN 22.73g
FAT 4.67g SATURATED FAT 0.65g
CARBOHYDRATE 68.75g
FIBRE 11.9g SUGAR 9.89g
SODIUM 272mg

1 Soak the beans overnight in cold water. Drain and rinse well. Pour 1 litre/1¾ pints/4 cups of water into a large, heavy-based saucepan together with the beans and bay leaf and boil rapidly for 10 minutes. Lower the heat, cover and simmer for 35–40 minutes, or until the beans are tender.

2 Add the onion, garlic clove, celery, cumin, chilli powder, chopped tomatoes, tomato purée and dried mixed herbs. Half-cover the pan with a lid and simmer for a further 10 minutes.

3 Stir in the lemon juice, yellow pepper and seasoning. Simmer for a further 8-10 minutes, stirring occasionally, until the vegetables are just tender. Discard the bay leaf and spoon the mixture into a large casserole.

4 Pre-heat the oven to 220°C/425°F/Gas 7. For the topping, put the corn meal, flour, baking powder and a pinch of salt into a bowl and mix together. Make a well in the centre and add the egg and milk. Mix and pour over the bean mixture. Bake in the pre-heated oven for 20 minutes, or until brown.

Cheese and Onion Slice

This inexpensive supper dish is made substantial with the addition of porridge oats.

Serves 4

INGREDIENTS
2 large onions, thinly sliced
1 garlic clove, crushed
150 ml/¼ pint/⅔ cup vegetable stock
5 ml/1 tsp vegetable extract
250 g/9 oz/3 cups porridge oats
115 g/4 oz/1 cup grated Edam cheese
30 ml/2 tbsp chopped fresh parsley
2 eggs, lightly beaten
1 medium potato, peeled
salt and freshly ground black pepper
coleslaw and tomatoes, halved,
   to serve

porridge oats

Edam cheese

eggs

parsley

onion

potato

NUTRITIONAL NOTES
PER PORTION:

ENERGY 436 K Cals / 1833 KJ **PROTEIN** 20.68 g
FAT 15.81 g **SATURATED FAT** 6.50 g
CARBOHYDRATE 56.38 g **FIBRE** 6.18 g
ADDED SUGAR 0 **SALT** 1.05 g

1 Pre-heat the oven to 180°C/350°F/ Gas 4. Line the base of a 20 cm/8 in sandwich tin with non-stick baking paper. Put the onions, garlic clove and stock into a heavy-based saucepan and simmer until the stock has reduced entirely. Stir in the vegetable extract.

2 Spread the oats on a baking sheet and toast in the oven for 10 minutes. Mix with the onions, cheese, parsley, eggs, salt and freshly ground black pepper.

3 Thinly slice the potato and use it to line the base of the tin. Spoon in the oat mixture. Cover with a piece of foil.

4 Bake in the pre-heated oven for 35 minutes. Turn out onto a baking sheet and remove the lining paper. Put under a pre-heated hot grill to brown the potatoes. Cut into wedges and serve hot with coleslaw and halved tomatoes.

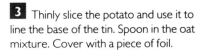

Carrot Mousse with Mushroom Sauce

The combination of fresh vegetables in this impressive yet easy-to-make mousse makes healthy eating a pleasure.

NUTRITIONAL NOTES

Per portion:

ENERGY 179.75Kcals/753.25KJ PROTEIN 13.43g
FAT 6.53g SATURATED FAT 1.85g
CARBOHYDRATE 17.77g
FIBRE 2.81g SUGAR 11.29g
SODIUM 170.73mg

Serves 4

INGREDIENTS

350 g/12 oz carrots, roughly chopped
1 small red pepper, seeded and
  roughly chopped
45 ml/3 tbsp vegetable stock or water
2 eggs
1 egg white
115 g/4 oz/½ cup quark or low fat soft
  cheese
15 ml/1 tbsp chopped fresh tarragon
salt and freshly ground black pepper
sprig of fresh tarragon, to garnish
boiled rice and leeks, to serve

FOR THE MUSHROOM SAUCE

25 g/1 oz/2 tbsp low fat spread
175 g/6 oz mushrooms, sliced
30 ml/2 tbsp plain flour
250 ml/8 fl oz/1 cup skimmed milk

carrots

egg white

mushrooms

pepper

eggs

flour

soft cheese

low fat spread

1 Pre-heat the oven to 190°C/375°F/ Gas 5. Line the bases of four 150 ml/ ¼ pint/⅔ cup dariole moulds or ramekin dishes with non-stick baking paper. Put the carrots and red pepper in a small saucepan with the vegetable stock or water. Cover and cook for 5 minutes, or until tender. Drain well.

2 Lightly beat the eggs and egg white together. Mix with the quark or low fat soft cheese. Season to taste. Purée the cooked vegetables in a food processor or blender. Add the cheese mixture and process for a few seconds more until smooth. Stir in the chopped tarragon.

3 Divide the carrot mixture between the prepared dariole moulds or ramekin dishes and cover with foil. Place the dishes in a roasting tin half-filled with hot water. Bake in the pre-heated oven for 35 minutes, or until set.

4 For the mushroom sauce, melt 15 g/½ oz/1 tbsp of the low fat spread in a frying pan. Add the mushrooms and gently sauté for 5 minutes, until soft.

5 Put the remaining low fat spread in a small saucepan together with the flour and milk. Cook over a medium heat, stirring all the time, until the sauce thickens. Stir in the mushrooms and season to taste.

6 Turn out each mousse onto a serving plate. Spoon over a little sauce and serve the remainder separately. Garnish with a sprig of fresh tarragon and serve with boiled rice and leeks.

Ratatouille Pancakes

These pancakes are made slightly thicker than usual to hold the juicy vegetable filling.

Serves 4

INGREDIENTS
75 g/3 oz/¾ cup plain flour
25 g/1 oz/¼ cup medium oatmeal
1 egg
300 ml/½ pint/1¼ cups
  skimmed milk
mixed salad, to serve

FOR THE FILLING
1 large aubergine, cut into 2.5 cm/1 in
  cubes
1 garlic clove, crushed
2 medium courgettes, sliced
1 green pepper, seeded and sliced
1 red pepper, seeded and sliced
75 ml/5 tbsp vegetable stock
200 g/7 oz can chopped tomatoes
5 ml/1 tsp cornflour
salt and freshly ground black pepper

courgettes

oatmeal

pepper

cornflour

chopped tomatoes

aubergine

flour

egg

1 Sift the flour and a pinch of salt into a bowl. Stir in the oatmeal. Make a well in the centre, add the egg and half the milk and mix to a smooth batter. Gradually beat in the remaining milk. Cover the bowl and leave to stand for 30 minutes.

2 Spray a 18 cm/7 in pancake pan or heavy-based frying pan with non-stick cooking spray. Heat the pan, then pour in just enough batter to cover the base of the pan thinly. Cook for 2-3 minutes, until the underside is golden brown. Flip over and cook for a further 1-2 minutes.

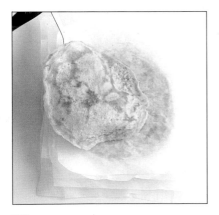

3 Slide the pancake out onto a plate lined with non-stick baking paper. Stack the other pancakes on top as they are made, interleaving each with non-stick baking paper. Keep warm.

4 For the filling, put the aubergine in a colander and sprinkle well with salt. Leave to stand on a plate for 30 minutes. Rinse thoroughly and drain well.

5 Put the garlic clove, courgettes, peppers, stock and tomatoes into a large saucepan. Simmer uncovered and stir occasionally for 10 minutes. Add the aubergine and cook for a further 15 minutes. Blend the cornflour with 10 ml/ 2 tsp water and add to the saucepan. Simmer for 2 minutes. Season to taste.

NUTRITIONAL NOTES

PER PORTION:

ENERGY 182 K Cals / 767 KJ **PROTEIN** 9.36 g
FAT 3.07 g **SATURATED FAT** 0.62 g
CARBOHYDRATE 31.40 g **FIBRE** 4.73 g
ADDED SUGAR 0 **SALT** 0.22 g

6 Spoon the ratatouille mixture into the middle of each pancake. Fold each one in half, then in half again to make a cone shape. Serve hot with a mixed salad.

Vegetable Biryani

This exotic dish made from everyday ingredients will be appreciated by vegetarians and meat eaters alike.

Serves 4–6

NUTRITIONAL NOTES

PER PORTION:

ENERGY 152Kcals/644KJ PROTEIN 4.5g
FAT 1.18g SATURATED FAT 0.1g
CARBOHYDRATE 34.16g
FIBRE 1.86g SUGAR 3.22g
SODIUM 0.05mg

INGREDIENTS

175 g/6 oz/1 cup long-grain rice
2 whole cloves
seeds of 2 cardamom pods
450 ml/¾ pint/scant 2 cups
   vegetable stock
2 garlic cloves
1 small onion, roughly chopped
5 ml/1 tsp cumin seeds
5 ml/1 tsp ground coriander
2.5 ml/½ tsp ground turmeric
2.5 ml/½ tsp chilli powder
1 large potato, peeled and cut into
   2.5 cm/1 in cubes
2 carrots, sliced
½ cauliflower, broken into florets
50 g/2 oz French beans, cut into
   2.5 cm/1 in lengths
30 ml/2 tbsp chopped fresh coriander
30 ml/2 tbsp lime juice
salt and freshly ground black pepper
sprig of fresh coriander, to garnish

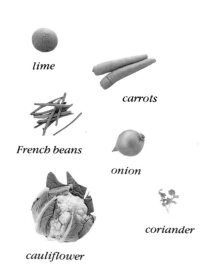

lime

carrots

French beans

onion

coriander

cauliflower

1 Put the rice, cloves and cardamom seeds into a large, heavy-based saucepan. Pour over the stock and bring to the boil.

2 Reduce the heat, cover and simmer for 20 minutes, or until all the stock has been absorbed.

3 Meanwhile put the garlic cloves, onion, cumin seeds, coriander, turmeric, chilli powder and seasoning into a blender or coffee grinder together with 30 ml/ 2 tbsp water. Blend to a paste.

4 Preheat the oven to 180°C/350°F/ Gas 4. Spoon the spicy paste into a flameproof casserole and cook over a low heat for 2 minutes, stirring occasionally.

5 Add the potato, carrots, cauliflower, beans and 90 ml/6 tbsp water. Cover and cook over a low heat for a further 12 minutes, stirring occasionally. Add the chopped coriander.

6 Spoon the rice over the vegetables. Sprinkle over the lime juice. Cover and cook in the oven for 25 minutes, or until the vegetables are tender. Fluff up the rice with a fork before serving and garnish with a sprig of fresh coriander.

Mixed Mushroom Ragout

These mushrooms are delicious served hot or cold and can be made up to two days in advance.

Serves 4

NUTRITIONAL NOTES

Per portion:

ENERGY 36Kcals/152KJ PROTEIN 2.25g
FAT 0.63g SATURATED FAT 0.07g
CARBOHYDRATE 4.92g
FIBRE 0.94g SUGAR 4.04g
SODIUM 32.75mg

INGREDIENTS
1 small onion, finely chopped
1 garlic clove, crushed
5 ml/1 tsp coriander seeds, crushed
30 ml/2 tbsp red wine vinegar
15 ml/1 tbsp soy sauce
15 ml/1 tbsp dry sherry
10 ml/2 tsp tomato purée
10 ml/2 tsp soft light brown sugar
150 ml/¼ pint/⅔ cup vegetable stock
115 g/4 oz baby button mushrooms
115 g/4 oz chestnut mushrooms,
    quartered
115 g/4 oz oyster mushrooms, sliced
salt and freshly ground black pepper
sprig of fresh coriander, to garnish

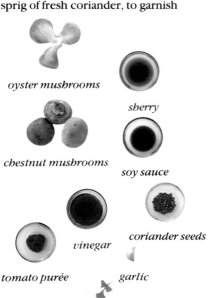

oyster mushrooms

sherry

chestnut mushrooms

soy sauce

coriander seeds

vinegar

tomato purée   *garlic*

coriander

*button
mushrooms*

onion

1 Put the first nine ingredients into a large saucepan. Bring to the boil and reduce the heat. Cover and simmer for 5 minutes.

2 Uncover the saucepan and simmer for 5 more minutes, or until the liquid has reduced by half.

3 Add the baby button and chestnut mushrooms and simmer for 3 minutes. Stir in the oyster mushrooms and cook for a further 2 minutes.

4 Remove the mushrooms with a slotted spoon and transfer them to a serving dish.

5 Boil the juices for about 5 minutes, or until reduced to about 75 ml/5 tbsp. Season to taste.

6 Allow to cool for 2-3 minutes, then pour over the mushrooms. Serve hot or well chilled, garnished with a sprig of fresh coriander.

Le
wi

Tend
and a

Serve

INGRED
675 g/
  piec
150 m
  or w
45 ml/
5 ml/1
pinch
275 m
  requ
25 g/1
25 g/1

FOR T
115 g/
  brea
115 g/
30 ml
75 g/3
  grat
25 g/1

par

brea

Vegetable and Macaroni Bake

A tasty change from macaroni cheese, this recipe is delicious served with steamed fresh vegetables.

COOK'S TIP
Use another reduced-fat hard cheese such as Red Leicester or Double Gloucester in place of the Cheddar cheese.

Serves 6

INGREDIENTS
225 g/8 oz/2¼ cups
   wholewheat macaroni
225 g/8 oz/2 cups leeks, sliced
45 ml/3 tbsp vegetable stock
225 g/8 oz broccoli florets
50 g/2 oz/4 tbsp half-fat spread
50 g/2 oz/½ cup plain
   wholemeal flour
900 ml/1½ pints/3¾ cups
   skimmed milk
150 g/5 oz/1¼ cups reduced-fat
   mature Cheddar cheese, grated
5 ml/1 tsp prepared
   English mustard
350 g/12 oz can sweetcorn kernels
25 g/1 oz/½ cup fresh
   wholemeal breadcrumbs
30 ml/2 tbsp chopped fresh parsley
2 tomatoes, cut into eighths
salt and ground black pepper

wholewheat macaroni

vegetable stock

leeks

half-fat spread

plain wholemeal flour

broccoli

reduced-fat mature Cheddar cheese

English mustard

skimmed milk

fresh wholemeal breadcrumbs

sweetcorn

fresh parsley

tomatoes

1 Preheat the oven to 200°C/400°F/Gas 6. Cook the macaroni in lightly salted, boiling water for about 10 minutes, until just tender, then drain and keep warm.

2 Cook the leeks in the stock for about 10 minutes, until tender, then strain and set aside. Blanch the broccoli for 2 minutes, drain and set aside.

3 Put the half-fat spread, flour and milk in a saucepan. Heat gently, whisking continuously, until the sauce comes to the boil and thickens. Simmer gently for 3 minutes, stirring.

4 Remove the pan from the heat, add 115 g/4 oz/1 cup cheese and stir until melted and well blended.

5 Add the macaroni, leeks, broccoli, mustard, drained sweetcorn and seasoning and mix well. Transfer the mixture to an ovenproof dish.

6 Mix the remaining cheese, breadcrumbs and parsley together and sprinkle over the top. Arrange the tomatoes on top and then bake for 30–40 minutes, until golden brown and bubbling.

NUTRITIONAL NOTES
PER PORTION:

ENERGY 376Kcals/1593KJ PROTEIN 23.30g
FAT 9.68g SATURATED FAT 3.82g
CARBOHYDRATE 52.34g FIBRE 7.12g
ADDED SUGAR 0.01g SODIUM 0.53g

Courgette, Sweetcorn and Plum Tomato Wholewheat Pizza

This tasty wholewheat pizza can be served hot or cold with a mixed bean salad and fresh crusty bread or baked potatoes. It is also ideal as a takeaway snack.

NUTRITIONAL NOTES

Per portion:

ENERGY 291Kcals/1222KJ PROTEIN 12.56g
FAT 12.35g SATURATED FAT 3.69g
CARBOHYDRATE 34.54g FIBRE 4.93g
ADDED SUGAR 0.00g SODIUM 0.25g

Serves 6

INGREDIENTS
225 g/8 oz/2 cups plain
  wholemeal flour
pinch of salt
10 ml/2 tsp baking powder
50 g/2 oz/4 tbsp polyunsaturated
  margarine
150 ml/¼ pint/⅔ cup skimmed milk
30 ml/2 tbsp tomato purée
10 ml/2 tsp dried *herbes
  de Provence*
10 ml/2 tsp olive oil
1 onion, sliced
1 garlic clove, crushed
2 small courgettes, sliced
115 g/4 oz/1½ cups
  mushrooms, sliced
115 g/4 oz/⅔ cup frozen
  sweetcorn kernels
2 plum tomatoes, sliced
50 g/2 oz/½ cup reduced-fat Red
  Leicester cheese, finely grated
50 g/2 oz/½ cup mozzarella cheese,
  finely grated
salt and ground black pepper
basil sprigs, to garnish

plain wholemeal flour

salt

baking powder

mushrooms

courgettes

polyunsaturated margarine

skimmed milk

tomato purée

dried herbes de Provence

olive oil

onion

garlic

plum tomatoes

reduced-fat Red Leicester cheese

sweetcorn

mozzarella cheese

1 Preheat the oven to 220°C/425°F/ Gas 7. Line a baking sheet with non-stick baking paper. Put the flour, salt and baking powder in a bowl and rub the fat lightly into the flour until the mixture resembles breadcrumbs.

2 Add enough milk to form a soft dough and knead lightly. Roll the dough out on a lightly floured surface, to a circle about 25 cm/10 in in diameter.

3 Place the dough on the prepared baking sheet and make the edges slightly thicker than the centre. Spread the tomato purée over the base and sprinkle the herbs on top.

4 Heat the oil in a frying pan, add the onion, garlic, courgettes and mushrooms and cook gently for 10 minutes, stirring occasionally.

5 Spread the vegetable mixture over the pizza base and sprinkle over the sweetcorn and seasoning. Arrange the tomato slices on top.

6 Mix together the cheeses and sprinkle over the pizza. Bake for 25–30 minutes, until cooked and golden brown. Serve the pizza hot or cold in slices, garnished with basil sprigs.

COOK'S TIP
This pizza is ideal for freezing in portions or slices. Freeze for up to 3 months.

Vegetable Paella

A delicious change from the more traditional seafood-based paella, this recipe is full of flavour and nutrients, including fibre.

Serves 6

INGREDIENTS
1 onion, chopped
2 garlic cloves, crushed
225 g/8 oz/2 cups leeks, sliced
3 sticks celery, chopped
1 red pepper, seeded and sliced
2 courgettes, sliced
175 g/6 oz/2¼ cups brown cap
  mushrooms, sliced
175 g/6 oz/1½ cups frozen peas
450 g/1 lb/2 cups long grain
  brown rice
400 g/14 oz can cannellini beans,
  rinsed and drained
900 ml/1½ pints/3¾ cups
  vegetable stock
60 ml/4 tbsp dry white wine
few saffron strands
225 g/8 oz/2 cups cherry
  tomatoes, halved
45–60 ml/3–4 tbsp chopped fresh
  mixed herbs
salt and ground black pepper
lemon wedges and celery leaves,
  to garnish

onion · garlic · leeks · celery · red pepper · cannellini beans · vegetable stock · courgettes · dry white wine · fresh mixed herbs · salt

1 Put the onion, garlic, leeks, celery, pepper, courgettes and mushrooms in a large saucepan and mix together.

2 Add the peas, rice, cannellini beans, stock, wine and saffron.

brown cap mushrooms · frozen peas · brown rice · saffron strands · cherry tomatoes · black pepper

3 Bring to the boil, stirring, then simmer uncovered for about 35 minutes, until almost all the liquid has been absorbed and the rice is tender, stirring occasionally.

4 Stir in the tomatoes, chopped herbs and seasoning. Serve garnished with lemon wedges and celery leaves.

NUTRITIONAL NOTES

PER PORTION:

ENERGY 416Kcals/1759KJ PROTEIN 13.69g
FAT 3.95g SATURATED FAT 0.86g
CARBOHYDRATE 84.87g FIBRE 8.85g
ADDED SUGAR 0.03g SODIUM 0.54g

Vegetable Chilli

This alternative to traditional chilli con carne is delicious served with brown rice.

Serves 4

INGREDIENTS
2 onions, chopped
1 garlic clove, crushed
3 sticks celery, chopped
1 green pepper, seeded and diced
225 g/8 oz/3 cups
  mushrooms, sliced
2 courgettes, diced
400 g/14 oz can red kidney beans,
  rinsed and drained
400 g/14 oz can chopped tomatoes
150 ml/¼ pint/⅔ cup passata
30 ml/2 tbsp tomato purée
15 ml/1 tbsp tomato ketchup
5 ml/1 tsp each hot chilli powder,
  ground cumin and ground
  coriander
salt and ground black pepper
fresh coriander sprigs, to garnish
natural yogurt and cayenne pepper,
  to serve

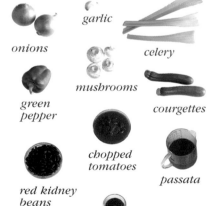

onions *garlic* *celery*
green pepper *mushrooms* *courgettes*
red kidney beans *chopped tomatoes* *passata*
tomato purée *tomato ketchup* *hot chilli powder*
ground cumin *ground coriander*

1 Put the onions, garlic, celery, pepper, mushrooms and courgettes in a large saucepan and mix together.

2 Add the kidney beans, tomatoes, passata, tomato purée and the tomato ketchup.

NUTRITIONAL NOTES
PER PORTION:
ENERGY 158Kcals/667KJ PROTEIN 9.96g
FAT 1.59g SATURATED FAT 0.27g
CARBOHYDRATE 27.55g FIBRE 8.58g
ADDED SUGAR 0.57g SODIUM 0.39g

3 Add the spices and seasoning and mix well.

4 Cover, bring to the boil and simmer for 20–30 minutes, stirring occasionally, until the vegetables are tender. Serve with natural yogurt, sprinkled with cayenne pepper. Garnish with fresh coriander sprigs.

Sweet and Sour Mixed Bean Hot-pot

An appetizing mixture of beans and vegetables in a tasty sweet and sour sauce, topped with potato.

Serves 6

INGREDIENTS

450 g/1 lb unpeeled potatoes
15 ml/1 tbsp olive oil
40 g/1½ oz/3 tbsp half-fat spread
40 g/1½ oz/⅓ cup plain
  wholemeal flour
300 ml/½ pint/1¼ cups passata
150 ml/¼ pint/⅔ cup unsweetened
  apple juice
60 ml/4 tbsp each light soft brown
  sugar, tomato ketchup, dry sherry,
  cider vinegar and light soy sauce
400 g/14 oz can butter beans
400 g/14 oz can red kidney beans
400 g/14 oz can flageolet beans
400 g/14 oz can chick-peas
175 g/6 oz green beans, chopped
  and blanched
225 g/8 oz shallots, sliced and
  blanched
225 g/8 oz/3 cups mushrooms,
  sliced
15 ml/1 tbsp each chopped fresh
thyme and marjoram
salt and ground black pepper
fresh herb sprigs, to garnish

1 Preheat the oven to 200°C/400°F/ Gas 6. Thinly slice the potatoes and par-boil them for 4 minutes. Drain thoroughly, toss them in the oil so they are lightly coated all over and set aside.

2 Place the half-fat spread, flour, passata, apple juice, sugar, tomato ketchup, sherry, vinegar and soy sauce in a saucepan. Heat gently, whisking continuously, until the sauce comes to the boil and thickens. Simmer gently for 3 minutes, stirring.

3 Rinse and drain the beans and chick-peas and add to the sauce with all the remaining ingredients, except the herb garnish. Mix well.

potatoes

olive oil

half-fat spread

plain wholemeal flour

passata

unsweetened apple juice

light soft brown sugar

tomato ketchup

dry sherry

cider vinegar

light soy sauce

butter beans

red kidney beans

flageolet beans

chick-peas

green beans   *shallots*   *mushrooms*   *fresh thyme*   *fresh marjoram*

4 Spoon the bean mixture into a casserole.

5 Arrange the potato slices over the top, completely covering the bean mixture.

6 Cover the dish with foil and bake for about 1 hour, until the potatoes are cooked and tender. Remove the foil for the last 20 minutes of the cooking time, to lightly brown the potatoes. Serve garnished with fresh herb sprigs.

NUTRITIONAL NOTES
PER PORTION:

ENERGY 410Kcals/1733KJ PROTEIN 17.36g
FAT 7.43g SATURATED FAT 1.42g
CARBOHYDRATE 70.40g FIBRE 12.52g
ADDED SUGAR 15.86g SODIUM 1.54g

NUTRITIONAL NOTES
PER PORTION:
ENERGY 484 Kcals/2048 KJ **FAT** 10.9 g
SATURATED FAT 1.5 g

Pasta Shells with Tomatoes and Rocket

This pretty-coloured pasta dish relies for its success on a salad green called rocket (arugula). Available in large supermarkets, it is a leaf easily grown in the garden or a window box and tastes slightly peppery.

Serves 4

INGREDIENTS
450 g/1 lb/4 cups pasta shells
salt and pepper
450 g/1 lb ripe cherry tomatoes
45 ml/3 tbsp olive oil
Parmesan cheese, to serve
75 g/3 oz fresh rocket

olive oil

pasta shells

cherry tomatoes

Parmesan cheese

rocket

1 Cook the pasta in plenty of boiling salted water according to the manufacturer's instructions. Drain well.

2 Halve the tomatoes. Trim, wash and dry the rocket (arugula).

3 Heat the oil in a large saucepan, add the tomatoes and cook for barely 1 minute. The tomatoes should only just heat through and not disintegrate.

4 Shave the Parmesan cheese using a rotary vegetable peeler.

5 Add the pasta, then the rocket. Carefully stir to mix and heat through. Season well with salt and freshly ground black pepper. Serve immediately with plenty of shaved Parmesan cheese.

Creamy Pea Sauce with Pasta, Asparagus and Broad Beans

A creamy pea sauce makes a wonderful combination with crunchy young vegetables.

Serves 4

INGREDIENTS

15 ml/1 tbsp olive oil
1 garlic clove, crushed
6 spring onions, sliced
225 g/8 oz/1 cup frozen peas,
  defrosted
350 g/12 oz fresh young asparagus
30 ml/2 tbsp chopped fresh sage, plus
extra leaves to garnish
finely grated rind of 2 lemons
450 ml/¾ pint/1¾ cups vegetable
  stock or water
225 g/8 oz frozen broad beans,
  defrosted
450 g/1 lb tagliatelle
60 ml/4 tbsp low-fat yogurt

lemon

garlic

asparagus

broad beans

peas

yogurt

tagliatelle

sage

spring onion

1 Heat the oil in a pan. Add the garlic and spring onions and cook gently for 2–3 minutes until softened.

2 Add the peas and ⅓ of the asparagus, together with the sage, lemon rind and stock or water. Bring to the boil, reduce the heat and simmer for 10 minutes until tender. Purée in a blender until smooth.

3 Meanwhile remove the outer skins from the broad beans and discard.

4 Cut the remaining asparagus into 5 cm/2 in lengths trimming off any tough fibrous stems, and blanch in boiling water for 2 minutes.

5 Cook the tagliatelle following the instructions on the side of the packet until *al dente*. Drain well.

NUTRITIONAL NOTES
PER PORTION:

CALORIES 522 **FAT** 6.9 g
SATURATED FAT 0.9 g **PROTEIN** 23.8 g
CARBOHYDRATE 97.1 g **FIBRE** 11.2 g

COOK'S TIP

Frozen peas and beans have been used here to cut down the preparation time, but the dish tastes even better if you use fresh young vegetables when in season.

6 Add the cooked asparagus and shelled beans to the sauce and reheat. Stir in the yogurt and toss into the tagliatelle. Garnish with a few extra sage leaves and serve.

Pasta Primavera

Serves 4

INGREDIENTS
225 g/8 oz thin asparagus spears, cut in half
115 g/4 oz mange-tout, topped and tailed
115 g/4 oz whole baby corn-on-the-cob
225 g/8 oz whole baby carrots, trimmed
1 small red pepper, seeded and chopped
8 spring onions, sliced
225 g/8 oz torchietti
150 ml/¼ pint/⅔ cup low-fat cottage cheese
150 ml/¼ pint/⅔ cup low-fat yogurt
15 ml/1 tbsp lemon juice
15 ml/1 tbsp chopped parsley
15 ml/1 tbsp snipped chives
skimmed milk (optional)
salt and ground black pepper
sun-dried tomato bread, to serve

spring onions

baby corn-on-the-cob

red pepper

parsley

baby carrots

lemon

chives

torchietti

mange-tout

asparagus spears

1 Cook the asparagus spears in a pan of boiling, salted water for 3–4 minutes. Add the mange-tout halfway through the cooking time. Drain and rinse both under cold water.

2 Cook the baby corn, carrots, red pepper and spring onions in the same way until tender. Drain and rinse.

low-fat yogurt   *low-fat cottage cheese*

3 Cook the pasta in a large pan of boiling, salted water until *al dente*. Drain thoroughly.

NUTRITIONAL NOTES
PER PORTION:

ENERGY 320Kcals/1344KJ **FAT** 3.1g
SATURATED FAT 0.4g **CHOLESTEROL** 3mg
CARBOHYDRATE 58g **FIBRE** 6.2g

4 Put the cottage cheese, yogurt, lemon juice, parsley, chives and seasoning into a food processor or blender and process until smooth. Thin the sauce with skimmed milk, if necessary. Put into a large pan with the pasta and vegetables, heat gently and toss carefully. Transfer to a serving plate and serve with sun-dried tomato bread.

Tagliatelle with Mushrooms

Serves 4

INGREDIENTS

1 small onion, finely chopped
2 garlic cloves, crushed
150 ml/¼ pint/⅔ cup
    vegetable stock
225 g/8 oz mixed fresh mushrooms,
    such as field, chestnut, oyster,
    or chanterelles
60 ml/4 tbsp white or red wine
10 ml/2 tsp concentrated
    tomato purée
15 ml/1 tbsp soy sauce
5 ml/1 tsp chopped fresh thyme
30 ml/2 tbsp chopped fresh parsley
225 g/8 oz fresh sun-dried tomato
    and herb tagliatelle
salt and ground black pepper
shavings of Parmesan cheese,
    to serve (optional)

tomato purée   *Parmesan cheese*   *onion*

mixed mushrooms

thyme   *parsley*

vegetable stock

garlic

soy sauce

white wine

tagliatelle

NUTRITIONAL NOTES

PER PORTION:

ENERGY 241Kcals/1010KJ **FAT** 2.4g
SATURATED FAT 0.7g **CHOLESTEROL** 3mg
CARBOHYDRATE 45g **FIBRE** 3g

1 Put the onion and garlic into a pan with the stock. Then cover and cook for 5 minutes or until tender.

2 Add the mushrooms (quartered or sliced if large or left whole if small), wine, purée and soy sauce. Cover and cook for 5 minutes.

3 Remove the lid from the pan and boil until the liquid has reduced by half. Stir in the chopped fresh herbs and season to taste.

4 Cook the pasta in a large pan of boiling, salted water until *al dente*. Drain thoroughly and toss lightly with the mushrooms. Serve at once with shavings of Parmesan cheese, if using.

Vegetarian Lasagne

Serves 6–8

INGREDIENTS

1 small aubergine
1 large onion, finely chopped
2 garlic cloves, crushed
150 ml/¼ pint/⅔ cup
    vegetable stock
225 g/8 oz mushrooms, sliced
400 g/14 oz can chopped tomatoes
30 ml/2 tbsp tomato purée
150 ml/¼ pint/⅔ cup red wine
1.5 ml/¼ tsp ground ginger
5 ml/1 tsp mixed dried herbs
10–12 sheets lasagne
salt and pepper
25 g/1 oz low-fat margarine
25 g/1 oz plain flour
300 ml/½ pint/1¼ cups
    skimmed milk
large pinch of grated nutmeg
200 g/7 oz low-fat cottage cheese
1 egg, beaten
15 g/½ oz grated Parmesan cheese
25 g/1 oz reduced-fat Cheddar
    cheese, grated
salt and ground black pepper

1 Wash the aubergine and cut it into 2.5 cm/1 in cubes. Put the onion and garlic into a saucepan with the stock, cover and cook for about 5 minutes or until tender.

2 Add the diced aubergine, sliced mushrooms, tomatoes, tomato purée, wine, ginger, seasoning and herbs. Bring to the boil, cover and cook for 15–20 minutes. Remove the lid and cook rapidly to evaporate the liquid by half.

3 To make the sauce, put the margarine, flour, skimmed milk and nutmeg into a pan. Whisk together over the heat until thickened and smooth. Season to taste.

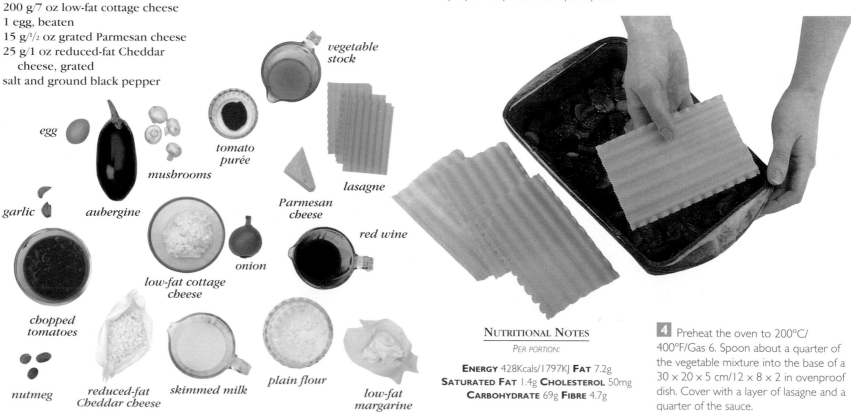

vegetable stock

egg

tomato purée

mushrooms

lasagne

garlic

aubergine

Parmesan cheese

red wine

onion

low-fat cottage cheese

chopped tomatoes

nutmeg

reduced-fat Cheddar cheese

skimmed milk

plain flour

low-fat margarine

NUTRITIONAL NOTES

PER PORTION:

ENERGY 428Kcals/1797KJ **FAT** 7.2g
SATURATED FAT 1.4g **CHOLESTEROL** 50mg
CARBOHYDRATE 69g **FIBRE** 4.7g

4 Preheat the oven to 200°C/400°F/Gas 6. Spoon about a quarter of the vegetable mixture into the base of a 30 × 20 × 5 cm/12 × 8 × 2 in ovenproof dish. Cover with a layer of lasagne and a quarter of the sauce.

5 Repeat with two more layers, then cover with the cottage cheese. Beat the egg into the remaining sauce and pour over the top. Sprinkle with the two grated cheeses.

6 Bake for 25–30 minutes or until the top is golden brown.

Crescent Spinach Ravioli

Serves 4–6

INGREDIENTS
bunch of spring onions,
    finely chopped
1 carrot, coarsely grated
2 garlic cloves, crushed
200 g/7 oz low-fat cottage cheese
15 ml/1 tbsp chopped dill
4 halves sun-dried tomatoes,
    finely chopped
25 g/1 oz grated Parmesan cheese
1 quantity of basic pasta dough,
    with 115 g/4 oz frozen chopped
    spinach added
egg white, beaten, for brushing
flour, for dusting
salt and ground black pepper
2 halves sun-dried tomatoes, finely
    chopped, and fresh dill,
    to garnish

carrot

dill

sun-dried tomatoes

garlic

spring onions

Parmesan cheese

spinach

low-fat cottage cheese

1 Put the spring onions, carrot, garlic and cottage cheese into a bowl. Add the chopped dill, tomatoes, seasoning and Parmesan cheese.

2 Roll the spinach pasta into thin sheets, cut into 7.5 cm/3 in rounds with a fluted pastry cutter.

3 Place a dessertspoon of filling in the centre of each circle. Brush the edges with egg white.

4 Fold each in half to make crescents. Press the edges together to seal. Transfer to a floured dish towel to rest for 1 hour before cooking. Makes about 80 crescents.

5 Cook the pasta in a large pan of boiling, salted water for 5 minutes (cook in batches to stop them sticking together). Drain well.

6 Put the crescents on to warmed serving plates and garnish with sun-dried tomatoes and dill.

NUTRITIONAL NOTES
PER PORTION:

ENERGY 312Kcals/1309KJ **FAT** 7.3g
SATURATED FAT 2.4g **CHOLESTEROL** 119mg
CARBOHYDRATE 43g **FIBRE** 3.4g

Vegetarian Cannelloni

Serves 4–6

INGREDIENTS

1 onion, finely chopped
2 garlic cloves, crushed
2 carrots, coarsely grated
2 sticks celery, finely chopped
150 g/¼ pint/⅔ cup vegetable stock
115 g/4 oz red or green lentils
400 g/14 oz can chopped tomatoes
30 ml/2 tbsp tomato purée
2.5 ml/½ tsp ground ginger
5 ml/1 tsp fresh thyme
5 ml/1 tsp chopped fresh rosemary
40 g/1½ oz low-fat margarine
40 g/1½ oz plain flour
600 ml/1 pint/2½ cups
    skimmed milk
1 bay leaf
large pinch grated nutmeg
16–18 cannelloni
25 g/1 oz reduced-fat Cheddar
    cheese, grated
25 g/1 oz grated Parmesan cheese
25 g/1 oz fresh white breadcrumbs
salt and ground black pepper
flat leaf parsley, to garnish

1 To make the filling put the onion, garlic, carrots and celery into a large saucepan, add half the stock, cover and cook for 5 minutes or until tender.

2 Add the lentils, chopped tomatoes, tomato purée, ginger, thyme, rosemary and seasoning. Bring to the boil, cover and cook for 20 minutes. Remove the lid and cook for about 10 minutes until thick and soft. Leave to cool.

3 To make the sauce, put the margarine, flour, skimmed milk and bay leaf into a pan and whisk over the heat until thick and smooth. Season with salt, pepper and nutmeg. Discard the bay leaf.

plain flour

low-fat margarine

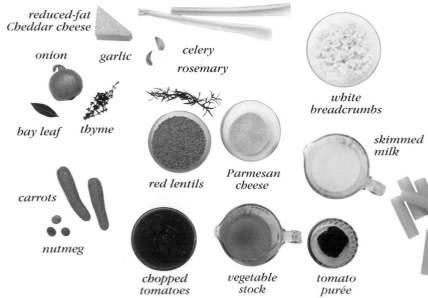

reduced-fat Cheddar cheese
onion *garlic* *celery* *rosemary*
white breadcrumbs
bay leaf *thyme*
skimmed milk
carrots *red lentils* *Parmesan cheese*
nutmeg
cannelloni tubes
chopped tomatoes *vegetable stock* *tomato purée*

4 Fill the uncooked cannelloni by piping the filling into each tube. (It is easiest to hold them upright with one end flat on a board, while piping into the other end.)

5 Preheat the oven to 180°C/350°F/ Gas 4. Spoon half the sauce into the bottom of a 20 cm/8 in square ovenproof dish. Lay two rows of filled cannelloni on top and spoon over the remaining sauce.

6 Scatter over the cheeses and breadcrumbs. Bake in the preheated oven for 30–40 minutes. Grill to brown the top, if necessary. Garnish with flat leaf parsley.

NUTRITIONAL NOTES
PER PORTION:

ENERGY 579Kcals/2432KJ **FAT** 9.8g
SATURATED FAT 2.7g **CHOLESTEROL** 13mg
CARBOHYDRATE 100g **FIBRE** 5.7g

Tagliatelle with Spinach Gnocchi

Serves 4–6

INGREDIENTS
450 g/1 lb mixed flavoured
    tagliatelle
flour, for dusting
shavings of Parmesan cheese,
    to garnish

SPINACH GNOCCHI
450 g/1 lb frozen chopped spinach
1 small onion, finely chopped
1 garlic clove, crushed
1.5 ml/¼ tsp ground nutmeg
400 g/14 oz low-fat cottage cheese
115 g/4 oz dried white breadcrumbs
75 g/3 oz semolina or plain flour
50 g/2 oz grated Parmesan cheese
3 egg whites
salt and pepper

TOMATO SAUCE
1 onion, finely chopped
1 stick celery, finely chopped
1 red pepper, seeded and diced
1 garlic clove, crushed
150 ml/¼ pint/⅔ cup
    vegetable stock
400 g/14 oz can tomatoes
15 ml/1 tbsp tomato purée
10 ml/2 tsp caster sugar
5 ml/1 tsp dried oregano

1 To make the tomato sauce, put the chopped onion, celery, pepper and garlic into a non-stick pan. Add the stock, bring to the boil and cook for 5 minutes or until tender.

2 Add the tomatoes, tomato purée, sugar and oregano. Season to taste, bring to the boil and simmer for 30 minutes until thick, stirring occasionally.

3 Meanwhile, put the frozen spinach, onion and garlic into a saucepan, cover and cook until the spinach is defrosted. Remove the lid and increase the heat to drive off any moisture. Season with salt, pepper and nutmeg. Cool the spinach in a bowl, add the remaining ingredients and mix thoroughly.

celery

egg _nutmeg_ _garlic_

onion

low-fat cottage cheese

flavoured tagliatelle _red pepper_

grated Parmesan cheese _spinach_

dried white breadcrumbs

vegetable stock

tomato purée _tomatoes_ _semolina_

4 Shape the mixture into about 24 ovals with two dessertspoons and place them on a lightly floured tray. Place in the fridge for 30 minutes.

5 Have a large shallow pan of boiling, salted water ready. Cook the gnocchi in batches, for about 5 minutes (the water should simmer gently and not boil). As soon as the gnocchi rise to the surface, remove them with a slotted spoon and drain thoroughly.

6 Cook the tagliatelle in a large pan of boiling, salted water until *al dente*. Drain thoroughly. Transfer to warmed serving plates, top with gnocchi and spoon over the tomato sauce. Scatter with shavings of Parmesan cheese and serve at once.

NUTRITIONAL NOTES
PER PORTION:

ENERGY 789Kcals/3315KJ **FAT** 10.9g
SATURATED FAT 3.7g **CHOLESTEROL** 20mg
CARBOHYDRATE 135g **FIBRE** 8.1g

Tofu Stir-fry with Egg Noodles

Serves 4

INGREDIENTS

225 g/8 oz firm smoked tofu
45 ml/3 tbsp dark soy sauce
30 ml/2 tbsp sherry or vermouth
3 leeks, sliced thinly
2.5 cm/1 in piece root ginger, peeled and finely grated
1–2 red chillies, seeded and sliced in rings
1 small red pepper, seeded and sliced thinly
150 ml/¼ pint/⅔ cup vegetable stock
10 ml/2 tsp runny honey
10 ml/2 tsp cornflour
225 g/8 oz medium egg noodles
salt and ground black pepper

leeks

egg noodles

root ginger

smoked tofu

red chillies

red pepper

soy sauce

vegetable stock

vermouth

1 Cut the tofu into 2 cm/¾ in cubes. Put it into a bowl with the soy sauce and sherry or vermouth. Toss to coat each piece and leave to marinate for about 30 minutes.

2 Put the leeks, ginger, chilli, pepper and stock into a frying pan. Bring to the boil and cook quickly for 2–3 minutes until just soft.

3 Strain the tofu, reserving the marinade. Mix the honey and cornflour into the marinade.

4 Put the egg noodles into a large pan of boiling water and leave to stand for about 6 minutes until cooked (or follow the instructions on the packet).

5 Heat a non-stick frying pan and quickly fry the tofu until lightly golden brown on all sides.

6 In a saucepan, add the vegetable mixture to the tofu with the marinade, and stir well until the liquid is thick and glossy. Spoon on to the egg noodles and serve at once.

NUTRITIONAL NOTES

PER PORTION

ENERGY 345Kcals/1448KJ **FAT** 8.2g
SATURATED FAT 0.7g **CHOLESTEROL** 0mg
CARBOHYDRATE 55g **FIBRE** 2.5g

Ratatouille Penne Bake

Serves 6

INGREDIENTS
1 small aubergine
2 courgettes, thickly sliced
200 g/7 oz firm tofu, cubed
45 ml/3 tbsp dark soy sauce
1 garlic clove, crushed
10 ml/2 tsp sesame seeds
1 small red pepper, seeded
    and sliced
1 onion, finely chopped
1–2 garlic cloves, crushed
150 ml/¼ pint/⅔ cup
    vegetable stock
3 firm ripe tomatoes, skinned,
    seeded and quartered
15 ml/1 tbsp chopped mixed herbs
225 g/8 oz penne
salt and ground black pepper
crusty bread, to serve

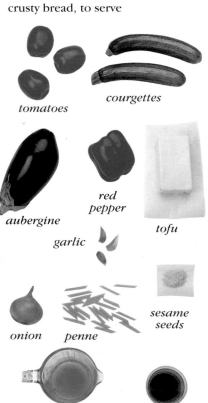

tomatoes

courgettes

aubergine

red
pepper

garlic

tofu

onion   penne

sesame
seeds

vegetable stock   soy sauce

1 Wash and cut the aubergine into 2.5 cm/1 in cubes. Put into a colander with the courgettes, sprinkle with salt and leave to drain for 30 minutes.

2 Mix the tofu with the soy sauce, garlic and sesame seeds. Cover and marinate for 30 minutes.

NUTRITIONAL NOTES
PER PORTION:

ENERGY 208Kcals/873KJ **FAT** 3.7g
SATURATED FAT 0.5g **CHOLESTEROL** 0mg
CARBOHYDRATE 36g **FIBRE** 3.9g

3 Put the pepper, onion and garlic into a saucepan, with the stock. Bring to the boil, cover and cook for 5 minutes until tender. Remove the lid and boil until all the stock has evaporated. Add the tomatoes and herbs and cook for a further 3 minutes. Season to taste.

4 Meanwhile cook the pasta in a large pan of boiling, salted water until *al dente*. Drain thoroughly. Toss the pasta with the vegetables and tofu. Transfer to a shallow 25 cm/10 in square ovenproof dish and grill until lightly toasted. Transfer to a serving dish and serve with fresh crusty bread.

Fettuccine with Broccoli and Garlic

Serves 4

INGREDIENTS
3–4 garlic cloves, crushed
350 g/12 oz broccoli florets
150 ml/¼ pint/⅔ cup chicken stock
60 ml/4 tbsp white wine
30 ml/2 tbsp chopped fresh basil
60 ml/4 tbsp grated
   Parmesan cheese
350 g/12 oz fettuccine or tagliatelle
salt and pepper
fresh basil leaves, to garnish

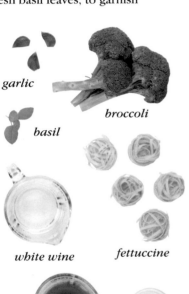

garlic

broccoli

basil

white wine

fettuccine

chicken stock

grated Parmesan cheese

1 Put the garlic, broccoli and stock into a saucepan. Bring to the boil and cook for 5 minutes until tender, stirring from time to time.

2 Mash with a fork or potato masher, until roughly chopped. Return to the pan with the white wine, basil and Parmesan cheese. Season to taste.

NUTRITIONAL NOTES

PER PORTION:

ENERGY 477Kcals/2002KJ **FAT** 8.3g
SATURATED FAT 3.4g **CHOLESTEROL** 15mg
CARBOHYDRATE 71g **FIBRE** 5g

3 Cook the fettuccine in a large pan of boiling, salted water until *al dente*. Drain thoroughly.

4 Return to the pan with half the broccoli sauce, toss to coat the pasta and transfer to serving plates. Top with the remaining broccoli sauce and garnish with basil leaves.

Salsas, Salads & Side Dishes

Roasted Pepper and Ginger Salsa

Char-grilling to remove the skins will take away any bitterness from the peppers.

NUTRITIONAL NOTES

PER PORTION:

ENERGY 33 Kcals/138 KJ **FAT** 0.6 g
SATURATED FAT 0 **PROTEIN** 1.4 g
CARBOHYDRATE 5.9 g **FIBRE** 1.6 g

Serves 6

INGREDIENTS
1 large red pepper
1 large yellow pepper
1 large orange pepper
2.5 cm/1 in piece root ginger
2.5 ml/$^1/_2$ tsp coriander seeds
5 ml/1 tsp cumin seeds
1 small garlic clove
30 ml/2 tbsp lime or lemon juice
1 small red onion, finely chopped
30 ml/2 tbsp chopped fresh
    coriander
5 ml/1 tsp chopped fresh thyme
salt and pepper

red pepper

thyme

yellow pepper

coriander and cumin seeds

orange pepper

garlic

lime

root ginger

coriander

1 Quarter the peppers and remove the stalk, seeds and membranes.

2 Grill the quarters, skin side up, until charred and blistered. Rub away the skins and slice very finely.

3 Peel or scrape the root ginger and chop roughly.

4 Over a moderate heat, gently dry-fry the spices for 30 seconds to 1 minute, making sure they don't scorch.

5 Crush the spices in a pestle and mortar. Add the ginger and garlic and continue to work to a pulp. Work in the lime or lemon juice.

6 Mix together the peppers, spice mixture, onion and herbs. Season to taste and spoon into a serving bowl. Chill for 1–2 hours before serving as an accompaniment to barbecued meats or kebabs.

Mango and Red Onion Salsa

A very simple salsa, which is livened up by the addition of passion-fruit pulp.

NUTRITIONAL NOTES

PER PORTION:

ENERGY 61 Kcals/255 KJ **FAT** 0.3 g
SATURATED FAT 0 **PROTEIN** 1.1 g
CARBOHYDRATE 14.5 g **FIBRE** 2.9 g

Serves 4

INGREDIENTS
1 large ripe mango
1 red onion
2 passion fruit
6 large fresh basil leaves
juice of 1 lime, to taste
sea salt

mango

red onion

passion fruit

basil

lime juice

1 Holding the mango upright on a chopping board, use a large knife to slice the flesh away from either side of the large flat stone in two portions.

2 Using a smaller knife, trim away any flesh still clinging to the top and bottom of the stone.

3 Score the flesh of the mango halves deeply, taking care to avoid cutting through the skin: make parallel incisions about 1 cm/½ in apart; turn and cut lines in the opposite direction. Carefully turn the skin inside out so the flesh stands out like hedgehog spikes. Slice the dice away from the skin.

4 Finely chop the red onion and place it in a bowl with the mango.

5 Halve the passion fruit, scoop out the seeds and pulp, and add to the mango mixture.

6 Tear the basil leaves coarsely and stir them into the salsa with lime juice and a little sea salt to taste. Serve immediately.

VARIATION
Sweetcorn kernels are a delicious addition to this salsa.

Tuna, Chick-pea and Cherry Tomato Salad

A quick and easy salad that makes a satisfying light meal when served with thick slices of wholemeal bread.

NUTRITIONAL NOTES

PER PORTION:

ENERGY 198Kcals/839KJ PROTEIN 20.98g
FAT 4.30g SATURATED FAT 0.62g
CARBOHYDRATE 20.70g FIBRE 5.88g
ADDED SUGAR 0.00g SODIUM 0.45g

Serves 6

INGREDIENTS

5 ml/1 tsp olive oil
1 garlic clove, crushed
5 ml/1 tsp ground coriander
5 ml/1 tsp garam masala
5 ml/1 tsp hot chilli powder
120 ml/4 fl oz/½ cup tomato juice
30 ml/2 tbsp balsamic vinegar
dash of Tabasco sauce
675 g/1½ lb cherry tomatoes, halved
½ cucumber, sliced
1 bunch radishes, sliced
1 bunch spring onions, chopped
50 g/2 oz watercress, chopped
2 x 400 g/14 oz cans chick-peas,
  rinsed and drained
400 g/14 oz can tuna in brine,
  drained and flaked
15 ml/1 tbsp chopped fresh parsley
15 ml/1 tbsp chopped fresh chives
salt and ground black pepper

1 Heat the oil in a small saucepan. Add the garlic and spices and cook gently for 1 minute, stirring.

2 Stir in the tomato juice, vinegar and Tabasco sauce, and heat gently until the mixture is boiling. Remove the pan from the heat and set aside to cool slightly.

3 Put the tomatoes and cucumber in a serving bowl.

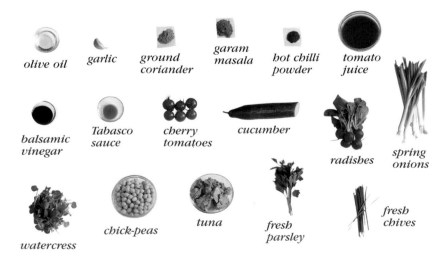

olive oil   garlic   ground coriander   garam masala   hot chilli powder   tomato juice

balsamic vinegar   Tabasco sauce   cherry tomatoes   cucumber   radishes   spring onions

watercress   chick-peas   tuna   fresh parsley   fresh chives

4 Add the radishes, spring onions and watercress.

5 Stir in the chick-peas, the tuna and the herbs.

6 Pour the tomato dressing over the salad and toss the ingredients together to mix. Season to taste and serve.

Fruit and Fibre Salad

Fresh, fast and filling, this salad makes a great starter, supper or snack.

Serves 4–6

INGREDIENTS
225 g/8 oz red or white cabbage or a
   mixture of both
3 medium carrots
1 pear
1 red-skinned eating apple
200 g/7 oz can green flageolet beans,
   drained
50 g/2 oz/¼ cup chopped dates

FOR THE DRESSING
2.5 ml/½ tsp dry English mustard
10 ml/2 tsp clear honey
30 ml/2 tbsp orange juice
5 ml/1 tsp white wine vinegar
2.5 ml/½ tsp paprika
salt and freshly ground black pepper

carrot

dates

orange

flageolet beans

cabbage   *pear*   *apple*

1 Shred the cabbage very finely, discarding any tough stalks.

2 Cut the carrots into very thin strips, about 5 cm/2 in long.

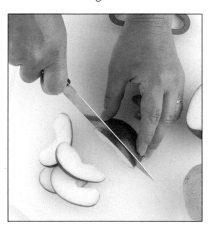

3 Quarter, core and slice the pear and apple, leaving the skin on.

4 Put the fruit and vegetables in a bowl with the beans and dates. Mix well.

5 For the dressing, blend the mustard with the honey until smooth. Add the orange juice, vinegar, paprika and seasoning and mix well.

NUTRITIONAL NOTES

Per portion:

ENERGY 137 K Cals / 574 KJ **PROTEIN** 4.56 g
FAT 0.87 g **SATURATED FAT** 0.03 g
CARBOHYDRATE 29.43 g **FIBRE** 6.28 g
ADDED SUGAR 1.91 g **SALT** 0.30 g

6 Pour the dressing over the salad and toss to coat. Chill in the refrigerator for 30 minutes before serving.

Apple Coleslaw

The term coleslaw stems from the Dutch *koolsla*, meaning 'cool cabbage'. There are many variations of this salad; this recipe combines the sweet flavours of apple and carrot with celery salt. Coleslaw is traditionally served with cold ham.

Serves 4

INGREDIENTS

450 g/1 lb white cabbage
1 medium onion
2 apples, peeled and cored
175 g/6 oz carrots, peeled
150 ml/5 fl oz/⅔ cup low-fat
   mayonnaise
5 ml/1 tsp celery salt
black pepper

carrots

onion

apple

white cabbage

2 Feed the cabbage and the onion through a food processor fitted with a slicing blade. Change to a grating blade and grate the apples and carrots. Alternatively use a hand grater and vegetable slicer.

3 Combine the salad ingredients in a large bowl. Fold in the mayonnaise and season with celery salt and freshly ground black pepper.

1 Discard the outside leaves of the cabbage if they are dirty, cut the cabbage into 5 cm/2 in wedges, then remove the stem section.

NUTRITIONAL NOTES

PER PORTION:

ENERGY 91 Kcals/380.5 KJ **FAT** 3.9 g
SATURATED FAT 0.09 g

COOK'S TIP

This recipe can be adapted easily to suit different tastes. You could add 125 g/4 oz/½ cup chopped walnuts or raisins for added texture. For a richer coleslaw, add 125 g/4 oz/½ cup grated Cheddar cheese. You may find you will need smaller portions, as the cheese makes a more filling dish.

Carrot, Raisin and Apricot Coleslaw

A tasty high fibre coleslaw, combining cabbage, carrots and dried fruit in a light yogurt dressing.

Serves 6

INGREDIENTS

350 g/12 oz/3 cups white cabbage, finely shredded
225 g/8 oz/1½ cups carrots, coarsely grated
1 red onion, sliced
3 celery sticks, sliced
175 g/6 oz/1 cup raisins
75 g/3 oz ready-to-eat dried apricots, chopped
120 ml/8 tbsp reduced-calorie mayonnaise
90 ml/6 tbsp low-fat plain yogurt
30 ml/2 tbsp chopped fresh mixed herbs
salt and ground black pepper

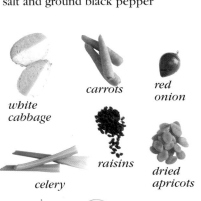

white cabbage *carrots* *red onion*

celery *raisins* *dried apricots*

reduced-calorie mayonnaise *low-fat plain yogurt*

fresh mixed herbs

 *salt*  *black pepper*

1 Put the cabbage and carrot in a large bowl.

2 Add the onion, celery, raisins and apricots and mix well.

3 In a small bowl, mix together the mayonnaise, yogurt, herbs and seasoning.

COOK'S TIP

Use other dried fruit such as sultanas and ready-to-eat dried pears or peaches in place of the raisins and apricots.

4 Add the mayonnaise dressing to the bowl and toss the ingredients together to mix. Cover and chill for several hours before serving.

NUTRITIONAL NOTES

PER PORTION:

ENERGY 204Kcals/858KJ PROTEIN 3.71g
FAT 6.37g SATURATED FAT 0.93g
CARBOHYDRATE 35.04g FIBRE 4.25g
ADDED SUGAR 0.50g SODIUM 0.24g

Marinated Cucumber Salad

Sprinkling the cucumber with salt draws out some of
the water and makes them crisper.

Serves 4–6

INGREDIENTS
2 medium cucumbers
15 ml/1 tbsp salt
90 g/3½ oz/½ cup granulated sugar
175 ml/6 fl oz/¾ cup dry cider
15 ml/1 tbsp cider vinegar
45 ml/3 tbsp chopped fresh dill
pinch of pepper

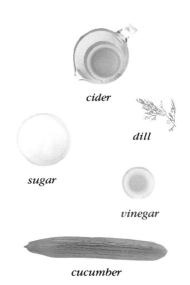

cider

dill

sugar

vinegar

cucumber

NUTRITIONAL NOTES
PER PORTION:

ENERGY 111 K Cals/465 KJ **PROTEIN** 0.52 g
FAT 0.14 g **SATURATED FAT** 0.01 g
CARBOHYDRATE 25.59 g **FIBRE** 0.62 g
ADDED SUGAR 23.62 g **SALT** 0.02 g

1 Slice the cucumbers thinly and place
them in a colander, sprinkling salt
between each layer. Put the colander
over a bowl and leave to drain for 1 hour.

2 Thoroughly rinse the cucumber
under cold running water to remove
excess salt, then pat dry on absorbent
kitchen paper.

3 Gently heat the sugar, cider and
vinegar in a saucepan, until the sugar has
dissolved. Remove from the heat and
leave to cool. Put the cucumber slices in a
bowl, pour over the cider mixture and
leave to marinate for 2 hours.

4 Drain the cucumber and sprinkle
with the dill and pepper to taste. Mix well
and transfer to a serving dish. Chill in the
refrigerator until ready to serve.

Cachumbar

Cachumbar is a salad relish most commonly served with Indian curries. There are many versions, although this one will leave your mouth feeling cool and fresh after a spicy meal.

Serves 4

INGREDIENTS
3 ripe tomatoes
2 spring onions (scallions), chopped
¼ tsp caster (superfine) sugar
salt
45 ml/3 tbsp chopped fresh coriander

tomatoes

coriander

spring onion

COOK'S TIP
Cachumbar also makes a fine accompaniment to fresh crab, lobster and shellfish.

NUTRITIONAL NOTES
PER PORTION:

ENERGY 61 Kcals/259 KJ FAT 1.1 g
SATURATED FAT 0.3 g

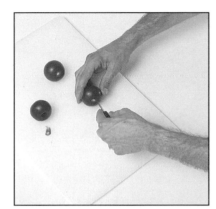

1 Remove the tough cores from the tomatoes with a small knife.

2 Halve the tomatoes, remove the seeds and dice the flesh.

3 Combine the tomatoes with the spring onions, sugar, salt and chopped coriander. Serve at room temperature.

Vegetables à la Grecque

This simple side salad is made with winter vegetables, but you can vary it according to the season.

Serves 4

INGREDIENTS
175 ml/6 fl oz/¾ cup white wine
5 ml/1 tsp olive oil
30 ml/2 tbsp lemon juice
2 bay leaves
sprig of fresh thyme
4 juniper berries
450 g/1 lb leeks, trimmed and cut into
   2.5 cm/1 in lengths
1 small cauliflower, broken into
   florets
4 celery sticks, sliced on the diagonal
30 ml/2 tbsp chopped fresh parsley
salt and freshly ground black pepper

wine

celery

cauliflower

parsley

olive oil

leeks

NUTRITIONAL NOTES
PER PORTION:

ENERGY 88.25Kcals/349KJ PROTEIN 3.61g
FAT 2.32g SATURATED FAT 0.37g
CARBOHYDRATE 5.32g
FIBRE 3.86g SUGAR 4.23g
SODIUM 28mg

1 Put the wine, oil, lemon juice, bay leaves, thyme and juniper berries into a large, heavy-based saucepan and bring to the boil. Cover and leave to simmer for 20 minutes.

2 Add the leeks, cauliflower and celery. Simmer very gently for 5–6 minutes or until just tender.

COOK'S TIP
Choose a dry or medium-dry white wine for this dish.

3 Remove the vegetables with a slotted spoon and transfer them to a serving dish. Briskly boil the cooking liquid for 15-20 minutes, or until reduced by half. Strain.

4 Stir the parsley into the liquid and season to taste. Pour over the vegetables and leave to cool. Chill in the refrigerator for at least 1 hour before serving.

Green Bean Salad with Egg Topping

When green beans are fresh and plentiful, serve them lightly cooked as a salad starter topped with butter-fried breadcrumbs, egg and parsley.

Serves 6

INGREDIENTS

700 g/1½ lb green beans, topped and tailed
salt
30 ml/2 tbsp garlic oil
30 ml/2 tbsp polyunsaturated margarine
50 g/2 oz/1 cup fresh white breadcrumbs
60 ml/4 tbsp chopped fresh parsley
1 egg, hard-boiled and shelled

parsley

egg

green beans

2 Heat the margarine in a large frying-pan, add the breadcrumbs and fry until golden. Remove from the heat, add the parsley, then grate in the hard-boiled egg.

3 Place the beans in a shallow serving dish and spoon on the breadcrumb topping. Serve at room temperature.

1 Bring a large saucepan of salted water to the boil. Add the beans and cook for 6 minutes. Drain well, toss in garlic oil and allow to cool.

NUTRITIONAL NOTES
Per portion:

ENERGY 132 Kcals/546 KJ **FAT** 9.5 g
SATURATED FAT 1.8 g

COOK'S TIP

Few cooks need reminding how to boil an egg, but many are faced with the problem of a dark ring around the yolk when cooked. This is caused by boiling for longer than the optimum period of 12 minutes. Allow boiled eggs to cool in water for easy peeling.

Sweet Turnip Salad with Horseradish and Caraway

The robust-flavoured turnip partners well with the taste of horseradish and caraway seeds. This salad is delicious with cold roast beef or smoked trout.

Serves 4

INGREDIENTS
350 g/12 oz medium turnips
2 spring onions (scallions), white part only, chopped
15 ml/1 tbsp caster (superfine) sugar
salt
30 ml/2 tbsp horseradish cream
10 ml/2 tsp caraway seeds

turnips

NUTRITIONAL NOTES
PER PORTION:

ENERGY 48 Kcals/202 KJ **FAT** 0.9 g
SATURATED FAT 0.08 g

COOK'S TIP

If turnips are not available, giant white radish (mooli) can be used as a substitute.

1 Peel, slice and shred the turnips – or grate them if you wish.

2 Add the spring onions (scallions), sugar and salt, then rub together with your hands to soften the turnip.

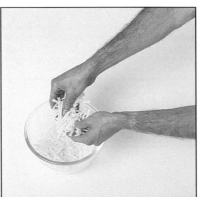

3 Fold in the horseradish cream and caraway seeds.

spring onions

Lentil and Cabbage Salad

This warm crunchy salad makes a satisfying meal if served with crusty French bread or wholemeal rolls.

Serves 4–6

INGREDIENTS
225 g/8 oz/1 cup puy lentils
1 garlic clove
1 bay leaf
1 small onion, peeled and studded
   with 2 cloves
15 ml/1 tbsp olive oil
1 red onion, finely sliced
2 garlic cloves, crushed
15 ml/1 tbsp thyme leaves
350 g/12 oz cabbage, finely shredded
finely grated rind and juice of 1 lemon
15 ml/1 tbsp raspberry vinegar
salt and freshly ground black pepper

NUTRITIONAL NOTES
Per portion:

ENERGY 230 Kcals/970 KJ **FAT** 4.1 g
SATURATED FAT 0.5 g

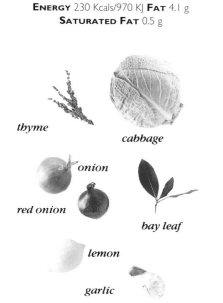

thyme

cabbage

onion

red onion

bay leaf

lemon

garlic

cloves

peppercorns

1 Rinse the lentils in cold water and place in a large pan with 1.3 litres/ 2¼ pints/6 cups cold water, peeled garlic clove, bay leaf and clove-studded onion. Bring to the boil and cook for 10 minutes. Reduce the heat, cover and simmer gently for 15-20 minutes. Drain; remove the onion, garlic and bay leaf.

2 Heat the oil in a large pan. Add the red onion, garlic and thyme and cook for 5 minutes until softened.

3 Add the cabbage and cook for 3–5 minutes until just cooked but still crunchy.

4 Stir in the cooked lentils, lemon rind and juice and the raspberry vinegar. Season to taste and serve.

Curried New Potato and Green Bean Salad

Tender new potatoes and green beans tossed together in a subtly flavoured light dressing make this salad ideal for serving with chargrilled vegetables and fresh wholemeal bread.

Serves 6

INGREDIENTS

225 g/8 oz/1½ cups green beans, trimmed and halved
675 g/1½ lb cooked baby new potatoes
2 bunches spring onions, chopped
115 g/4 oz/⅔ cup sultanas
75 g/3 oz ready-to-eat dried pears, finely chopped
90 ml/6 tbsp reduced-calorie mayonnaise
60 ml/4 tbsp low fat plain yogurt
30 ml/2 tbsp Greek yogurt
15 ml/1 tbsp tomato purée
15 ml/1 tbsp curry paste
30 ml/2 tbsp snipped fresh chives
salt and ground black pepper

green beans

baby new potatoes

spring onions

sultanas

dried pears

reduced-calorie mayonnaise

low fat plain yogurt

Greek yogurt

tomato purée

curry paste

chives

black pepper

 salt

1 Cook the beans in boiling water for about 5 minutes, until tender. Rinse under cold running water to cool them quickly, drain and set aside.

2 Put the potatoes, beans, spring onions, sultanas and pears in a bowl and mix together.

3 In a small bowl, mix together the mayonnaise, yogurts, tomato purée, curry paste, chives and seasoning.

4 Add the dressing to the bowl and toss the ingredients together to mix. Cover and leave to stand for at least 1 hour before serving.

NUTRITIONAL NOTES

PER PORTION:

ENERGY 235Kcals/994KJ PROTEIN 5.17g
FAT 6.10 SATURATED FAT 1.06g
CARBOHYDRATE 42.62g FIBRE 3.87g
ADDED SUGAR 0.83g SODIUM 0.22g

White Bean and Celery Salad

This simple bean salad is a delicious alternative to the potato salad that seems to appear on every salad menu. If you do not have time to soak and cook dried beans, use canned ones.

Serves 4

INGREDIENTS

450 g/1 lb dried white beans (haricot, canellini, navy or butter beans) or 3 × 400 g/14 oz cans white beans
1 litre/1¾ pints/4½ cups vegetable stock, made from a cube
3 stalks celery, cut into 1 cm/½ in strips
125 ml/4 fl oz French Dressing
45 ml/3 tbsp chopped fresh parsley
salt and pepper

parsley

white beans

celery

1 If using dried beans, cover with plenty of cold water and soak for at least 4 hours. Discard the soaking water, then place the beans in a heavy saucepan. Cover with fresh water, bring to the boil and simmer without a lid for 1½ hours, or until the skins are broken. Cooked beans will squash readily between a thumb and forefinger. Drain the beans. If using canned beans, drain, rinse and use from this stage in the recipe.

NUTRITIONAL NOTES
PER PORTION:

ENERGY 231 Kcals/969 KJ **FAT** 9.05 g
SATURATED FAT 1.9 g

COOK'S TIP

Dried beans that have been kept for longer than 6 months will need soaking overnight to lessen their cooking time. As a rule, the less time beans have been kept in store, the shorter the soaking and cooking time they need. The times given here are suited to freshly purchased beans.

2 Place the cooked beans in a large saucepan. Add the vegetable stock and celery, bring to the boil, cover and simmer for 15 minutes. Drain thoroughly. Moisten the beans with the dressing and leave to cool.

3 Add the chopped parsley and season to taste with salt and pepper.

Roast Pepper and Wild Mushroom Pasta Salad

A combination of grilled peppers and wild mushrooms makes this pasta salad colourful as well as nutritious.

Serves 6

INGREDIENTS
1 red pepper, halved
1 yellow pepper, halved
1 green pepper, halved
350 g/12 oz/3 cups wholewheat
  pasta shells or twists
30 ml/2 tbsp olive oil
45 ml/3 tbsp balsamic vinegar
75 ml/5 tbsp tomato juice
30 ml/2 tbsp chopped fresh basil
15 ml/1 tbsp chopped fresh thyme
175 g/6 oz/2⅓ cups shiitake
  mushrooms, sliced
175 g/6 oz/2⅓ cups oyster
  mushrooms, sliced
400 g/14 oz can black-eyed
  beans, rinsed and drained
115 g/4 oz/⅔ cup sultanas
2 bunches spring onions,
  finely chopped
salt and ground black pepper

red pepper

yellow pepper

green pepper

wholewheat pasta shells

olive oil

balsamic vinegar

tomato juice

fresh basil

fresh thyme

shiitake mushrooms

oyster mushrooms

black-eyed beans

sultanas

spring onions

1 Preheat the grill. Put the peppers cut-side down on a grillpan rack and place under a hot grill for 10–15 minutes, until the skins are charred. Cover the peppers with a clean, damp tea towel and set aside to cool.

2 Meanwhile, cook the pasta in lightly salted, boiling water for 10–12 minutes until *al dente*, then drain thoroughly.

3 Mix together the oil, vinegar, tomato juice, basil and thyme, add to the warm pasta and toss together.

4 Remove and discard the skins from the peppers. Seed and slice the peppers and add to the pasta with the mushrooms, beans, sultanas, spring onions and seasoning. Toss the ingredients to mix and serve immediately or cover and chill in the fridge before serving.

NUTRITIONAL NOTES
PER PORTION:

ENERGY 334Kcals/1425KJ PROTEIN 13.58g
FAT 6.02g SATURATED FAT 0.89g
CARBOHYDRATE 60.74g FIBRE 9.37g
ADDED SUGAR 0.00g SODIUM 0.11g

Sweet and Sour Peppers with Bows

Serves 4–6

INGREDIENTS

1 red, 1 yellow and 1 orange pepper
1 garlic clove, crushed
30 ml/2 tbsp capers
30 ml/2 tbsp raisins
5 ml/1 tsp wholegrain mustard
rind and juice of 1 lime
5 ml/1 tsp runny honey
30 ml/2 tbsp chopped
    fresh coriander
225 g/8 oz pasta bows (farfalle)
salt and ground black pepper
shavings of Parmesan cheese,
    to serve (optional)

raisins

red pepper

yellow pepper

coriander

orange pepper

pasta bows

Parmesan cheese

capers

honey

garlic

1 Quarter the peppers, remove the stalk and seeds. Put into boiling water and cook for 10–15 minutes until tender. Drain and rinse under cold water. Peel away the skin and cut the flesh into strips lengthways.

2 Put the garlic, capers, raisins, mustard, lime rind and juice, honey, coriander and seasoning into a bowl and whisk together.

NUTRITIONAL NOTES

PER PORTION:

ENERGY 268Kcals/1125KJ **FAT** 2.0g
SATURATED FAT 0.5g **CHOLESTEROL** 1.3mg
CARBOHYDRATE 57g **FIBRE** 4.3g

3 Cook the pasta in a large pan of boiling, salted water for 10–12 minutes until tender. Drain thoroughly.

4 Return the pasta to the pan, add the reserved peppers and dressing. Heat gently and toss to mix. Transfer to a warm serving bowl. Serve with a few shavings of Parmesan cheese, if using.

Fruity Rice Salad

An appetizing and colourful rice salad combining many different flavours, ideal for a packed lunch.

Serves 4–6

INGREDIENTS
225 g/8 oz/1 cup mixed brown and
  wild rice
1 yellow pepper, seeded and diced
1 bunch spring onions, chopped
3 sticks celery, chopped
1 large beefsteak tomato, chopped
2 green-skinned eating
  apples, chopped
175 g/6 oz/¾ cup ready-to-eat dried
  apricots, chopped
115 g/4 oz/⅔ cup raisins
30 ml/2 tbsp unsweetened
  apple juice
30 ml/2 tbsp dry sherry
30 ml/2 tbsp light soy sauce
dash of Tabasco sauce
30 ml/2 tbsp chopped fresh parsley
15 ml/1 tbsp chopped fresh rosemary
salt and ground black pepper

mixed brown and wild rice *yellow pepper* *spring onions*

celery *beefsteak tomato* *eating apples*

dried apricots *raisins* *light soy sauce*

unsweetened apple juice *dry sherry*

Tabasco sauce *fresh parsley* *fresh rosemary*

1 Cook the rice in a large saucepan of lightly salted, boiling water for about 30 minutes (or according to the instructions on the packet) until tender. Rinse the rice under cold running water to cool quickly and drain thoroughly.

2 Place the pepper, spring onions, celery, tomato, apples, apricots, raisins and the cooked rice in a serving bowl and mix well.

3 In a small bowl, mix together the apple juice, sherry, soy sauce, Tabasco sauce, herbs and seasoning.

NUTRITIONAL NOTES

PER PORTION:

ENERGY 428Kcals/1817KJ PROTEIN 8.15g
FAT 2.50g SATURATED FAT 0.52g
CARBOHYDRATE 97.15g FIBRE 7.17g
ADDED SUGAR 0.31g SODIUM 0.58g

4 Pour the dressing over the rice mixture and toss the ingredients together to mix. Serve immediately or cover and chill in the fridge before serving.

Bulgur Wheat and Broad Bean Salad

This appetizing salad is ideal served with fresh crusty wholemeal bread and home-made chutney or pickle, and for non-vegetarians it can be served as an accompaniment to grilled lean meat or fish.

Serves 6

INGREDIENTS

350 g/12 oz/2 cups bulgur wheat
225 g/8 oz frozen broad beans
115 g/4 oz/1 cup frozen petit pois
225 g/8 oz cherry tomatoes, halved
1 sweet onion, chopped
1 red pepper, seeded and diced
50 g/2 oz mangetouts, chopped
50 g/2 oz watercress
15 ml/1 tbsp chopped fresh parsley
15 ml/1 tbsp chopped fresh basil
15 ml/1 tbsp chopped fresh thyme
fat-free French dressing
salt and ground black pepper

bulgur wheat *frozen broad beans* *frozen petit pois*

cherry tomatoes *sweet onion* *red pepper*

mangetouts *watercress* *fresh parsley*

fresh basil *fresh thyme* *fat-free French dressing*

salt *black pepper*

1 Soak and cook the bulgur wheat according to the packet instructions. Drain thoroughly and put into a serving bowl.

2 Meanwhile, cook the broad beans and petits pois in boiling water for about 3 minutes, until tender. Drain thoroughly and add to the prepared bulgur wheat.

3 Add the cherry tomatoes, onion, pepper, mangetouts and watercress to the bulgur wheat mixture and mix.

NUTRITIONAL NOTES
PER PORTION:

ENERGY 277Kcals/1162KJ PROTEIN 11.13g
FAT 1.81g SATURATED FAT 0.17g
CARBOHYDRATE 55.34g FIBRE 4.88g
ADDED SUGAR 0.00g SODIUM 0.02g

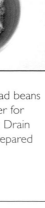

4 Add the herbs, seasoning and enough French dressing to taste, tossing the ingredients together. Serve immediately or cover and chill in the fridge before serving.

COOK'S TIP
Use cooked couscous, boiled brown rice or wholewheat pasta in place of the bulgur wheat.

Thai Fragrant Rice

A lovely, soft, fluffy rice dish, perfumed with fresh lemon grass.

Serves 4

INGREDIENTS
1 piece of lemon grass
2 limes
225 g/8 oz/1 cup brown basmati rice
15 ml/1 tbsp olive oil
1 onion, chopped
2.5 cm/1 in piece of fresh ginger root, peeled and finely chopped
7.5 ml/1½ tsp coriander seeds
7.5 ml/1½ tsp cumin seeds
700 ml/1¼ pints/3 cups vegetable stock
60 ml/4 tbsp chopped fresh coriander
lime wedges, to serve

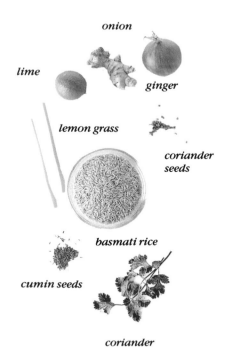

onion

lime

ginger

lemon grass

coriander seeds

basmati rice

cumin seeds

coriander

1 Finely chop the lemon grass.

2 Remove the zest from the limes using a zester or fine grater.

3 Rinse the rice in plenty of cold water until the water runs clear. Drain through a sieve.

4 Heat the oil in a large pan and add the onion, spices, lemon grass and lime zest and cook gently for 2–3 minutes.

5 Add the rice and cook for another minute, then add the stock and bring to the boil. Reduce the heat to very low and cover the pan. Cook gently for 30 minutes then check the rice. If it is still crunchy, cover the pan again and leave for a further 3–5 minutes. Remove from the heat.

6 Stir in the fresh coriander, fluff up the grains, cover and leave for 10 minutes. Serve with lime wedges.

COOK'S TIP
Other varieties of rice, such as white basmati or long grain, can be used for this dish but you will need to adjust the cooking times accordingly.

NUTRITIONAL NOTES
PER PORTION:

ENERGY 232 Kcals/982 KJ **FAT** 4.4 g
SATURATED FAT 0.8 g

Rice with Mushrooms and Prawns

Although mushrooms are not a very common vegetable in India, this dish provides a perfect combination of flavours.

Serves 4

INGREDIENTS
150g/5oz basmati rice
15ml/1 tbsp corn oil
1 medium onion, chopped
4 black peppercorns
2.5cm/1in cinnamon stick
1 bay leaf
1.5ml/¼ tsp black cumin seeds
2 cardamom pods
5ml/1 tsp garlic pulp
5ml/1 tsp ginger pulp
5ml/1 tsp garam masala
5ml/1 tsp chilli powder
7.5ml/1½ tsp salt
115g/4oz frozen cooked, peeled
   prawns, thawed
115g/4oz mushrooms, cut into
   large pieces
30ml/2 tbsp chopped
   fresh coriander
120ml/4fl oz/½ cup natural
   low fat yogurt
15ml/1 tbsp lemon juice
50g/2oz frozen peas
250ml/8fl oz/1 cup water
1 red chilli, seeded and sliced,
   to garnish

basmati rice
mushrooms
prawns
chilli powder
garam masala
onion
salt

yogurt
peppercorns
cinnamon stick
cardamom
ginger pulp
cumin seeds
bay leaf
red chilli
garlic pulp
lemon juice
peas
fresh coriander

1 Wash the rice well and leave to soak in water.

2 Heat the oil in a non-stick wok or frying pan and add the onion, peppercorns, cinnamon, bay leaf, cumin seeds, cardamoms, garlic pulp, ginger pulp, garam masala, chilli powder and salt. Lower the heat and stir-fry for about 2 minutes.

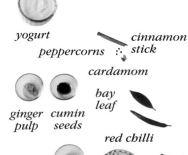

3 Add the prawns and cook for 2 minutes, before adding the mushrooms.

4 Add the coriander and the yogurt, followed by the lemon juice and peas.

NUTRITIONAL NOTES

Per portion:

ENERGY 248 K Cals/1050 K J **PROTEIN** 13.12g
FAT 5.20g **SATURATED FAT** 0.99g
CARBOHYDRATE 40.04g **FIBRE** 1.85g
ADDED SUGAR 0
SALT 1.23g

5 Drain the rice and add it to the prawn mixture. Pour in the water, cover the pan and cook over a medium heat for about 15 minutes, checking once.

6 Remove from the heat and leave to stand, still covered, for about 5 minutes. Transfer to a serving dish and serve garnished with the sliced red chilli.

Vegetable
Dishes

Vegetables Provençal

The flavours of the Mediterranean are created in this delicious vegetable dish, ideal for a starter or lunchtime snack, served with fresh crusty wholemeal bread.

Serves 6

INGREDIENTS
1 onion, sliced
2 leeks, sliced
2 garlic cloves, crushed
1 red pepper, seeded and sliced
1 green pepper, seeded and sliced
1 yellow pepper, seeded and sliced
350 g/12 oz courgettes, sliced
225 g/8 oz/3 cups
  mushrooms, sliced
400 g/14 oz can chopped tomatoes
30 ml/2 tbsp ruby port
30 ml/2 tbsp tomato purée
15 ml/1 tbsp tomato ketchup
400 g/14 oz can chick-peas
115 g/4 oz/1 cup pitted black olives
45 ml/3 tbsp chopped fresh
  mixed herbs
salt and ground black pepper
chopped fresh mixed herbs,
  to garnish

onion   *leeks*

garlic   *red pepper*

yellow pepper   *green pepper*

courgettes   *mushrooms*

chopped tomatoes   *ruby port*   *tomato purée*

tomato ketchup   *chick-peas*   *pitted black olives*   *fresh mixed herbs*

1 Put the onion, leeks, garlic, peppers, courgettes and mushrooms into a large saucepan.

2 Add the tomatoes, port, tomato purée and tomato ketchup and mix well.

3 Rinse and drain the chick-peas and add to the pan.

4 Cover, bring to the boil and simmer gently for 20–30 minutes, until the vegetables are cooked and tender but not overcooked, stirring occasionally.

5 Remove the lid and increase the heat slightly for the last 10 minutes of the cooking time, to thicken the sauce, if liked.

6 Stir in the olives, herbs and seasoning. Serve hot or cold garnished with chopped mixed herbs.

NUTRITIONAL NOTES
PER PORTION:

ENERGY 155Kcals/654KJ PROTEIN 8.26g
FAT 4.56g SATURATED FAT 0.67g
CARBOHYDRATE 20.19g FIBRE 6.98g
ADDED SUGAR 0.52g SODIUM 0.62g

Baked Squash

A creamy, sweet and nutty filling makes the perfect topping for tender buttery squash.

Serves 4

INGREDIENTS
2 butternut or acorn squash, 500 g/
 1¼ lb each
15 ml/1 tbsp olive oil
175 g/6 oz/¾ cup canned sweetcorn
 kernels, drained
115 g/4 oz/½ cup unsweetened
 chestnut purée
75 ml/5 tbsp low-fat yogurt
salt and freshly ground black pepper
50 g/2 oz/¼ cup fresh goat's cheese
snipped chives, to garnish

yogurt

chestnut purée

sweetcorn

butternut squash

goat's cheese

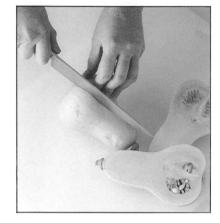

1 Preheat the oven to 180°C/350°F/ Gas 4. Cut the squash in half lengthwise.

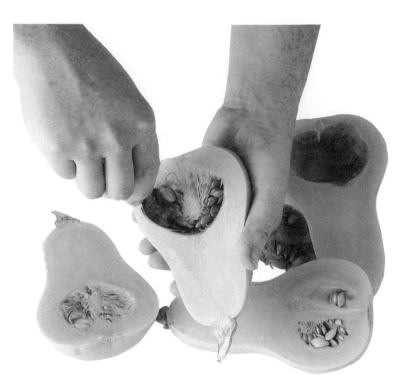

2 Scoop out the seeds with a spoon and discard.

3 Place the squash halves on a baking sheet and brush the flesh lightly with the oil. Bake in the oven for 30 minutes.

4 Mix together the sweetcorn, chestnut purée and yogurt in a bowl. Season to taste.

5 Remove the squash from the oven and divide the chestnut mixture between them, spooning it into the hollows.

COOK'S TIP

Use mozzarella or other mild, soft cheeses in place of goat's cheese. The cheese can be omitted entirely for a lower-fat alternative.

6 Top each half with ¼ of the goat's cheese and return to the oven for a further 10–15 minutes. Garnish with snipped chives.

NUTRITIONAL NOTES
Per portion:

ENERGY 212 Kcals/887.5 KJ **FAT** 5.5 g
SATURATED FAT 1.8 g

Red Cabbage in Port and Red Wine

A sweet and sour, spicy red cabbage dish, with the added crunch of pears and walnuts.

Serves 8

INGREDIENTS
10 ml/2 tsp walnut oil
1 onion, sliced
2 whole star anise
5 ml/1 tsp ground cinnamon
pinch of ground cloves
450 g/1 lb red cabbage, finely
   shredded
25 g/1 oz/2 tbsp dark brown sugar
45 ml/3 tbsp red wine vinegar
300 ml/½ pint/1¼ cups red wine
150 ml/¼ pint/⅔ cup port
2 pears, cut into 1 cm/½ in cubes
115 g/4 oz/½ cup raisins
salt and freshly ground black pepper
50 g/2 oz/¼ cup walnut halves

brown sugar

red cabbage

pears

onion   raisins

walnut halves

star anise

red wine vinegar

port

red wine

1 Heat the oil in a large pan. Add the onion and cook gently for about 5 minutes until softened.

2 Add the star anise, cinnamon, cloves and cabbage and cook for about 3 minutes more.

NUTRITIONAL NOTES
PER PORTION:
ENERGY 245 Kcals/1018 KJ **FAT** 11.5 g
SATURATED FAT 1 g

3 Stir in the sugar, vinegar, red wine and port. Cover the pan and simmer gently for 10 minutes, stirring occasionally.

4 Stir in the cubed pears and raisins and cook for a further 10 minutes or until the cabbage is tender. Season to taste. Mix in the walnut halves and serve.

Herby Baked Tomatoes

Dress up sliced, sweet tomatoes with fresh herbs and a crisp breadcrumb topping.

Serves 4–6

INGREDIENTS

675 g/1½ lb (about 8) large red and yellow tomatoes
10 ml/2 tsp red wine vinegar
2.5 ml/½ tsp wholegrain mustard
1 garlic clove, crushed
10 ml/2 tsp chopped fresh parsley
10 ml/2 tsp snipped fresh chives
25 g/1 oz/½ cup fresh fine white breadcrumbs
salt and freshly ground black pepper
sprigs of flat-leaf parsley, to garnish

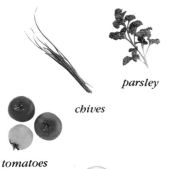

parsley

chives

tomatoes

mustard

vinegar

breadcrumbs

NUTRITIONAL NOTES

PER PORTION:

ENERGY 47 K Cals/196 KJ PROTEIN 1.97 g
FAT 0.73 g SATURATED FAT 0.08 g
CARBOHYDRATE 8.63 g FIBRE 1.98 g
ADDED SUGAR 0 SALT 0.15 g

1 Pre-heat the oven to 200°C/400°F/Gas 6. Thickly slice the tomatoes and arrange half of them in a 900 ml/1½ pint/3¾ cup ovenproof dish.

2 Mix the vinegar, mustard, garlic clove and seasoning together. Stir in 10 ml/2 tsp of cold water. Sprinkle the tomatoes with half the parsley and chives, then drizzle over half the dressing.

3 Lay the remaining tomato slices on top, overlapping them slightly. Drizzle with the remaining dressing.

4 Sprinkle over the breadcrumbs. Bake in the pre-heated oven for 25 minutes or until the topping is golden. Sprinkle with the remaining parsley and chives. Serve immediately garnished with sprigs of flat-leaf parsley.

Courgettes and Asparagus en Papillote

An impressive dinner party accompaniment, these puffed paper parcels should be broken open at the table by each guest, so that the wonderful aroma can be fully appreciated.

Serves 4

INGREDIENTS

2 medium courgettes
1 medium leek
225 g/8 oz young asparagus, trimmed
4 tarragon sprigs
4 whole garlic cloves, unpeeled
salt and freshly ground black pepper
1 egg, beaten

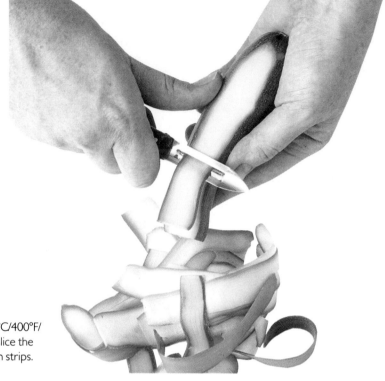

1 Preheat the oven to 200°C/400°F/Gas 6. Using a potato peeler slice the courgettes lengthwise into thin strips.

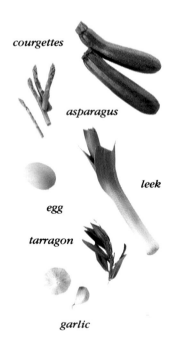

courgettes

asparagus

leek

egg

tarragon

garlic

2 Cut the leek into very fine julienne strips and cut the asparagus evenly into 5 cm/2 in lengths.

3 Cut out 4 sheets of greaseproof paper measuring 30 × 38 cm/12 × 15 in and fold in half. Draw a large curve to make a heart shape when unfolded. Cut along the inside of the line and open out.

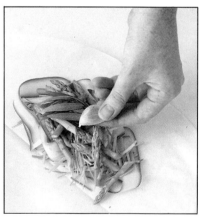

4 Divide the courgettes, asparagus and leek evenly between each paper heart, positioning the filling on one side of the fold line, and topping each with a sprig of tarragon and an unpeeled garlic clove. Season to taste.

NUTRITIONAL NOTES
PER PORTION:

ENERGY 53 Kcals/221 KJ **FAT** 2.3 g
SATURATED FAT 0.5 g

COOK'S TIP

Experiment with other vegetables and herbs such as sugar-snap peas and mint or baby carrots and rosemary. The possibilities are endless.

5 Brush the edges lightly with the beaten egg and fold over.

6 Pleat the edges together so that each parcel is completely sealed. Lay the parcels on a baking tray and cook for 10 minutes. Serve immediately.

Pok Choi and Mushroom Stir-fry

Try to buy all the varieties of mushroom for this dish; the wild oyster and shitake mushrooms have particularly distinctive, delicate flavours.

Serves 4 as an accompaniment

INGREDIENTS
4 dried black Chinese mushrooms
450 g/1 lb pok choi
50 g/2 oz oyster mushrooms
50 g/2 oz shitake mushrooms
15 ml/1 tbsp vegetable oil
1 clove garlic, crushed
30 ml/2 tbsp oyster sauce

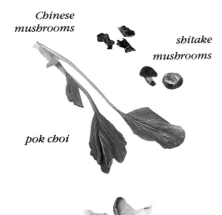

Chinese mushrooms

shitake mushrooms

pok choi

oyster mushrooms

1 Soak the black Chinese mushrooms in 150 ml/¼ pint/⅔ cup boiling water for 15 minutes to soften.

2 Tear the pok choi into bite-size pieces with your fingers.

3 Halve any large oyster or shitake mushrooms, using a sharp knife.

4 Strain the Chinese mushrooms. Heat the wok, then add the oil. When the oil is hot, stir-fry the garlic until softened but not coloured.

5 Add the pok choi and stir-fry for 1 minute. Mix in all the mushrooms and stir-fry for 1 minute.

6 Add the oyster sauce, toss well and serve immediately.

NUTRITIONAL NOTES
PER PORTION:

ENERGY 155 Kcals/643 KJ **FAT** 4.2 g
SATURATED FAT 0.5 g

Mixed Roasted Vegetables

Frying Parmesan cheese in this unusual way gives a wonderful crusty coating to the vegetables and creates a truly Mediterranean flavour.

Serves 4 as an accompaniment

INGREDIENTS
1 large aubergine, about 225 g/8 oz
salt, for sprinkling
175 g/6 oz plum tomatoes
2 red peppers
1 yellow pepper
30 ml/2 tbsp olive oil
25 g/1 oz Parmesan cheese
30 ml/2 tbsp fresh parsley, chopped
freshly ground black pepper

peppers

plum tomatoes

aubergine

1 Cut the aubergine into segments lengthwise. Place in a colander and sprinkle with salt. Leave for 30 minutes, to allow the salt to draw out the bitter juices.

2 Rinse off the salt under cold water and pat dry on kitchen towels.

3 Cut the plum tomatoes into segments lengthwise.

4 Cut the red and yellow peppers into quarters lengthwise and deseed.

5 Heat the wok, then add 5 ml/1 tsp of the olive oil. When the oil is hot, add the Parmesan and stir-fry until golden brown. Remove from the wok, allow to cool and chop into fine flakes.

6 Heat the wok, and then add the remaining oil. When the oil is hot stir-fry the aubergine and peppers for 4–5 minutes. Stir in the tomatoes and stir-fry for a further 1 minute. Toss the vegetables in the Parmesan, parsley and black pepper and serve.

NUTRITIONAL NOTES
Per portion:

ENERGY 104 Kcals/435 KJ **FAT** 5.7 g
SATURATED FAT 1.9 g

Beetroot and Celeriac Gratin

Beautiful ruby-red slices of beetroot and celeriac make a stunning light accompaniment to any main course dish.

Serves 6

INGREDIENTS
350 g/12 oz raw beetroot
350 g/12 oz celeriac
4 thyme sprigs
6 juniper berries, crushed
salt and freshly ground black pepper
100 ml/4 fl oz/½ cup fresh orange juice
100 ml/4 fl oz/½ cup vegetable stock

celeriac

orange juice

juniper berries

beetroot

thyme

1 Preheat the oven to 190°C/375°F/ Gas 5. Peel and slice the beetroot very finely. Quarter and peel the celeriac and slice very finely.

2 Fill a 25 cm/10 in diameter, cast iron, ovenproof or flameproof frying pan with alternate layers of beetroot and celeriac slices, sprinkling with the thyme, juniper and seasoning between each layer.

3 Mix the orange juice and stock together and pour over the gratin. Place over a medium heat and bring to the boil. Boil for 2 minutes.

4 Cover with foil and place in the oven for 15–20 minutes. Remove the foil and raise the oven temperature to 200°C/ 400°F/Gas 6. Cook for a further 10 minutes.

NUTRITIONAL NOTES
Per portion:

ENERGY 56 Kcals/234 KJ **FAT** 0.4 g
SATURATED FAT 0

Courgettes in Citrus Sauce

If baby courgettes are unavailable, you can use larger ones, but they should be cooked whole so that they don't absorb too much water. Halve them lengthways and cut into 10 cm/4 in lengths.

Serves 4

INGREDIENTS

350 g/12 oz baby courgettes
4 spring onions, finely sliced
2.5 cm/1 in fresh root ginger, grated
30 ml/2 tbsp cider vinegar
15 ml/1 tbsp light soy sauce
5 ml/1 tsp soft light brown sugar
45 ml/3 tbsp vegetable stock
finely grated rind and juice of ½
    lemon and ½ orange
5 ml/1 tsp cornflour

orange

lemon   *courgettes*

ginger

spring onions

NUTRITIONAL NOTES
Per portion:

ENERGY 33 K Cals/138 KJ **PROTEIN** 2.18 g
FAT 0.42 g **SATURATED FAT** 0.09 g
CARBOHYDRATE 5.33 g **FIBRE** 0.92 g
ADDED SUGAR 1.31 g **SALT** 0.55 g

1 Cook the courgettes in lightly salted boiling water for 3-4 minutes, or until just tender. Drain well.

2 Meanwhile put all the remaining ingredients, except the cornflour, into a small saucepan and bring to the boil. Simmer for 3 minutes.

3 Blend the cornflour with 10 ml/2 tsp of cold water and add to the sauce. Bring to the boil, stirring continuously, until the sauce has thickened.

4 Pour the sauce over the courgettes and gently heat, shaking the pan to coat evenly. Transfer to a warmed serving dish and serve.

Balti Mushrooms in a Creamy Garlic Sauce

This is a simple and delicious recipe which could be accompanied by any of the rice dishes from this book.

Serves 4

INGREDIENTS
350g/12oz button mushrooms
45ml/3 tbsp olive oil
1 bay leaf
3 garlic cloves, roughly chopped
2 green chillies, seeded
  and chopped
225g/8oz/1 cup fromage frais
15ml/1 tbsp chopped fresh mint
15ml/1 tbsp chopped
  fresh coriander
5ml/1 tsp salt
fresh mint and coriander leaves,
  to garnish

garlic

button mushrooms

bay leaf

coriander

mint

green chillies

salt

fromage frais

NUTRITIONAL NOTES
Per portion:
ENERGY 75 K Cals/314 K J **PROTEIN** 6.50g
FAT 3.38g **SATURATED FAT** 0.54g
CARBOHYDRATE 4.93g **FIBRE** 1.12g
ADDED SUGAR 0.01g
SALT 0.52g

1 Cut the mushrooms in half and set them aside.

2 Heat the oil in a non-stick wok or frying pan, then add the bay leaf, garlic and chillies and cook for about 1 minute.

COOK'S TIP
Cook the mushrooms for longer if you like them well cooked and browned.

3 Add the mushrooms. Stir-fry for about 2 minutes.

4 Remove from the heat and stir in the fromage frais followed by the mint, coriander and salt. Stir-fry for about 2 minutes, then transfer to a warmed serving dish and garnish with mint and coriander leaves.

Potato Gratin

Don't rinse the potato slices before layering because the starch makes a thick sauce during cooking.

Serves 4

INGREDIENTS
1 garlic clove
5 large baking potatoes, peeled
45 ml/3 tbsp freshly grated Parmesan
    cheese
600 ml/1 pint/2½ cups vegetable or
    chicken stock
pinch of freshly grated nutmeg
salt and freshly ground black pepper

potatoes

Parmesan cheese

stock

NUTRITIONAL NOTES
PER PORTION:

ENERGY 221 K Cals/927 KJ **PROTEIN** 7.88 g
FAT 2.71 g **SATURATED FAT** 1.30 g
CARBOHYDRATE 43.77 g **FIBRE** 3.30 g
ADDED SUGAR 0 **SALT** 0.21 g

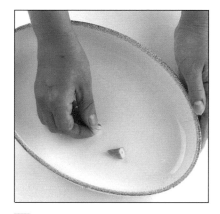

1 Pre-heat the oven to 200°C/400°F/ Gas 6. Halve the garlic clove and rub over the base and sides of a gratin dish measuring about 20 × 30 cm/8 × 12 in.

2 Slice the potatoes very thinly and arrange a third of them in the dish. Sprinkle with a little grated cheese, salt and freshly ground black pepper. Pour over some of the stock to prevent the potatoes from discolouring.

3 Continue layering the potatoes and cheese as before, then pour over the rest of the stock. Sprinkle with the grated nutmeg.

4 Bake in the oven for 1¼-1½ hours or until the potatoes are tender and the tops well browned.

VARIATION
For a potato and onion gratin, thinly slice one medium onion and layer with the potato.

Breads &
Baking

Wholemeal Herb Triangles

Stuffed with cooked chicken and salad these make a good lunchtime snack and are also an ideal accompaniment to a bowl of steaming soup.

Makes 8

INGREDIENTS

225 g/8 oz/2 cups wholemeal flour
115 g/4 oz/1 cup strong plain flour
5 ml/1 tsp salt
2.5 ml/¹/₂ tsp bicarbonate of soda
5 ml/1 tsp cream of tartar
2.5 ml/¹/₂ tsp chilli powder
50 g/2 oz/¹/₄ cup soft margarine
60 ml/4 tbsp chopped mixed
    fresh herbs
250 ml/8 fl oz/1 cup skimmed milk
15 ml/1 tbsp sesame seeds

mixed fresh
herbs

sesame
seeds

chilli
powder

wholemeal
flour

bicarbonate
of soda

cream of
tartar

soft
margarine

skimmed
milk

salt

strong plain
flour

1 Preheat the oven to 220°C/425°F/ Gas 7. Lightly flour a baking sheet. Put the wholemeal flour in a mixing bowl. Sift in the remaining dry ingredients, including the chilli powder, then rub in the soft margarine.

2 Add the herbs and milk and mix quickly to a soft dough. Turn on to a lightly floured surface. Knead only very briefly or the dough will become tough. Roll out to a 23 cm/9 in round and place on the prepared baking sheet. Brush lightly with water and sprinkle evenly with the sesame seeds.

3 Carefully cut the dough round into 8 wedges, separate them slightly and bake for 15–20 minutes. Transfer to a wire rack to cool. Serve warm or cold.

NUTRITIONAL NOTES

PER PORTION:

ENERGY 222 Kcals/932 KJ
FAT 7.22 g **SATURATED FAT** 1.25 g
CHOLESTEROL 1.06 mg **FIBRE** 3.54 g

VARIATION

To make Sun-dried Tomato Triangles, replace the fresh mixed herbs with 30 ml/2 tbsp drained chopped sun-dried tomatoes in oil, and add 15 ml/1 tbsp each mild paprika, chopped fresh parsley and chopped fresh marjoram.

Caraway Bread Sticks

Ideal to nibble with drinks, these can be made with all sorts of other seeds – try cumin seeds, poppy seeds or celery seeds.

Makes about 20

INGREDIENTS
150 ml/¹/₄ pint/²/₃ cup warm water
2.5 ml/¹/₂ tsp dried yeast
pinch of sugar
225 g/8 oz/2 cups plain flour
2.5 ml/¹/₂ tsp salt
10 ml/2 tsp caraway seeds

caraway seeds

dried yeast

plain flour

water

salt

NUTRITIONAL NOTES
PER PORTION:

ENERGY 45 Kcals/189 KJ
FAT 0.24 g **SATURATED FAT** 0.02 g
CHOLESTEROL 0 **FIBRE** 0.39 g

VARIATION
To make Coriander and Sesame Sticks, replace the caraway seeds with 15 ml/1 tbsp crushed coriander seeds. Dampen the bread sticks lightly and sprinkle them with sesame seeds before baking.

1 Grease two baking sheets. Put the warm water in a jug. Sprinkle the yeast on top. Add the sugar, mix well and leave for 10 minutes.

2 Sift the flour and salt into a mixing bowl, stir in the caraway seeds and make a well in the centre. Add the yeast mixture and gradually incorporate the flour to make a soft dough, adding a little extra water if necessary.

3 Turn on to a lightly floured surface and knead for 5 minutes until smooth. Divide the mixture into 20 pieces and roll each one into a 30 cm/12 in stick. Arrange on the baking sheets, leaving room to allow for rising, then leave for 30 minutes until well risen. Meanwhile, preheat the oven to 220°C/425°F/Gas 7.

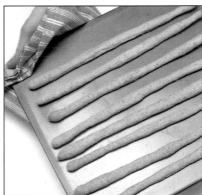

4 Bake the bread sticks for about 10–12 minutes until golden brown. Cool on the baking sheets.

Chive and Potato Scones

These little scones should be fairly thin, soft and crisp on the outside. Serve them for breakfast.

Makes 20

INGREDIENTS
450 g/1 lb potatoes
115 g/4 oz/1 cup plain flour, sifted
30 ml/2 tbsp olive oil
30 ml/2 tbsp snipped chives
salt and freshly ground black pepper
low fat spread, for topping
   (optional)

potatoes

black pepper

olive oil

chives

plain flour

salt

1 Cook the potatoes in a saucepan of boiling salted water for 20 minutes or until tender, then drain thoroughly. Return the potatoes to the clean pan and mash them. Preheat a griddle.

2 Add the flour, olive oil and snipped chives with a little salt and pepper to the hot mashed potato in the pan. Mix to a soft dough.

COOK'S TIP
Cook the scones over a low heat so that the outsides do not burn before the insides are cooked through.

3 Roll out the dough on a well-floured surface to a thickness of 5 mm/¹/₄ in and stamp out rounds with a 5 cm/2 in plain pastry cutter. Lightly grease the griddle or frying pan.

4 Cook the scones, in batches, on the hot griddle or frying pan for about 10 minutes, turning once, until they are golden brown on both sides. Keep the heat low. Top with a little low fat spread, if you like, and serve immediately.

Ham and Tomato Scones

These make an ideal accompaniment for soup. Choose a strongly flavoured ham and chop it fairly finely, so that a little goes a long way.

Makes 12

INGREDIENTS

225 g/8 oz/2 cups self-raising flour
5 ml/1 tsp dry mustard
5 ml/1 tsp paprika, plus extra for sprinkling
2.5 ml/½ tsp salt
25 g/1 oz/2 tbsp soft margarine
15 ml/1 tbsp snipped fresh basil
50 g/2 oz/⅓ cup drained sun-dried tomatoes in oil, chopped
50 g/2 oz Black Forest ham, chopped
90–120 ml/3–4 fl oz/½–⅔ cup skimmed milk, plus extra for brushing

soft margarine
paprika
salt
skimmed milk
self-raising flour
fresh basil
dry mustard
sun-dried tomatoes
Black Forest ham

1 Preheat the oven to 200°C/400°F/ Gas 6. Flour a large baking sheet. Sift the flour, mustard, paprika and salt into a bowl. Rub in the margarine until the mixture resembles breadcrumbs.

2 Stir in the basil, sun-dried tomatoes and ham, and mix lightly. Pour in enough milk to mix to a soft dough.

3 Turn the dough out on to a lightly floured surface, knead lightly and roll out to a 20 × 15 cm/8 × 6 in rectangle. Cut into 5 cm/2 in squares and arrange on the baking sheet.

4 Brush lightly with milk, sprinkle with paprika and bake for 12–15 minutes. Transfer to a wire rack to cool.

NUTRITIONAL NOTES

PER PORTION:

ENERGY 113 Kcals/474 KJ
FAT 4.23 g **SATURATED FAT** 0.65 g
CHOLESTEROL 2.98 mg **FIBRE** 0.65 g

Soda Bread

Finding the bread bin empty need never be a problem when your repertoire includes a recipe for soda bread. It takes only a few minutes to make and needs no rising or proving. If possible eat soda bread while still warm from the oven as it does not keep well.

Serves 8

INGREDIENTS
450 g/1 lb/4 cups plain flour
5 ml/1 tsp salt
5 ml/1 tsp bicarbonate of soda
5 ml/1 tsp cream of tartar
350 ml/12 fl oz/1¹/₂ cups buttermilk

salt

buttermilk

bicarbonate of soda

plain flour

cream of tartar

1 Preheat the oven to 220°C/425°F/ Gas 7. Flour a baking sheet. Sift all the dry ingredients into a mixing bowl and make a well in the centre.

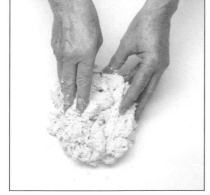

2 Add the buttermilk and mix quickly to a soft dough. Turn on to a floured surface and knead lightly. Shape into a round about 18 cm/7 in in diameter and place on the baking sheet.

3 Cut a deep cross on top of the loaf and sprinkle with a little flour. Bake for 25–30 minutes, then transfer the soda bread to a wire rack to cool.

NUTRITIONAL NOTES
PER PORTION:

ENERGY 230 Kcals/967 KJ
FAT 1.03 g **SATURATED FAT** 0.24 g
CHOLESTEROL 0.88 mg **FIBRE** 1.94 g

COOK'S TIP
Soda bread needs a light hand. The ingredients should be bound together quickly in the bowl and kneaded very briefly. The aim is just to get rid of the largest cracks, as the dough will become tough if it is handled for too long.

Parma Ham and Parmesan Bread

This nourishing bread is almost a meal in itself.

Serves 8

INGREDIENTS
225 g/8 oz/2 cups self-raising
   wholemeal flour
225 g/8 oz/2 cups self-raising
   white flour
5 ml/1 tsp baking powder
5 ml/1 tsp salt
5 ml/1 tsp freshly ground
   black pepper
75 g/3 oz Parma ham, chopped
25 g/1 oz/2 tbsp freshly grated
   Parmesan cheese
30 ml/2 tbsp chopped fresh parsley
45 ml/3 tbsp Meaux mustard
350 ml/12 fl oz/1½ cups buttermilk
skimmed milk, to glaze

parsley

salt

Parmesan cheese

black pepper

self-raising wholemeal flour

self-raising white flour

Meaux mustard

buttermilk

Parma ham

baking powder

1 Preheat the oven to 200°C/400°F/ Gas 6. Flour a baking sheet. Place the wholemeal flour in a bowl and sift in the white flour, baking powder and salt. Add the pepper and the ham. Set aside about 15 ml/1 tbsp of the grated Parmesan and stir the rest into the flour mixture. Stir in the parsley. Make a well in the centre.

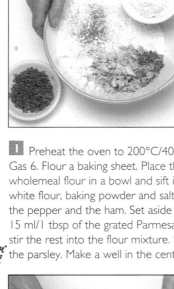

2 Mix the mustard and buttermilk in a jug, pour into the flour mixture and quickly mix to a soft dough.

3 Turn the dough on to a floured surface and knead briefly. Shape into an oval loaf, brush with milk and sprinkle with the remaining cheese. Place the loaf on the prepared baking sheet.

4 Bake the loaf for 25–30 minutes, or until golden brown. Transfer to a wire rack to cool.

NUTRITIONAL NOTES

PER PORTION:

ENERGY 250 Kcals/1053 KJ
FAT 3.65 g **SATURATED FAT** 1.30 g
CHOLESTEROL 7.09 mg **FIBRE** 3.81 g

Banana and Cardamom Bread

The combination of banana and cardamom is delicious in this soft-textured moist loaf. It is perfect for tea time, served with low fat spread and jam.

NUTRITIONAL NOTES

PER PORTION:

ENERGY 299 Kcals/1254 KJ
FAT 1.55 g **SATURATED FAT** 0.23 g
CHOLESTEROL 0 **FIBRE** 2.65 g

COOK'S TIP
Make sure the bananas are really ripe, so that they impart maximum flavour to the bread.

If you prefer, place the dough in one piece in a 450 g/1 lb loaf tin and bake for an extra 5 minutes.

Serves 6

INGREDIENTS
150 ml/¹/₄ pint/²/₃ cup warm water
5 ml/1 tsp dried yeast
pinch of sugar
10 cardamom pods
400 g/14 oz/3¹/₂ cups strong
　white flour
5 ml/1 tsp salt
30 ml/2 tbsp malt extract
2 ripe bananas, mashed
5 ml/1 tsp sesame seeds

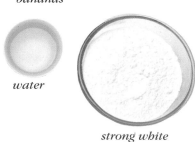

malt extract　*dried yeast*　*sesame seeds*

cardamom pods

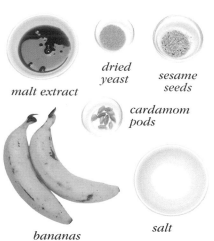

bananas　*salt*

water

strong white flour

1 Put the water in a small bowl. Sprinkle the yeast on top, add the sugar and mix well. Leave for 10 minutes.

2 Split the cardamom pods. Remove the seeds and chop them finely.

3 Sift the flour and salt into a mixing bowl and make a well in the centre. Add the yeast mixture with the malt extract, chopped cardamom seeds and bananas.

4 Gradually incorporate the flour and mix to a soft dough, adding a little extra water if necessary. Turn the dough on to a floured surface and knead for about 5 minutes until smooth and elastic. Return to the clean bowl, cover with a damp dish towel and leave to rise for about 2 hours until doubled in bulk.

5 Grease a baking sheet. Turn the dough on to a floured surface, knead briefly, then shape into a plait. Place the plait on the baking sheet and cover loosely with a plastic bag (ballooning it to trap the air). Leave until well risen. Preheat the oven to 220°C/425°F/Gas 7.

6 Brush the plait lightly with water and sprinkle with the sesame seeds. Bake for 10 minutes, then lower the oven temperature to 200°C/400°F/Gas 6. Cook for 15 minutes more, or until the loaf sounds hollow when it is tapped underneath. Cool on a wire rack.

Swedish Sultana Bread

A lightly sweetened bread that is delicious served warm. It is also excellent toasted and topped with low fat spread.

NUTRITIONAL NOTES

PER PORTION:

ENERGY 273 Kcals/1145 KJ
FAT 4.86 g SATURATED FAT 0.57 g
CHOLESTEROL 0.39 mg FIBRE 3.83 g

Serves 8–10

INGREDIENTS

150 ml/¼ pint/⅔ cup warm water
5 ml/1 tsp dried yeast
15 ml/1 tbsp clear honey
225 g/8 oz/2 cups wholemeal flour
225 g/8 oz/2 cups strong white flour
5 ml/1 tsp salt
115 g/4 oz/⅔ cup sultanas
50 g/2 oz/½ cup walnuts, chopped
175 ml/6 fl oz/¾ cup warm skimmed milk, plus extra for glazing

salt

walnuts

strong white flour

clear honey

water

skimmed milk

sultanas

dried yeast

wholemeal flour

VARIATION

To make Apple and Hazelnut Bread, replace the sultanas with 2 chopped eating apples and use chopped toasted hazelnuts instead of the walnuts. Add 5 ml/1 tsp ground cinnamon with the flour.

1 Put the water in a small bowl. Sprinkle the yeast on top. Add a few drops of the honey to help activate the yeast, mix well and leave for 10 minutes.

2 Put the flours in a bowl with the salt and sultanas. Set aside 15 ml/1 tbsp of the walnuts and add the rest to the bowl. Mix together lightly and make a well in the centre.

3 Add the yeast mixture to the flour mixture with the milk and remaining honey. Gradually incorporate the flour, mixing to a soft dough; add a little extra water if you need to.

4 Turn the dough on to a floured surface and knead for 5 minutes until smooth and elastic. Return to the clean bowl, cover with a damp dish towel and leave in a warm place to rise for about 2 hours until doubled in bulk. Grease a baking sheet.

5 Turn the dough on to a floured surface and knead for 2 minutes, then shape into a 28 cm/11 in long sausage shape. Place the loaf on the prepared baking sheet. Make some diagonal cuts down the whole length of the loaf.

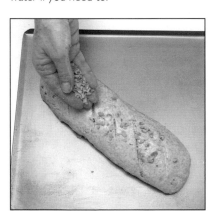

6 Brush the loaf with milk, sprinkle with the reserved walnuts and leave to rise for about 40 minutes. Preheat the oven to 220°C/425°F/Gas 7. Bake the loaf for 10 minutes. Lower the oven temperature to 200°C/400°F/Gas 6 and bake for about 20 minutes more, or until the loaf sounds hollow when it is tapped underneath.

Rye Bread

Rye bread is popular in Northern Europe and makes an excellent base for open sandwiches – add a low fat topping of your choice.

Makes 2 loaves, each serving 6

INGREDIENTS
475 ml/16 fl oz/2 cups warm water
10 ml/2 tsp dried yeast
pinch of sugar
350 g/12 oz/3 cups wholemeal flour
225 g/8 oz/2 cups rye flour
115 g/4 oz/1 cup strong white flour
7.5 ml/1½ tsp salt
30 ml/2 tbsp caraway seeds
30 ml/2 tbsp molasses
30 ml/2 tbsp sunflower oil

molasses
dried yeast
strong white flour
rye flour
wholemeal flour
salt
caraway seeds
sunflower oil
water

1 Put half the water in a jug. Sprinkle the yeast on top. Add the sugar, mix well and leave for 10 minutes.

2 Put the flours and salt in a bowl. Set aside 5 ml/1 tsp of the caraway seeds and add the rest to the bowl.

3 Make a well in the flour mixture, then add the yeast mixture with the molasses, oil and the remaining water. Gradually incorporate the flour and mix to a soft dough, adding a little extra water if necessary.

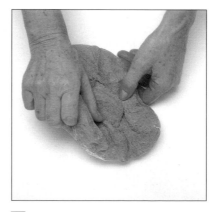

4 Turn the dough on to a floured surface and knead for 5 minutes until smooth and elastic. Return to the clean bowl, cover with a damp dish towel and leave in a warm place to rise for about 2 hours until doubled in bulk. Grease a baking sheet.

5 Turn the dough on to a floured surface and knead for 2 minutes, then divide the dough in half, shape into two 23 cm/9 in long oval loaves. Flatten the loaves slightly and place them on the baking sheet.

6 Brush the loaves with water and sprinkle with the remaining caraway seeds. Cover and leave in a warm place for about 40 minutes until well risen. Preheat the oven to 200°C/400°F/Gas 6. Bake the loaves for 30 minutes, or until they sound hollow when they are tapped underneath. Cool on a wire rack. Serve the bread plain, or slice and add a low fat topping.

NUTRITIONAL NOTES
PER PORTION:

ENERGY 224 Kcals/941 KJ
FAT 3.43 g **SATURATED FAT** 0.33 g
CHOLESTEROL 0 **FIBRE** 6.04 g

VARIATION
Shape the dough into two loaves and bake in two greased 450 g/1 lb loaf tins, if you prefer.

Olive and Oregano Bread

This is an excellent accompaniment to all salads and is particularly good served warm.

Serves 8–10

NUTRITIONAL NOTES
PER PORTION:

ENERGY 202 Kcals/847 KJ
FAT 3.28 g SATURATED FAT 0.46 g
CHOLESTEROL 0 FIBRE 22.13 g

INGREDIENTS
300 ml/10 fl oz/1¼ cups warm water
5 ml/1 tsp dried yeast
pinch of sugar
15 ml/1 tbsp olive oil
1 onion, chopped
450 g/1 lb/4 cups strong white flour
5 ml/1 tsp salt
1.5 ml/¼ tsp freshly ground
   black pepper
50 g/2 oz/⅓ cup stoned black olives,
   roughly chopped
15 ml/1 tbsp black olive paste
15 ml/1 tbsp chopped fresh oregano
15 ml/1 tbsp chopped fresh parsley

fresh oregano *fresh parsley* *black olives*

black pepper *strong white flour*

olive oil *black olive paste*

water

dried yeast *salt* *onion*

1 Put half the warm water in a jug. Sprinkle the yeast on top. Add the sugar, mix well and leave for 10 minutes.

2 Heat the olive oil in a frying pan and fry the onion until golden brown.

3 Sift the flour into a mixing bowl with the salt and pepper. Make a well in the centre. Add the yeast mixture, the fried onion (with the oil), the olives, olive paste, herbs and remaining water. Gradually incorporate the flour and mix to a soft dough, adding a little extra water if necessary.

4 Turn the dough on to a floured surface and knead for 5 minutes until smooth and elastic. Place in a mixing bowl, cover with a damp dish towel and leave in a warm place to rise for about 2 hours until doubled in bulk. Lightly grease a baking sheet.

5 Turn the dough on to a floured surface and knead again for a few minutes. Shape into a 20 cm/8 in round and place on the prepared baking sheet. Using a sharp knife, make criss-cross cuts over the top, cover and leave in a warm place for 30 minutes until well risen. Preheat the oven to 220°C/425°F/Gas 7.

6 Dust the loaf with a little flour. Bake for 10 minutes then lower the oven temperature to 200°C/400°F/Gas 6. Bake for 20 minutes more, or until the loaf sounds hollow when it is tapped underneath. Transfer to a wire rack to cool slightly before serving.

Sun-dried Tomato Plait

This is a marvellous Mediterranean-flavoured bread to serve at a summer buffet or barbecue.

Serves 8–10

INGREDIENTS

300 ml/½ pint/1¼ cups warm water
5 ml/1 tsp dried yeast
pinch of sugar
225 g/8 oz/2 cups wholemeal flour
225 g/8 oz/2 cups strong white flour
5 ml/1 tsp salt
1.5 ml/¼ tsp freshly ground
  black pepper
115 g/4 oz/⅔ cup drained sun-dried
  tomatoes in oil, chopped, plus
  15 ml/1 tbsp oil from the jar
25 g/1 oz/¼ cup freshly grated
  Parmesan cheese
30 ml/2 tbsp red pesto
5 ml/1 tsp coarse sea salt

Parmesan cheese
red pesto
black pepper
wholemeal flour
salt
dried yeast
sun-dried tomatoes
water
strong white flour
coarse sea salt
tomato oil

NUTRITIONAL NOTES

PER PORTION:

ENERGY 294 Kcals/1233 KJ
FAT 12.12 g **SATURATED FAT** 2.13 g
CHOLESTEROL 3.40 mg **FIBRE** 3.39 g

COOK'S TIP

If you are unable to locate red pesto, use 30 ml/2 tbsp chopped fresh basil mixed with 15 ml/1 tbsp sun-dried tomato paste.

1 Put half the warm water in a jug. Sprinkle the yeast on top. Add the sugar, mix well and leave for 10 minutes.

2 Put the wholemeal flour in a mixing bowl. Sift in the white flour, salt and pepper. Make a well in the centre and add the yeast mixture, oil, sun-dried tomatoes, Parmesan, pesto and the remaining water. Gradually incorporate the flour and mix to a soft dough, adding a little extra water if necessary.

3 Turn the dough on to a floured surface and knead for 5 minutes until smooth and elastic. Return to the clean bowl, cover with a damp dish towel and leave in a warm place to rise for about 2 hours until doubled in bulk. Lightly grease a baking sheet.

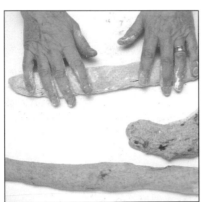

4 Turn the dough on to a lightly floured surface and knead for a few minutes. Divide the dough into three equal pieces and shape each into a 33 cm/13 in long sausage.

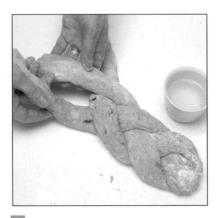

5 Dampen the ends of the three "sausages". Press them together at one end, plait them loosely, then press them together at the other end. Place on the baking sheet, cover and leave in a warm place for 30 minutes until well risen. Preheat the oven to 220°C/425°F/Gas 7.

6 Sprinkle the plait with the coarse sea salt. Bake for 10 minutes, then lower the temperature to 200°C/400°F/Gas 6 and bake for a further 15–20 minutes, or until the loaf sounds hollow when tapped underneath. Cool on a wire rack.

Focaccia

This flat Italian bread is best served warm. It makes a delicious snack with low fat cheese and chunks of fresh tomato.

Serves 8

INGREDIENTS

300 ml/½ pint/1¼ cups warm water
5 ml/1 tsp dried yeast
pinch of sugar
450 g/1 lb/4 cups strong white flour
5 ml/1 tsp salt
1.5 ml/¼ tsp freshly ground
  black pepper
15 ml/1 tbsp pesto
115 g/4 oz/⅔ cup stoned black
  olives, chopped
25 g/1 oz/3 tbsp drained sun-dried
  tomatoes in oil, chopped, plus
  15 ml/1 tbsp oil from the jar
5 ml/1 tsp coarse sea salt
5 ml/1 tsp roughly chopped
  fresh rosemary

1 Put the water in a bowl. Sprinkle the yeast on top. Add the sugar, mix well and leave for 10 minutes. Lightly grease a 33 × 23 cm/13 × 9 in Swiss roll tin.

2 Sift the flour, salt and pepper into a bowl and make a well in the centre.

3 Add the yeast mixture with the pesto, olives and sun-dried tomatoes (reserve the oil). Mix to a soft dough, adding a little extra water if necessary.

black pepper *sun-dried tomatoes* *pesto*

strong white flour

black olives *coarse sea salt* *salt*

water

dried yeast

fresh rosemary

tomato oil

4 Turn the dough on to a floured surface and knead for 5 minutes until smooth and elastic. Return to the clean bowl, cover with a damp dish towel and leave in a warm place to rise for about 2 hours until doubled in bulk.

5 Turn the dough on to a floured surface, knead briefly, then roll out to a 33 × 23 cm/13 × 9 in rectangle. Lift the dough over the rolling pin and place in the prepared tin. Preheat the oven to 220°C/425°F/Gas 7.

NUTRITIONAL NOTES
PER PORTION:

ENERGY 247 Kcals/1038 KJ
FAT 6.42 g **SATURATED FAT** 0.93 g
CHOLESTEROL 0.35 mg **FIBRE** 2.18 g

 Using your fingertips, make small indentations all over the dough. Brush with the reserved oil from the sun-dried tomatoes, then sprinkle with the salt and rosemary. Leave to rise for 20 minutes, then bake for 20–25 minutes, or until golden. Transfer to a wire rack, but serve while still warm.

VARIATION
To make Oregano and Onion Focaccia, omit the pesto, olives and sun-dried tomatoes. Add 15 ml/ 1 tbsp chopped fresh oregano or 5 ml/1 tsp dried oregano to the flour. Slice 1 onion very thinly into rounds and scatter over the rolled out dough. Drizzle with olive oil and sprinkle with sea salt before baking.

Coffee Sponge Drops

These are delicious on their own, but taste even better with a filling made by mixing low fat soft cheese with drained and chopped stem ginger.

Makes 12

INGREDIENTS
50 g/2 oz/¹/₂ cup plain flour
15 ml/1 tbsp instant coffee powder
2 eggs
75 g/3 oz/6 tbsp caster sugar

FOR THE FILLING
115 g/4 oz/¹/₂ cup low fat soft cheese
40 g/1¹/₂ oz/¹/₄ cup chopped
    stem ginger

instant coffee powder

eggs

plain flour

caster sugar

low fat soft cheese

stem ginger

NUTRITIONAL NOTES
PER PORTION:

ENERGY 69 Kcals/290 KJ
FAT 1.36 g SATURATED FAT 0.50 g
CHOLESTEROL 33.33 mg FIBRE 0.29 g

1 Preheat the oven to 190°C/375°F/Gas 5. Line two baking sheets with non-stick baking paper. Make the filling by beating together the soft cheese and stem ginger. Chill until required. Sift the flour and instant coffee powder together.

2 Combine the eggs and caster sugar in a bowl. Beat with a hand-held electric whisk until thick and mousse-like (when the whisk is lifted a trail should remain on the surface of the mixture for at least 15 seconds).

3 Carefully add the sifted flour and coffee mixture and gently fold in with a metal spoon, being careful not to knock out any air.

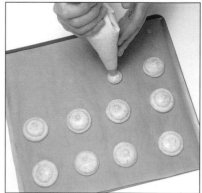

4 Spoon the mixture into a piping bag fitted with a 1 cm/¹/₂ in plain nozzle. Pipe 4 cm/1¹/₂ in rounds on the baking sheets. Bake for 12 minutes. Cool on a wire rack. Sandwich together with the filling.

Oaty Crisps

These biscuits are very crisp and crunchy – ideal to serve with morning coffee.

Makes 18

INGREDIENTS
175 g/6 oz/1³/₄ cups rolled oats
75 g/3 oz/¹/₂ cup light muscovado
 sugar
1 egg
60 ml/4 tbsp sunflower oil
30 ml/2 tbsp malt extract

malt extract   *sunflower oil*

rolled oats

light muscovado sugar   *egg*

NUTRITIONAL NOTES
PER PORTION:

ENERGY 86 Kcals/360 KJ
FAT 3.59 g **SATURATED FAT** 0.57 g
CHOLESTEROL 10.70 mg **FIBRE** 0.66 g

VARIATION
To give these crisp biscuits a coarser texture, substitute jumbo oats for some or all of the rolled oats.

1 Preheat the oven to 190°C/375°F/ Gas 5. Lightly grease two baking sheets. Mix the rolled oats and brown sugar in a bowl, breaking up any lumps in the sugar. Add the egg, sunflower oil and malt extract, mix well, then leave to soak for 15 minutes.

2 Using a teaspoon, place small heaps of the mixture well apart on the prepared baking sheets. Press the heaps into 7.5 cm/3 in rounds with the back of a dampened fork.

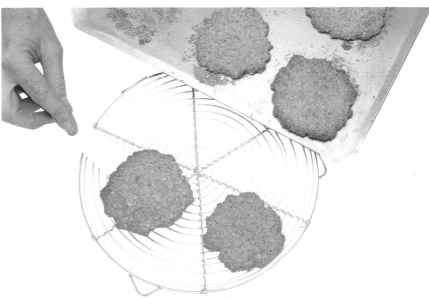

3 Bake the biscuits for 10–15 minutes until golden brown. Leave them to cool for 1 minute, then remove with a palette knife and cool on a wire rack.

Banana Gingerbread Slices

Bananas make this spicy bake delightfully moist. The flavour develops on keeping, so store the gingerbread for a few days before cutting into slices, if possible.

Makes 20 slices

INGREDIENTS
275 g/10 oz/2½ cups plain flour
5 ml/1 tsp bicarbonate of soda
20 ml/4 tsp ground ginger
10 ml/2 tsp mixed spice
115 g/4 oz/²⁄₃ cup soft light
   brown sugar
60 ml/4 tbsp sunflower oil
30 ml/2 tbsp molasses or
   black treacle
30 ml/2 tbsp malt extract
2 eggs
60 ml/4 tbsp orange juice
3 ripe bananas
115 g/4 oz/²⁄₃ cup raisins or sultanas

1 Preheat the oven to 180°C/350°F/ Gas 4. Lightly grease and line a 28 × 18 cm/11 × 7 in shallow baking tin.

2 Sift the flour, bicarbonate of soda and spices into a mixing bowl. Place the sugar in the sieve over the bowl, add some of the flour mixture and rub through the sieve with a wooden spoon.

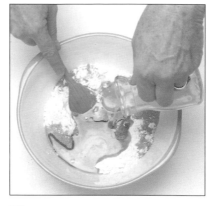

3 Make a well in the centre of the dry ingredients and add the oil, molasses or treacle, malt extract, eggs and orange juice. Mix thoroughly.

orange juice

malt extract

raisins

plain flour

mixed spice

soft light brown sugar

eggs

sunflower oil

bicarbonate of soda

ground ginger

bananas

molasses

5 Scrape the mixture into the prepared baking tin. Bake for about 35–40 minutes or until the centre of the gingerbread springs back when lightly pressed.

4 Mash the bananas on a plate. Add the raisins or sultanas to the gingerbread mixture then mix in the mashed bananas.

6 Leave the gingerbread in the tin to cool for 5 minutes, then turn out on to a wire rack to cool completely. Transfer to a board and cut into 20 slices to serve.

NUTRITIONAL NOTES
Per portion:

ENERGY 148 Kcals/621 KJ
FAT 3.07 g **SATURATED FAT** 0.53 g
CHOLESTEROL 19.30 mg **FIBRE** 0.79 g

COOK'S TIP
If your brown sugar is lumpy, mix it with a little flour and it will be easier to sift.

Pear and Sultana Bran Muffins

These tasty muffins are best eaten freshly baked and served warm or cold, on their own or spread with a little low-fat spread, reduced-sugar jam or honey.

NUTRITIONAL NOTES

PER PORTION:

ENERGY 108Kcals/455KJ PROTEIN 3.40g
FAT 2.68g SATURATED FAT 0.70g
CARBOHYDRATE 18.84g FIBRE 2.64g
ADDED SUGAR 4.37g SODIUM 0.15g

Makes 12

INGREDIENTS
75 g/3 oz/⅔ cup plain wholemeal
   flour, sifted
50 g/2 oz/½ cup plain white
   flour, sifted
50 g/2 oz/3 cups bran
15 ml/1 tbsp baking powder, sifted
pinch of salt
50 g/2 oz/4 tbsp half-fat spread
50 g/2 oz/¼ cup soft light
   brown sugar
1 egg
200 ml/7 fl oz/scant 1 cup
   skimmed milk
50 g/2 oz/½ cup ready-to-eat dried
   pears, chopped
50 g/2 oz/⅓ cup sultanas

plain wholemeal flour

plain white flour

bran

baking powder

salt

half-fat spread

light soft brown sugar

egg

skimmed milk

dried pears

sultanas

1 Preheat the oven to 200°C/400°F/ Gas 6. Lightly grease 12 muffin or deep-cup bun tins or line them with paper muffin cases. Mix together the flours, bran, baking powder and salt in a bowl.

4 Gently fold the ingredients together, only enough to combine. The mixture should look quite lumpy as over mixing will result in heavy muffins.

2 Gently heat the half-fat spread in a saucepan until melted.

5 Fold in the pears and sultanas.

COOK'S TIP
For a quick and easy way to chop dried fruit, snip with kitchen scissors.

3 Mix together the melted fat, sugar, egg and milk and pour over the dry ingredients.

6 Spoon the mixture into the prepared muffin or bun tins. Bake for 15–20 minutes, until well risen and golden brown. Turn out on to a wire rack to cool.

Fruity Muesli Bars

These fruity muesli bars make an appetizing treat for a takeaway snack.

Makes 10–12

INGREDIENTS
115 g/4 oz/8 tbsp half-fat spread
75 g/3 oz/⅓ cup soft light
  brown sugar
45 ml/3 tbsp golden syrup
150 g/5 oz/1¼ cups no-added sugar
  Swiss-style muesli
50 g/2 oz/½ cup rolled oats
5 ml/1 tsp ground mixed spice
50 g/2 oz/⅓ cup sultanas
50 g/2 oz/⅓ cup ready-to-eat dried
  pears, chopped

*half-fat
spread*

*light soft
brown sugar*

*golden
syrup*

*no-added-sugar
Swiss-style
muesli*

*rolled
oats*

*ground
mixed spice*

sultanas

*dried
pears*

1 Preheat the oven to 180°C/350°F/ Gas 4. Lightly grease an 18 cm/7 in square cake tin.

2 Put the half-fat spread, sugar and syrup in a saucepan and gently heat until melted and blended, stirring.

3 Remove the pan from the heat, add the muesli, oats, spice, sultanas and pears and mix well.

4 Transfer the mixture to the prepared tin and level the surface, pressing down.

5 Bake for 20–30 minutes, until golden brown. Cool slightly in the tin, then mark into bars using a sharp knife.

6 When firm, remove the muesli bars from the tin and cool on a wire rack.

NUTRITIONAL NOTES
PER PORTION:

ENERGY 191Kcals/804KJ PROTEIN 3.09g
FAT 6.26g SATURATED FAT 1.59g
CARBOHYDRATE 32.57g FIBRE 1.66g
ADDED SUGAR 10.14g SODIUM 0.11g

COOK'S TIP
A combination of rolled oats and oatmeal can be used in place of muesli for a delicious change.

Cheese and Pineapple Wholewheat Scones

These cheese and pineapple scones are delicious eaten freshly baked, warm or cold, with a little low-fat spread or reduced-sugar jam.

NUTRITIONAL NOTES

PER PORTION:

ENERGY 99Kcals/418KJ PROTEIN 4.22g
FAT 3.62g SATURATED FAT 1.05g
CARBOHYDRATE 13.28g FIBRE 1.74g
ADDED SUGAR 1.33g SODIUM 0.06g

Makes 14–16

INGREDIENTS

225 g/8 oz/2 cups self-raising
  wholemeal flour, sifted
5 ml/1 tsp baking powder, sifted
pinch of salt
40 g/1½ oz/3 tbsp polyunsaturated
  margarine
5 ml/1 tsp mustard powder
75 g/3 oz/¾ cup reduced-fat
  mature Cheddar cheese,
  finely grated
50 g/2 oz/¼ cup ready-to-eat dried
  pineapple, finely chopped
150 ml/¼ pint/⅔ cup skimmed milk

 baking powder   *salt*

self-raising wholemeal flour

mustard powder

polyunsaturated margarine

reduced-fat mature Cheddar cheese

ready-to-eat dried pineapple   *skimmed milk*

1 Preheat the oven to 220°C/425°F/ Gas 7. Line a baking sheet with non-stick baking paper. Sift the flour, baking powder and salt into a bowl.

2 Rub in the fat until the mixture resembles breadcrumbs.

3 Fold in the mustard powder, cheese, pineapple and enough milk to make a fairly soft dough.

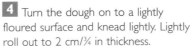

4 Turn the dough on to a lightly floured surface and knead lightly. Lightly roll out to 2 cm/¾ in thickness.

5 Using a 5 cm/2 in fluted cutter, stamp out rounds and place them on the prepared baking sheet.

6 Brush the tops with milk and bake for about 10 minutes, until well risen and golden brown. Transfer to a wire rack to cool and serve warm or cold.

COOK'S TIP
For economy, grate the cheese finely so it will go further and you will use less.

Malt Loaf

This is a rich and sticky loaf. If it lasts long enough to go stale, try toasting it for a delicious tea-time treat.

NUTRITIONAL NOTES

PER PORTION:

ENERGY 279 Kcals/1171 KJ
FAT 2.06 g **SATURATED FAT** 0.33 g
CHOLESTEROL 0.38 mg **FIBRE** 1.79 g

Serves 8

INGREDIENTS
150 ml/¼ pint/⅔ cup warm
  skimmed milk
5 ml/1 tsp dried yeast
pinch of caster sugar
350 g/12 oz/3 cups plain flour
1.5 ml/¼ tsp salt
30 ml/2 tbsp light muscovado sugar
175 g/6 oz/generous 1 cup sultanas
15 ml/1 tbsp sunflower oil
45 ml/3 tbsp malt extract

FOR THE GLAZE
30 ml/2 tbsp caster sugar
30 ml/2 tbsp water

malt extract

sultanas

salt

plain flour

skimmed milk

light muscovado sugar

dried yeast

sunflower oil

VARIATION

To make buns, divide the dough into 10 pieces, shape into rounds, leave to rise, then bake for about 15–20 minutes. Brush with the glaze while still hot.

1 Place the warm milk in a bowl. Sprinkle the yeast on top and add the sugar. Leave for 30 minutes until frothy. Sift the flour and salt into a mixing bowl, stir in the muscovado sugar and sultanas, and make a well in the centre.

2 Add the yeast mixture with the oil and malt extract. Gradually incorporate the flour and mix to a soft dough, adding a little extra milk if necessary.

3 Turn on to a floured surface and knead for about 5 minutes until smooth and elastic. Grease a 450 g/1 lb loaf tin.

4 Shape the dough and place it in the prepared tin. Cover with a damp dish towel and leave in a warm place for 1–2 hours until well risen. Preheat the oven to 190°C/375°F/Gas 5.

5 Bake the loaf for 30–35 minutes, or until it sounds hollow when it is tapped underneath.

6 Meanwhile, prepare the glaze by dissolving the sugar in the water in a small pan. Bring to the boil, stirring, then lower the heat and simmer for 1 minute. Place the loaf on a wire rack and brush with the glaze while still hot. Leave the loaf to cool before serving.

Pear and Sultana Teabread

This is an ideal teabread to make when pears are plentiful – an excellent use for windfalls.

Serves 6–8

INGREDIENTS

25 g/1 oz/scant ¹/₃ cup rolled oats
50 g/2 oz/¹/₃ cup light muscovado sugar
30 ml/2 tbsp pear or apple juice
30 ml/2 tbsp sunflower oil
1 large or 2 small pears
115 g/4 oz/1 cup self-raising flour
115 g/4 oz/²/₃ cup sultanas
2.5 ml/¹/₂ tsp baking powder
10 ml/2 tsp mixed spice
1 egg

small pears

egg

baking powder

sunflower oil

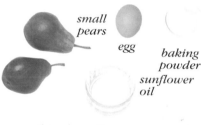
self-raising flour

rolled oats

sultanas

mixed spice

light muscovado sugar

pear juice

NUTRITIONAL NOTES
PER PORTION:

ENERGY 200 Kcals/841 KJ
FAT 4.61 g **SATURATED FAT** 0.79 g
CHOLESTEROL 27.50 mg **FIBRE** 1.39 g

1 Preheat the oven to 180°C/350°F/ Gas 4. Grease and line a 450 g/1 lb loaf tin with non-stick baking paper. Put the oats in a bowl with the sugar, pour over the pear or apple juice and oil, mix well and leave to stand for 15 minutes.

2 Quarter, core and grate the pear(s). Add to the oat mixture with the flour, sultanas, baking powder, mixed spice and egg, then mix together thoroughly.

3 Spoon the mixture into the prepared loaf tin and level the top. Bake for 50–60 minutes or until a skewer inserted into the centre comes out clean.

4 Transfer the teabread on to a wire rack and peel off the lining paper. Leave to cool completely.

COOK'S TIP
Health food shops sell concentrated pear and apple juice, ready for diluting as required.

Irish Whiskey Cake

This moist rich fruit cake is drizzled with whiskey as soon as it comes out of the oven.

Serves 12

INGREDIENTS
115 g/4 oz/²/₃ cup glacé cherries
175 g/6 oz/1 cup dark muscovado
   sugar
115 g/4 oz/²/₃ cup sultanas
115 g/4 oz/²/₃ cup raisins
115 g/4 oz/¹/₂ cup currants
300 ml/¹/₂ pint/1¹/₄ cups cold tea
300 g/10 oz/2¹/₂ cups self-raising
   flour, sifted
1 egg
45 ml/3 tbsp Irish whiskey

raisins

currants

sultanas

*muscovado
sugar*

glacé cherries

cold tea

*Irish
whiskey*

*self-raising
flour*

egg

COOK'S TIP

If time is short use hot tea and soak the fruit for just 2 hours.

1 Mix the cherries, sugar, dried fruit and tea in a large bowl. Leave to soak overnight until all the tea has been absorbed into the fruit.

2 Preheat the oven to 180°C/350°F/ Gas 4. Grease and line a 1 kg/2¹/₄ lb loaf tin. Add the flour, then the egg to the fruit mixture and beat thoroughly until well mixed.

NUTRITIONAL NOTES

PER PORTION:

ENERGY 265 Kcals/1115 K J
FAT 0.88 g **SATURATED FAT** 0.25 g
CHOLESTEROL 16.00 mg **FIBRE** 1.48 g

3 Pour the mixture into the prepared tin and bake for 1¹/₂ hours or until a skewer inserted into the centre of the cake comes out clean.

4 Prick the top of the cake with a skewer and drizzle over the whiskey while the cake is still hot. Allow to stand for about 5 minutes, then remove from the tin and cool on a wire rack.

Puddings & Desserts

Pineapple and Peach Upside Down Pudding

A tasty combination of pineapple and peaches, serve this old favourite with low-fat custard or ice cream.

Serves 6

INGREDIENTS

75 ml/5 tbsp golden syrup
227 g/8 oz can pineapple cubes in fruit juice
175 g/6 oz/¾ cup ready-to-eat dried peaches, chopped
115 g/4 oz/⅔ cup caster sugar
115 g/4 oz/8 tbsp half-fat spread
175 g/6 oz/1½ cups self-raising wholemeal flour
5 ml/1 tsp baking powder
2 eggs

golden syrup

pineapple cubes in fruit juice

dried peaches

caster sugar

half-fat spread

self-raising wholemeal flour

baking powder

eggs

NUTRITIONAL NOTES
PER PORTION:

ENERGY 410Kcals/1733KJ PROTEIN 8.36g
FAT 10.69g SATURATED FAT 2.82g
CARBOHYDRATE 74.73g FIBRE 4.94g
ADDED SUGAR 37.51g SODIUM 0.21g

COOK'S TIP
Other combinations of canned and dried fruit work just as well, such as apricots and pears or peaches and figs.

1 Preheat the oven to 180°C/350°F/Gas 4. Lightly grease an 18 cm/7 in, loose-bottomed round cake tin and line the base with non-stick baking paper.

2 Heat the golden syrup gently in a saucepan and pour over the bottom of the tin.

3 Strain the pineapple, reserving 45 ml/3 tbsp of the juice.

4 Mix together the pineapple and peaches and scatter them over the syrup layer.

5 Put the caster sugar, half-fat spread, flour, baking powder, eggs and reserved pineapple juice in a bowl and beat together until smooth.

6 Spread the cake mixture evenly over the fruit and level the surface. Bake for about 45 minutes until risen and golden brown. Turn out carefully on to a serving plate and serve hot or cold in slices.

Peach and Raspberry Crumble

A quick and easy tasty dessert, this crumble is good served hot or cold on its own or with low-fat custard.

Serves 4

INGREDIENTS
75 g/3 oz/⅔ cup plain
   wholemeal flour
75 g/3 oz/¾ cup medium oatmeal
75 g/3 oz/6 tbsp half-fat spread
50 g/2 oz/¼ cup soft light
   brown sugar
2.5 ml/½ tsp ground cinnamon
400 g/14 oz can peach slices in
   fruit juice
225 g/8 oz/1⅓ cups raspberries
30 ml/2 tbsp clear honey

plain wholemeal flour

medium oatmeal

half-fat spread

light soft brown sugar

ground cinnamon

peach slices in fruit juice

raspberries

clear honey

1 Preheat the oven to 180°C/350°F/Gas 4. Put the flour and oatmeal in a bowl and mix together.

2 Rub in the half-fat spread until the mixture resembles breadcrumbs, then stir in the sugar and cinnamon.

3 Drain the peach slices and reserve the juice.

4 Roughly chop the peaches and put them in an ovenproof dish, then scatter over the raspberries.

5 Mix together the reserved peach juice and honey, pour over the fruit and stir.

6 Spoon the crumble mixture over the fruit, pressing it down lightly. Bake for about 45 minutes, until golden brown on top. Serve hot or cold.

COOK'S TIP
Use other combinations of fruit, such as apples and blueberries, for a tasty change.

NUTRITIONAL NOTES
PER PORTION:
ENERGY 334Kcals/1413KJ PROTEIN 7.02g
FAT 9.9g SATURATED FAT 2.51g
CARBOHYDRATE 58.57g FIBRE 5.22g
ADDED SUGAR 12.66g SODIUM 0.14g

Baked Blackberry Cheesecake

This light, low-fat cheesecake is best made with wild blackberries, if they're available, but cultivated ones will do; or substitute other soft fruit, such as loganberries, raspberries or blueberries.

Serves 5

INGREDIENTS
175 g/6 oz/¾ cup cottage cheese
150 g/5 oz/⅔ cup low-fat natural yogurt
15 ml/1 tbsp plain wholemeal flour
25 g/1 oz/2 tbsp golden caster sugar
1 egg
1 egg white
finely grated rind and juice of ½ lemon
200 g/7 oz/2 cups fresh or frozen and thawed blackberries

cottage cheese

blackberries

wholemeal flour

lemon

natural yogurt

eggs

golden caster sugar

NUTRITIONAL NOTES
PER PORTION:

ENERGY 111 Kcals/468.6 KJ **FAT** 3.0 g
SATURATED FAT 1.4 g

COOK'S TIP
If you prefer to use canned blackberries, choose those canned in natural juice and drain the fruit well before adding it to the cheesecake mixture. The juice can be served with the cheesecake, but this will increase the total calories.

1 Preheat the oven to 180°C/350°F/Gas 4. Lightly grease and base-line an 18 cm/7 in sandwich tin.

2 Place the cottage cheese in a food processor and process until smooth. Alternatively, rub it through a sieve, to obtain a smooth mixture.

3 Add the yogurt, flour, sugar, egg and egg white and mix. Add the lemon rind, juice and blackberries, reserving a few for decoration.

4 Tip the mixture into the prepared tin and bake it for 30–35 minutes, or until it's just set. Turn off the oven and leave for a further 30 minutes.

5 Run a knife around the edge of the cheesecake, and then turn it out. Remove the lining paper and place the cheesecake on a warm serving plate.

6 Decorate the cheesecake with the reserved blackberries and serve it warm.

Mango and Amaretti Strudel

Fresh mango and crushed amaretti wrapped in wafer-thin filo pastry make a special treat that is equally delicious made with apricots or plums.

Serves 4

NUTRITIONAL NOTES
PER PORTION:

ENERGY 239 Kcals/1006 KJ
FAT 8.45 g **SATURATED FAT** 4.43 g
CHOLESTEROL 17.25 mg **FIBRE** 3.30 g

INGREDIENTS
1 large mango
grated rind of 1 lemon
2 amaretti biscuits
25 g/1 oz/3 tbsp demerara sugar
60 ml/4 tbsp wholemeal
    breadcrumbs
2 sheets of filo pastry, each 48 x
    28 cm/19 x 11 in
20 g/³/₄ oz/4 tsp soft margarine,
    melted
15 ml/1 tbsp chopped almonds
icing sugar, for dusting

filo pastry

mango

wholemeal breadcrumbs

lemon rind

amaretti biscuits

demerara sugar

chopped almonds

soft margarine

1 Preheat the oven to 190°C/375°F/Gas 5. Lightly grease a large baking sheet. Halve, stone and peel the mango. Cut the flesh into cubes, then place them in a bowl and sprinkle with the grated lemon rind.

2 Crush the amaretti biscuits and mix them with the demerara sugar and the wholemeal breadcrumbs.

3 Lay one sheet of filo on a flat surface and brush with a quarter of the melted margarine. Top with the second sheet, brush with one-third of the remaining margarine, then fold both sheets over, if necessary, to make a rectangle measuring 28 x 24 cm/11 x 9¹/₂ in. Brush with half the remaining margarine.

4 Sprinkle the filo with the amaretti mixture, leaving a 5 cm/2 in border on each long side. Arrange the mango cubes over the top.

5 Roll up the filo from one of the long sides, Swiss roll fashion. Lift the strudel on to the baking sheet with the join underneath. Brush with the remaining melted margarine and sprinkle with the chopped almonds.

6 Bake for 20–25 minutes until golden brown, then transfer to a board. Dust with the icing sugar, slice diagonally and serve warm.

COOK'S TIP
The easiest way to prepare a mango is to cut horizontally through the fruit, keeping the knife blade close to the stone. Repeat on the other side of the stone and peel off the skin. Remove the remaining skin and flesh from around the stone.

Filo and Apricot Purses

Filo pastry is very easy to use and is low in fat. Keep a packet in the freezer ready for rustling up a speedy tea-time treat.

Makes 12

INGREDIENTS

115 g/4 oz/³/₄ cup ready-to-eat
  dried apricots
45 ml/3 tbsp apricot compôte
  or conserve
3 amaretti biscuits, crushed
3 filo pastry sheets
20 ml/4 tsp soft margarine, melted
icing sugar, for dusting

filo pastry

*ready-to-eat
dried apricots*

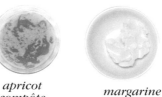

*apricot
compôte*   *margarine*

*amaretti
biscuits*

COOK'S TIP

The easiest way to crush amaretti biscuits is to put them in a plastic bag and roll with a rolling pin.

NUTRITIONAL NOTES
PER PORTION:

ENERGY 58 Kcals/245 KJ
FAT 1.85 g **SATURATED FAT** 0.40 g
CHOLESTEROL 0.12 mg **FIBRE** 0.74 g

1 Preheat the oven to 180°C/350°F/ Gas 4. Grease two baking sheets. Chop the apricots, put them in a bowl and stir in the apricot compôte. Add the crushed amaretti biscuits and mix well.

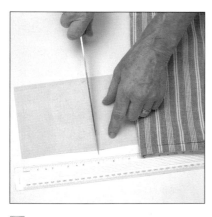

2 Cut the filo pastry into twenty-four 13 cm/5 in squares, pile the squares on top of each other and cover with a clean dish towel to prevent the pastry from drying out and becoming brittle.

3 Lay one pastry square on a flat surface, brush lightly with melted margarine and lay another square diagonally on top. Brush the top square with melted margarine. Spoon a small mound of apricot mixture in the centre of the pastry, bring up the edges and pinch together in a money-bag shape. Repeat with the remaining filo squares and filling to make 12 purses in all.

4 Arrange the purses on the prepared baking sheets and bake for 5–8 minutes until golden brown. Transfer to a wire rack and dust lightly with icing sugar. Serve warm.

Filo Scrunchies

Quick and easy to make, these pastries are ideal to serve at tea-time. Eat them warm or they will lose their crispness.

Makes 6

INGREDIENTS
5 apricots or plums
4 filo pastry sheets
20 ml/4 tsp soft margarine, melted
50 g/2 oz/⅓ cup demerara sugar
30 ml/2 tbsp flaked almonds
icing sugar, for dusting

flaked almonds

margarine

apricots

demerara sugar

filo pastry

COOK'S TIP
Filo pastry dries out very quickly. Keep it covered as much as possible with a dry cloth or clear film to limit exposure to the air, or it will become too brittle to use.

NUTRITIONAL NOTES
PER PORTION:

ENERGY 132 Kcals/555 KJ
FAT 4.19 g SATURATED FAT 0.63 g
CHOLESTEROL 0 FIBRE 0.67 g

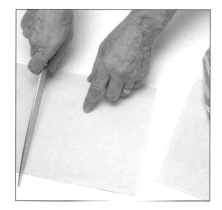

1 Preheat the oven to 190°C/375°F/Gas 5. Halve the apricots or plums, remove the stones and slice the fruit. Cut the filo pastry into twelve 18 cm/7 in squares. Pile the squares on top of each other and cover with a clean dish towel to prevent the pastry from drying out.

2 Remove one square of filo and brush it with melted margarine. Lay a second filo square on top, then, using your fingers, mould the pastry into folds. Make five more scrunchies in the same way, working quickly so that the pastry does not dry out.

3 Arrange a few slices of fruit in the folds of each scrunchie, then sprinkle generously with the demerara sugar and flaked almonds.

4 Place the scrunchies on a baking sheet. Bake for 8–10 minutes until golden brown, then loosen the scrunchies from the baking sheet with a palette knife and transfer to a wire rack. Dust with icing sugar and serve at once.

Muscovado Meringues

These light brown meringues are extremely low in fat and are delicious served on their own or sandwiched together with a fresh fruit and soft cheese filling.

Makes about 20

INGREDIENTS
115 g/4 oz/²/₃ cup light muscovado
   sugar
2 egg whites
5 ml/1 tsp finely chopped walnuts

eggs

light muscovado sugar

walnuts

NUTRITIONAL NOTES

PER PORTION:

ENERGY 30 Kcals/124 KJ
FAT 0.34 g **SATURATED FAT** 0.04 g
CHOLESTEROL 0 **FIBRE** 0.02 g

COOK'S TIP

For a sophisticated filling, mix 115 g/4 oz/¹/₂ cup low-fat soft cheese with 15 ml/1 tbsp icing sugar. Chop 2 slices of fresh pineapple and add to the mixture. Use to sandwich the meringues together in pairs.

1 Preheat the oven to 160°C/325°F/ Gas 3. Line two baking sheets with non-stick baking paper. Press the sugar through a metal sieve into a bowl.

2 Whisk the egg whites in a grease-free bowl until very stiff and dry, then whisk in the sugar, about 15 ml/1 tbsp at a time, until the meringue is very thick and glossy.

3 Spoon small mounds of the mixture on to the prepared baking sheets.

4 Sprinkle the meringues with the chopped walnuts. Bake for 30 minutes. Cool for 5 minutes on the baking sheets, then leave to cool on a wire rack.

Lemon Sponge Fingers

These sponge fingers are perfect for serving with fruit salads or light, creamy desserts.

Makes about 20

INGREDIENTS
2 eggs
75 g/3 oz/6 tbsp caster sugar
grated rind of 1 lemon
50 g/2 oz/½ cup plain flour, sifted
caster sugar, for sprinkling

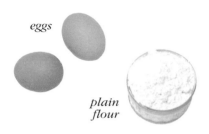

eggs

plain flour

caster sugar

lemon

VARIATION
To make Spicy Orange Fingers, substitute grated orange rind for the lemon rind and add 5 ml/1 tsp ground cinnamon with the flour.

1 Preheat the oven to 190°C/375°F/Gas 5. Line two baking sheets with non-stick baking paper. Whisk the eggs, sugar and lemon rind together with a hand-held electric whisk until thick and mousse-like (when the whisk is lifted, a trail should remain on the surface of the mixture for at least 15 seconds). Gently fold in the flour with a large metal spoon using a figure-of-eight action.

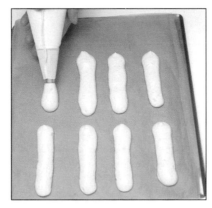

2 Place the mixture in a large piping bag fitted with a 1 cm/½ in plain nozzle. Pipe the mixture into finger lengths on the prepared baking sheets.

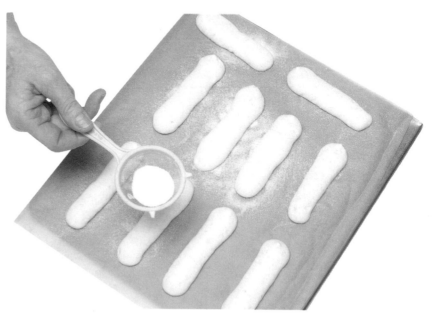

3 Sprinkle the fingers with caster sugar. Bake for about 6–8 minutes until golden brown, then transfer the sponge fingers to a wire rack to cool.

Cherry Pancakes

These pancakes are virtually fat-free, and lower in calories and higher in fibre than traditional ones. Serve with a spoonful of natural yogurt or fromage frais.

Serves 4

INGREDIENTS
FOR THE PANCAKES
50 g/2 oz/½ cup plain flour
50 g/2 oz/⅓ cup plain wholemeal
    flour
pinch of salt
1 egg white
150 ml/¼ pint/⅔ cup skimmed milk
150 ml/¼ pint/⅔ cup water
a little oil for frying

FOR THE FILLING
425 g/15 oz can black cherries in juice
7.5 ml/1½ tsp arrowroot

skimmed milk

wholemeal flour

plain flour

arrowroot

black cherries

egg

1 Sift the flours and salt into a bowl, adding any bran left in the sieve to the bowl at the end.

2 Make a well in the centre of the flour and add the egg white. Gradually beat in the milk and water, whisking hard until all the liquid is incorporated and the batter is smooth and bubbly.

3 Heat a non-stick pan with a small amount of oil until the pan is very hot. Pour in just enough batter to cover the base of the pan, swirling the pan to cover the base evenly.

4 Cook until the pancake is set and golden, and then turn to cook the other side. Remove to a sheet of absorbent paper and then cook the remaining batter, to make about eight pancakes.

5 Drain the cherries, reserving the juice. Blend about 30 ml/2 tbsp of the juice from the can of cherries with the arrowroot in a saucepan. Stir in the rest of the juice. Heat gently, stirring, until boiling. Stir over a moderate heat for about 2 minutes, until thickened and clear.

COOK'S TIP

If fresh cherries are in season, cook them gently in enough apple juice just to cover them, and then thicken the juice with arrowroot as in Step 5.

The basic pancakes will freeze very successfully. Interleave them with non-stick or absorbent paper, overwrap them in polythene and seal. Freeze for up to six months. Thaw at room temperature.

NUTRITIONAL NOTES
PER PORTION:

ENERGY 165 Kcals/698.5 KJ **FAT** 3.03 g
SATURATED FAT 0.4 g

6 Add the cherries and stir until thoroughly heated. Spoon the cherries into the pancakes and fold them in quarters.

Blueberry and Orange Crêpe Baskets

Impress your guests with these pretty, fruit-filled crêpes. When blueberries are out of season, replace them with other soft fruit, such as raspberries.

Serves 6

NUTRITIONAL NOTES
PER PORTION:

ENERGY 158 Kcals/1007 KJ **FAT** 0.85 g
SATURATED FAT 0.08 g

COOK'S TIP
Don't fill the pancake baskets until you're ready to serve them, because they will absorb the fruit juice and begin to soften.

INGREDIENTS
FOR THE PANCAKES
150 g/5 oz/1¼ cups plain flour
pinch salt
2 egg whites
200 ml/7 fl oz/⅞ cup skimmed milk
150 ml/¼ pint/⅔ cup orange juice

FOR THE FILLING
4 medium-size oranges
225 g/8 oz/2 cups blueberries

orange juice

oranges

eggs

blueberries

skimmed milk

1 Preheat the oven to 200°C/400°F/ Gas 6. To make the pancakes, sift the flour and salt into a bowl. Make a well in the centre of the flour and add the egg whites, milk and orange juice. Whisk hard, until all the liquid has been incorporated and the batter is smooth and bubbly.

2 Lightly grease a heavy or non-stick pancake pan and heat it until it is very hot. Pour in just enough batter to cover the base of the pan, swirling it to cover the pan evenly.

3 Cook until the pancake has set and is golden, and then turn it to cook the other side. Remove the pancake to a sheet of absorbent kitchen paper, and then cook the remaining batter, to make 6–8 pancakes.

4 Place six small ovenproof bowls or moulds on a baking sheet and arrange the pancakes over these. Bake them in the oven for about 10 minutes, until they are crisp and set into shape. Carefully lift the 'baskets' off the moulds.

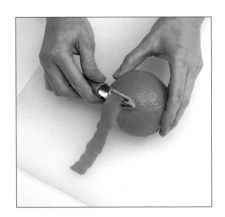

5 Pare a thin piece of orange rind from one orange and cut it in fine strips. Blanch the strips in boiling water for 30 seconds, rinse them in cold water and set them aside. Cut all the peel and white pith from all the oranges.

6 Divide the oranges into segments, catching the juice, combine with the blueberries and warm them gently. Spoon the fruit into the baskets and scatter the shreds of rind over the top. Serve with yogurt or light crème fraîche.

Baked Apples in Honey and Lemon

A classic mix of flavours in a healthy, traditional family pudding. Serve warm, with skimmed-milk custard.

Serves 4

INGREDIENTS
4 medium-size cooking apples
15 ml/1 tbsp clear honey
grated rind and juice of 1 lemon
15 ml/1 tbsp low-fat spread

clear honey

cooking apples

lemon

low-fat spread

1 Preheat the oven to 180°C/350°F/Gas 4. Remove the cores from the apples, leaving them whole.

2 With a cannelle or sharp knife, cut lines through the apple skin at intervals and place in an ovenproof dish.

COOK'S TIP

This recipe can also be cooked in the microwave to save time. Place the apples in a microwave-safe dish and cover them with a lid or pierced clear film. Microwave on **FULL POWER** (100%) for 9–10 minutes.

NUTRITIONAL NOTES
PER PORTION:

ENERGY 65 Kcals/276 KJ **FAT** 1.62 g
SATURATED FAT 0.42 g

3 Mix together the honey, lemon rind, juice and low-fat spread.

4 Spoon the mixture into the apples and cover the dish with foil or a lid. Bake for 40–45 minutes, or until the apples are tender. Serve with skimmed-milk custard.

Grilled Nectarines with Ricotta and Spice

This easy dessert is good at any time of year – use canned peach halves if fresh ones are not available.

Serves 4

INGREDIENTS
4 ripe nectarines or peaches
15 ml/1 tbsp light muscovado sugar
115 g/4 oz/½ cup ricotta cheese or
  fromage frais
2.5 ml/½ tsp ground star anise

nectarines

light muscovado sugar

ricotta cheese

ground star anise

1 Cut the nectarines in half and remove the stones.

2 Arrange the nectarines, cut-side upwards, in a wide flameproof dish or on a baking sheet.

NUTRITIONAL NOTES
Per portion:
ENERGY 95 Kcals/401 KJ **FAT** 3.3 g
SATURATED FAT 1.98 g

COOK'S TIP
Star anise has a warm, rich flavour – if you can't get it, try ground cloves or ground mixed spice instead.

3 Stir the sugar into the ricotta or fromage frais. Using a teaspoon, spoon the mixture into the hollow of each nectarine half.

4 Sprinkle with the star anise. Place under a moderately hot grill for 6–8 minutes, or until the nectarines are hot and bubbling. Serve warm.

Sultana and Couscous Puddings

Most couscous on the market now is the pre-cooked variety, which needs only the minimum of cooking, but check the pack instructions first to make sure. Serve hot, with yogurt or skimmed-milk custard.

Serves 4

INGREDIENTS
50 g/2 oz/⅓ cup sultanas
475 ml/16 fl oz/2 cups apple juice
90 g/3½ oz/1 cup couscous
2.5 ml/½ tsp mixed spice

apple juice

couscous

mixed spice

sultanas

1 Lightly grease four 250 ml/8 fl oz/1-cup pudding basins or one 1-litre/1¾-pint/4-cup pudding basin. Place the sultanas and apple juice in a pan.

2 Bring the apple juice to the boil, and then cover the pan and leave to simmer gently for 2–3 minutes, to plump up the fruit. Using a slotted spoon, lift out about half the fruit and place it in the bottom of the basins.

3 Add the couscous and mixed spice to the pan and bring back to the boil, stirring. Cover and leave over a low heat for 8–10 minutes, or until the liquid is absorbed.

4 Spoon the couscous into the basins, spread it level, and then cover the basins tightly with foil. Place the basins in a steamer over boiling water, cover and steam for about 30 minutes. Run a knife around the edges, turn the puddings out carefully and serve straight away.

Orange Yogurt Brûlées

A luxurious treat, but one that is much lower in fat than the classic brûlées, which are made with cream, eggs and large amounts of sugar.

Serves 4

INGREDIENTS
2 medium-size oranges
150 g/5 oz/⅔ cup Greek yogurt
50 g/2 oz/¼ cup crème fraîche
45 ml/3 tbsp golden caster sugar
30 ml/2 tbsp light muscovado sugar

golden caster sugar

light muscovado sugar

crème fraîche

oranges

Greek yogurt

1 With a sharp knife, cut away all the peel and white pith from the oranges and chop the fruit. Or, if there's time, segment the oranges, removing all the membrane.

2 Place the fruit in the bottom of four individual flameproof dishes. Mix together the yogurt and crème fraîche and spoon the mixture over the oranges.

COOK'S TIP
For a lighter version, simply use 200 g/7 oz/⅞ cup low-fat natural yogurt instead of the Greek yogurt and crème fraîche.

NUTRITIONAL NOTES
Per portion:

ENERGY 147 Kcals/620.5 KJ **FAT** 2.9 g
SATURATED FAT 1.75 g

3 Mix together the two sugars and sprinkle them evenly over the tops of the dishes.

4 Place the dishes under a preheated, very hot grill for 3–4 minutes or until the sugar melts and turns to a rich golden brown. Serve warm or cold.

Apricot and Banana Compote

This compote is delicious served on its own or with low-fat custard or ice cream. Served for breakfast, it makes a tasty start to the day.

Serves 4

INGREDIENTS
225 g/8 oz/1 cup ready-to-eat
  dried apricots
300 ml/½ pint/1¼ cups
  unsweetened orange juice
150 ml/¼ pint/⅔ cup unsweetened
  apple juice
5 ml/1 tsp ground ginger
3 medium bananas, sliced
25 g/1 oz/¼ cup toasted
  flaked almonds

dried apricots

unsweetened orange juice

unsweetened apple juice

ground ginger

bananas

toasted flaked almonds

NUTRITIONAL NOTES
PER PORTION:

ENERGY 241Kcals/1022KJ PROTEIN 4.92g
FAT 4.18g SATURATED FAT 0.37g
CARBOHYDRATE 48.98g FIBRE 4.91g
ADDED SUGAR 0.00g SODIUM 0.02g

1 Put the apricots in a saucepan with the fruit juices and ginger and stir. Cover, bring to the boil and simmer gently for 10 minutes, stirring occasionally.

2 Set aside to cool, leaving the lid on. Once cool, stir in the sliced bananas.

COOK'S TIP
Use other combinations of dried and fresh fruit such as prunes or figs and apples or peaches.

3 Spoon the fruit and juices into a serving dish.

4 Serve immediately, or cover and chill for several hours before serving. Sprinkle with flaked almonds just before serving.

Golden Ginger Compote

Warm, spicy and full of sun-ripened ingredients – this is the perfect winter dessert.

Serves 4

INGREDIENTS
200 g/7 oz/2 cups kumquats
200 g/7 oz/1¼ cups dried apricots
30 ml/2 tbsp sultanas
400 ml/14 fl oz/1⅔ cups water
1 orange
2.5 cm/1 in piece fresh root ginger
4 cardamom pods
4 cloves
30 ml/2 tbsp clear honey
15 ml/1 tbsp flaked almonds, toasted

orange

clear honey

kumquats

fresh root ginger

dried apricots

flaked almonds

cloves

cardamom pods

sultanas

1 Wash the kumquats, and, if they are large, cut them in half. Place them in a pan with the apricots, sultanas and water. Bring to the boil.

2 Pare the rind thinly from the orange and add to the pan. Peel and grate the ginger and add to the pan. Lightly crush the cardamom pods and add them to the pan, with the cloves.

3 Reduce the heat, cover the pan and leave to simmer gently for about 30 minutes, or until the fruit is tender, stirring occasionally.

4 Squeeze the juice from the orange and add to the pan with honey to sweeten to taste, sprinkle with flaked almonds and serve warm.

Winter Fruit Salad

A colourful, refreshing and nutritious fruit salad, which is ideal served with reduced-fat Greek-style yogurt or cream.

Serves 6

INGREDIENTS
225 g/8 oz can pineapple cubes in
  fruit juice
200 ml/7 fl oz/scant 1 cup freshly
  squeezed orange juice
200 ml/7 fl oz/scant 1 cup
  unsweetened apple juice
30 ml/2 tbsp orange or apple liqueur
30 ml/2 tbsp clear honey (optional)
2 oranges, peeled
2 green-skinned eating
  apples, chopped
2 pears, chopped
4 plums, stoned and chopped
12 fresh dates, stoned and chopped
115 g/4 oz/½ cup ready-to-eat
  dried apricots
fresh mint sprigs, to decorate

pineapple cubes in fruit juice *freshly squeezed orange juice*

unsweetened apple juice *orange or apple liqueur* *clear honey*

oranges *green-skinned eating apples* *pears*

plums *fresh dates* *dried apricots*

I Drain the pineapple, reserving the juice. Put the pineapple juice, orange juice, apple juice, liqueur and honey, if using, in a large serving bowl and stir.

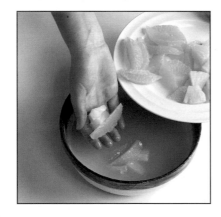

2 Segment the oranges, catching any juice in the bowl, and put the orange segments and pineapple in the fruit juice mixture.

NUTRITIONAL NOTES
PER PORTION:

ENERGY 227Kcals/967KJ PROTEIN 2.85g
FAT 0.37g SATURATED FAT 0.00g
CARBOHYDRATE 53.68g FIBRE 5.34g
ADDED SUGAR 1.33g SODIUM 0.01g

3 Add the apples and pears to the bowl.

COOK'S TIP
Use other unsweetened fruit juices such as pink grapefruit and pineapple juice in place of the orange and apple juice.

4 Stir in the plums, dates and apricots, cover and chill for several hours. Decorate with fresh mint sprigs to serve.

Watermelon, Ginger and Grapefruit Salad

This pretty, pink combination is very light and refreshing for any summer meal.

Serves 4

INGREDIENTS
500 g/1 lb/2 cups diced watermelon flesh
2 ruby or pink grapefruit
2 pieces stem ginger in syrup
30 ml/2 tbsp stem ginger syrup

watermelon flesh

ruby grapefruit

stem ginger in syrup

COOK'S TIP
Toss the fruits gently – grapefruit segments will break up easily and the appearance of the dish will be spoiled.

NUTRITIONAL NOTES
PER PORTION:

ENERGY 20 Kcals/342 KJ **FAT** 0.4 g
SATURATED FAT 0.1 g

1 Remove any seeds from the watermelon and cut into bite-sized chunks.

2 Using a small sharp knife, cut away all the peel and white pith from the grapefruits and carefully lift out the segments, catching any juice in a bowl.

3 Finely chop the stem ginger and place in a serving bowl with the melon cubes and grapefruit segments, adding the reserved juice.

4 Spoon over the ginger syrup and toss the fruits lightly to mix evenly. Chill before serving.

Cappuccino Coffee Cups

Coffee-lovers will love this one – and it tastes rich and creamy, even though it's very light.

Serves 4

INGREDIENTS
2 eggs
215 g/7.7 oz carton evaporated semi-skimmed milk
25 ml/5 tsp instant coffee granules or powder
30 ml/2 tbsp granulated sweetener
10 ml/2 tsp powdered gelatine
60 ml/4 tbsp light crème fraîche
extra cocoa powder or ground cinnamon, to decorate

evaporated semi-skimmed milk

powdered gelatine

granulated sweetener

instant coffee

eggs

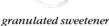
crème fraîche

cocoa powder

COOK'S TIP
It's important to ensure that the gelatine is completely dissolved before spooning the mixture into the dishes, otherwise the texture will not be smooth.

1 Separate one egg and reserve the white. Beat the yolk with the whole of the remaining egg.

2 Put the evaporated milk, coffee granules, sweetener and beaten eggs in a pan; whisk until evenly combined.

3 Put the pan over a low heat and stir constantly until the mixture is hot, but not boiling. Cook, stirring constantly, without boiling, until the mixture is slightly thickened and smooth.

4 Remove the pan from the heat. Sprinkle the gelatine over the pan and whisk until the gelatine has completely dissolved.

5 Spoon the coffee custard into four individual dishes or glasses and chill them until set.

6 Whisk the reserved egg white until stiff. Whisk in the crème fraîche and then spoon the mixture over the desserts. Sprinkle with cocoa or cinnamon and serve.

VARIATION
Greek yogurt can be used instead of the crème fraîche, if you prefer.

NUTRITIONAL NOTES
PER PORTION:

ENERGY 131 Kcals/546.5 KJ **FAT** 6.8 g
SATURATED FAT 2.3 g

Figs with Ricotta Cream

Fresh, ripe figs are full of natural sweetness, and need little adornment. This simple recipe makes the most of their beautiful, intense flavour.

Serves 4

INGREDIENTS
4 ripe, fresh figs
115 g/4 oz/½ cup ricotta or cottage
    cheese
45 ml/3 tbsp crème fraîche
15 ml/1 tbsp clear honey
2.5 ml/½ tsp vanilla essence
freshly grated nutmeg, to decorate

vanilla essence

clear honey

crème fraîche

ricotta cheese

figs

nutmeg

1 Trim the stalks from the figs. Make four cuts through each fig from the stalk-end, cutting them almost through but leaving them joined at the base.

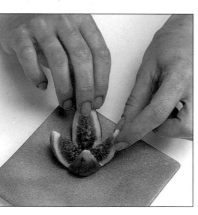

2 Place the figs on serving plates and open them out.

3 Mix together the ricotta or cottage cheese, crème fraîche, honey and vanilla.

4 Spoon a little ricotta cream on to each plate and sprinkle with grated nutmeg to serve.

NUTRITIONAL NOTES

PER PORTION:

ENERGY 99 Kcals/415 KJ **FAT** 5.5 g
SATURATED FAT 3.5 g

Pineapple Wedges with Allspice and Lime

Fresh pineapple is easy to prepare and always looks very festive, so this dish is perfect for easy entertaining.

Serves 4

INGREDIENTS
1 medium-size, ripe pineapple
1 lime
15 ml/1 tbsp dark muscovado sugar
5 ml/1 tsp ground allspice

ground allspice　　*pineapple*

muscovado sugar

lime

1 Cut the pineapple lengthways into quarters and remove the core.

2 Loosen the flesh, by sliding a knife between the flesh and the skin. Cut the flesh into slices, leaving it on the skin.

VARIATION

For a quick hot dish, place the pineapple slices on a baking sheet, sprinkle them with the lime juice, sugar and allspice and place them under a hot grill for 3–4 minutes, or until golden and bubbling. Sprinkle with shreds of lime zest and serve.

NUTRITIONAL NOTES
PER PORTION:

ENERGY 55 Kcals/237 KJ **FAT** 0.3 g
SATURATED FAT 0.03 g

3 Remove a few shreds of rind from the lime and then squeeze out the juice.

4 Sprinkle the pineapple with the lime juice and rind, sugar and allspice. Serve immediately, or chill for up to an hour.

Raspberry Muesli Layer

As well as being a delicious, low-fat, high-fibre dessert, this can also be served for a quick, healthy breakfast.

Serves 4

INGREDIENTS
225 g/8 oz/2¼ cups fresh or frozen
  and thawed raspberries
225 g/8 oz/1 cup low-fat natural
  yogurt
75 g/3 oz/½ cup Swiss-style muesli

raspberries

Swiss-style muesli

natural yogurt

NUTRITIONAL NOTES
PER PORTION:

ENERGY 122 Kcals/516.3 KJ **FAT** 2.7 g
SATURATED FAT 0.4 g

COOK'S TIP

This recipe can be made in advance and stored in the fridge for several hours, or overnight if you're serving it for breakfast.

1 Reserve four raspberries for decoration, and then spoon a few raspberries into four stemmed glasses or glass dishes.

2 Top the raspberries with a spoonful of yogurt in each glass.

3 Sprinkle a layer of muesli over the yogurt.

4 Repeat with the raspberries and other ingredients. Top each with a whole raspberry.

Brazilian Coffee Bananas

Rich, lavish and sinful-looking, this dessert takes only about 2 minutes to make!

Serves 4

INGREDIENTS

4 small ripe bananas
15 ml/1 tbsp instant coffee granules or
    powder
15 ml/1 tbsp hot water
30 ml/2 tbsp dark muscovado sugar
250 g/9 oz/1⅛ cups Greek yogurt
15 ml/1 tbsp toasted flaked almonds

bananas

Greek yogurt

flaked almonds

instant coffee

dark muscovado sugar

1 Peel and slice one banana and mash the remaining three with a fork.

2 Dissolve the coffee in the hot water and stir into the mashed bananas.

3 Spoon a little of the mashed banana mixture into four serving dishes and sprinkle with sugar. Top with a spoonful of yogurt, then repeat until all the ingredients are used up.

4 Swirl the last layer of yogurt for a marbled effect. Finish with a few banana slices and flaked almonds. Serve cold. Best eaten within about an hour of making.

VARIATION

For a special occasion, add a dash – just a dash – of dark rum or brandy to the bananas for extra richness. 15 ml/1 tbsp of rum or brandy adds about 30 calories.

NUTRITIONAL NOTES
Per portion:
ENERGY 169 Kcals/714.5 KJ **FAT** 2.7 g
SATURATED FAT 0.46 g

Minted Raspberry Bavarois

A sophisticated dessert that can be made a day in advance for a special dinner party.

Serves 6

INGREDIENTS
450 g/1 lb/5½ cups fresh or frozen
  and thawed raspberries
30 ml/2 tbsp icing sugar
30 ml/2 tbsp lemon juice
15 ml/1 tbsp finely chopped fresh mint
30 ml/2 tbsp/2 sachets powdered
  gelatine
75 ml/5 tbsp boiling water
300 ml/½ pint/1¼ cups custard,
  made with skimmed milk
250 g/9 oz/1⅛ cups Greek yogurt
fresh mint sprigs, to decorate

skimmed-milk custard

icing sugar

Greek yogurt

powdered gelatine

lemon

mint *raspberries*

NUTRITIONAL NOTES
PER PORTION:

ENERGY 113 Kcals/484.5 KJ **FAT** 0.6 g
SATURATED FAT 0.3 g

COOK'S TIP
You can make this dessert using frozen raspberries, which have a good colour and flavour. Allow them to thaw at room temperature, and use any juice in the jelly.

1 Reserve a few raspberries for decoration. Place the raspberries, icing sugar and lemon juice in a food processor and process them until smooth.

2 Press the purée through a sieve to remove the raspberry pips. Add the mint. You should have about 500 ml/1 pint/ 2½ cups of purée.

3 Sprinkle 5 ml/1 tsp of the gelatine over 30 ml/2 tbsp of the boiling water and stir until the gelatine has dissolved. Stir into 150 ml/¼ pint/⅔ cup of the fruit purée.

4 Pour this jelly into a 1-litre/1¾-pint/ 4-cup mould, and leave the mould to chill in the refrigerator until the jelly is just on the point of setting. Tip the tin to swirl the setting jelly around the sides, and then leave to chill until the jelly has set completely.

5 Stir the remaining fruit purée into the custard and yogurt. Dissolve the rest of the gelatine in the remaining water and stir it in quickly.

6 Pour the raspberry custard into the mould and leave it to chill until it has set completely. To serve, dip the mould quickly into hot water and then turn it out and decorate it with the reserved raspberries and the mint sprigs.

Lemon Hearts with Strawberry Sauce

These elegant little hearts are light as air, and they are best made the day before your dinner party – which saves on last-minute panics as well!

Serves 6

INGREDIENTS
FOR THE HEARTS
175 g/6 oz/¾ cup ricotta cheese
150 ml/¼ pint/⅔ cup crème fraîche
   or soured cream
15 ml/1 tbsp granulated sweetener
finely grated rind of ½ lemon
30 ml/2 tbsp lemon juice
10 ml/2 tsp powdered gelatine
2 egg whites

FOR THE SAUCE
225 g/8 oz/2 cups fresh or frozen and
   thawed strawberries
15 ml/1 tbsp lemon juice

crème fraîche

ricotta cheese

powdered gelatine

lemon

strawberries

eggs

granulated sweetener

1 Beat the ricotta cheese until smooth. Stir in the crème fraîche, sweetener and lemon rind.

2 Place the lemon juice in a small bowl and sprinkle the gelatine over it. Place the bowl over a pan of hot water and stir to dissolve the gelatine completely.

3 Quickly stir the gelatine into the cheese mixture, mixing it in evenly.

4 Beat the egg whites until they form soft peaks. Quickly fold them into the cheese mixture.

5 Spoon the mixture into six lightly oiled, individual heart-shaped moulds and chill the moulds until set.

VARIATION

These little heart-shaped desserts are
the perfect choice for a romantic
dinner, but they don't have to be
heart-shaped – try setting the mixture
in individual fluted moulds, or even in
ordinary teacups.

NUTRITIONAL NOTES
PER PORTION:

ENERGY 112 Kcals/463.6 KJ **FAT** 8.2 g
SATURATED FAT 5.14 g

6 Place the strawberries and lemon juice
in a blender and process until smooth.
Pour the sauce on to serving plates and
place the turned-out hearts on top.
Decorate with slices of strawberry.

Strawberry Rose-petal Pashka

This lighter version of a traditional Russian dessert is ideal for dinner parties – make it a day or two in advance for best results.

Serves 4

Calories per portion about 150

INGREDIENTS
350 g/12 oz/1½ cups cottage cheese
175 g/6 oz/¾ cup low-fat natural
   yogurt
30 ml/2 tbsp clear honey
2.5 ml/½ tsp rose-water
275 g/10 oz/2½ cups strawberries
handful of scented pink rose petals, to
   decorate

clear honey

cottage cheese

rose-water

strawberries

natural yogurt

NUTRITIONAL NOTES
PER PORTION:
ENERGY 151 Kcals/634.5 KJ **FAT** 3.8 g
SATURATED FAT 2.3 g

COOK'S TIP
The flowerpot shape is traditional for pashka, but you could make it in any shape – the small porcelain heart-shaped moulds with draining holes usually used for *coeurs à la crème* make a pretty alternative.

1 Drain any free liquid from the cottage cheese and tip the cheese into a sieve. Use a wooden spoon to rub it through the sieve into a bowl.

2 Stir the yogurt, honey and rose-water into the cheese.

3 Roughly chop about half the strawberries and stir them into the cheese mixture.

4 Line a new, clean flowerpot or a sieve with fine muslin and tip the cheese mixture in. Leave it to drain over a bowl for several hours, or overnight.

5 Invert the flowerpot or sieve on to a serving plate, turn out the pashka and remove the muslin.

6 Decorate with the reserved strawberries and rose petals. Serve chilled.

Chocolate Vanilla Timbales

You really can allow yourself the occasional chocolate treat, especially if it's a dessert as light as this one.

Serves 6

INGREDIENTS

FOR THE TIMBALES

350 ml/12 fl oz/1½ cups semi-
skimmed milk
30 ml/2 tbsp cocoa powder
2 eggs
5 ml/1 tsp vanilla essence
45 ml/3 tbsp granulated sweetener
15 ml/1 tbsp/1 sachet powdered
gelatine
45 ml/3 tbsp hot water

FOR THE SAUCE

115 g/4 oz/½ cup light Greek yogurt
2.5 ml/½ tsp vanilla essence
extra cocoa powder, to sprinkle

semi-skimmed milk

granulated sweetener

vanilla essence

eggs

cocoa powder

powdered gelatine

NUTRITIONAL NOTES

PER PORTION:

ENERGY 81 Kcals/340 KJ **FAT** 3.5 g
SATURATED FAT 0.14 g

1 Place the milk and cocoa in a saucepan and stir until the milk is boiling. Separate the eggs and beat the egg yolks with the vanilla and sweetener in a bowl, until the mixture is pale and smooth. Gradually pour in the chocolate milk, beating well.

2 Return the mixture to the pan and stir constantly over a gentle heat, without boiling, until it's slightly thickened and smooth. Dissolve the gelatine in the hot water and then quickly stir it into the milk mixture. Let it cool until it's on the point of setting.

3 Whisk the egg whites until they hold soft peaks. Fold the egg whites quickly into the milk mixture. Spoon the timbale mixture into six individual moulds and chill them until set.

4 To serve, run a knife around the edge, dip the moulds quickly into hot water and turn out the chocolate timbales on to serving plates. For the sauce, stir together the yogurt and vanilla, spoon on to the plates and sprinkle with a little more cocoa powder.

Wholemeal Bread and Banana Yogurt Ice

Serve this tempting yogurt ice with some fresh fruit such as strawberries, or with wafer biscuits for a light dessert.

Serves 6

INGREDIENTS
115 g/4 oz/2 cups fresh wholemeal breadcrumbs
50 g/2 oz/¼ cup soft light brown sugar
300 ml/½ pint/1¼ cups low fat ready-made cold custard
150 g/5 oz plain fromage frais, 8% fat
150 g/5 oz Greek-style yogurt
4 bananas
juice of 1 lemon
25 g/1 oz/¼ cup icing sugar, sifted
50 g/2 oz/⅓ cup raisins, chopped
pared lemon rind, to decorate

fresh wholemeal breadcrumbs

light soft brown sugar

plain fromage frais

low fat ready-made cold custard

Greek yogurt

lemon

bananas

icing sugar

raisins

NUTRITIONAL NOTES
PER PORTION:

ENERGY 277Kcals/1170KJ PROTEIN 7.55g
FAT 5.51g SATURATED FAT 2.99g
CARBOHYDRATE 52.27g FIBRE 2.01g
ADDED SUGAR 12.77g SODIUM 0.17g

1 Preheat the oven to 200°C/400°F/ Gas 6. Mix together the breadcrumbs and brown sugar and spread the mixture out on a non-stick baking sheet. Bake for about 10 minutes, until the crumbs are crisp, stirring occasionally. Set aside to cool, then break the mixture up into crumbs.

2 Meanwhile, put the custard, fromage frais and yogurt in a bowl and mix. Mash the bananas with the lemon juice and add to the custard mixture, mixing well. Fold in the icing sugar.

3 Pour the mixture into a shallow, plastic, freezerproof container and freeze for about 3 hours or until mushy in consistency. Spoon into a chilled bowl and quickly mash with a fork to break down the ice crystals.

4 Add the breadcrumbs and raisins and mix well. Return the mixture to the container, cover and freeze until firm. Transfer to the fridge about 30 minutes before serving, to soften a little. Serve in scoops, decorated with lemon rind.

Summer Fruit Salad Ice Cream

What could be more cooling on a hot summer day than fresh summer fruits, lightly frozen in this irresistible ice?

Serves 6

INGREDIENTS
900 g/2 lb/4½ cups mixed soft
   summer fruit, such as raspberries,
   strawberries, blackcurrants,
   redcurrants, etc
2 eggs
225 g/8 oz/1 cup Greek yogurt
175 ml/6 fl oz/¾ cup red grape juice
15 ml/1 tbsp/1 sachet powdered
   gelatine

red grape juice

powdered gelatine

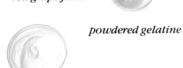

Greek yogurt

eggs

summer fruits

NUTRITIONAL NOTES
PER PORTION:
ENERGY 70 Kcals/296 KJ **FAT** 2.9 g
SATURATED FAT 0.12 g

COOK'S TIP
Red grape juice has a good flavour and improves the colour of the ice, but if it is not available, use cranberry, apple or orange juice instead.

1 Reserve half the fruit and purée the rest in a food processor, or rub it through a sieve to make a smooth purée.

2 Separate the eggs and whisk the yolks and the yogurt into the fruit purée.

3 Heat the grape juice until it's almost boiling, and then remove it from the heat. Sprinkle the gelatine over the grape juice and stir to dissolve the gelatine completely.

4 Whisk the dissolved gelatine mixture into the fruit purée and then pour the mixture into a freezer container. Freeze until half-frozen and slushy in consistency.

5 Whisk the egg whites until they are stiff. Quickly fold them into the half-frozen mixture.

6 Return to the freezer and freeze until almost firm. Scoop into individual dishes or glasses and add the reserved soft fruits.

Muscat Grape Frappé

The flavour and perfume of the Muscat grape is rarely more enticing than when captured in this icy-cool salad. Because of its alcohol content this dish is not suitable for young children.

Serves 4

INGREDIENTS
½ bottle Muscat wine, Beaumes de
   Venise, Frontignan or Rivsaltes
450 g/1 lb Muscat grapes

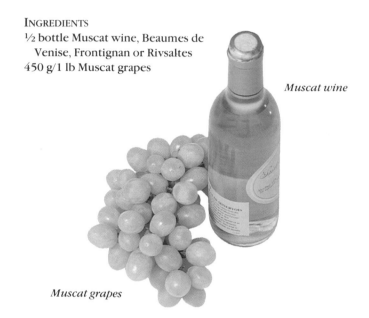

Muscat wine

Muscat grapes

1 Pour the wine into a stainless-steel or enamel tray, add 150 ml/5 fl oz/⅔ cup water and freeze for 3 hours or until completely solid.

2 Remove the seeds from the grapes with a pair of tweezers. If you have time, peel the grapes.

3 Scrape the frozen wine with a tablespoon to make a fine ice. Combine the grapes with the ice and spoon into 4 shallow glasses.

NUTRITIONAL NOTES
PER PORTION:

ENERGY 138 Kcals/584.8 KJ **FAT** 0.1 g
SATURATED FAT 0

Rhubarb and Orange Water-ice

Pretty pink rhubarb, with sweet oranges and honey – the perfect sweet ice.

Serves 4

INGREDIENTS
350 g/12 oz pink rhubarb
1 medium-size orange
15 ml/1 tbsp clear honey
5 ml/1 tsp powdered gelatine
orange slices, to decorate

clear honey

powdered gelatine

orange

rhubarb

NUTRITIONAL NOTES
PER PORTION:

ENERGY 70 Kcals/296 KJ **FAT** 2.9 g
SATURATED FAT 0.12 g

COOK'S TIP
Most pink, forced rhubarb is naturally quite sweet, but if yours is not, you can add a little more honey, sugar or artificial sweetener to taste.

1 Trim the rhubarb and slice into 2.5 cm/1 in lengths. Place the rhubarb in a pan.

2 Finely grate the rind from the orange and squeeze out the juice. Add about half the orange juice and the grated rind to the rhubarb in the pan and allow to simmer until the rhubarb is just tender. Stir in the honey.

3 Heat the remaining orange juice and stir in the gelatine to dissolve. Stir it into the rhubarb. Tip the whole mixture into a rigid freezer container and freeze it until it's slushy, about 2 hours.

4 Remove the mixture from the freezer and beat it well to break up the ice crystals. Return the water-ice to the freezer and freeze it again until firm. Allow the water-ice to soften slightly at room temperature before serving.

Frozen Apple and Blackberry Terrine

Apples and blackberries are a classic autumn combination; they really complement each other. This pretty, three-layered terrine can be frozen, so you can enjoy it at any time of year.

Serves 6

NUTRITIONAL NOTES
PER PORTION:

ENERGY 72 Kcals/307.5 KJ **FAT** 0.15 g
SATURATED FAT 0

VARIATION

For a quicker version the mixture can be set without the layering. Purée the apples and blackberries together, stir the dissolved gelatine and whisked egg whites into the mixture, turn the whole thing into the tin and leave the mixture to set.

INGREDIENTS
500 g/1 lb cooking or eating apples
300 ml/½ pint/1¼ cups sweet cider
15 ml/1 tbsp clear honey
5 ml/1 tsp vanilla essence
200 g/7 oz/2 cups fresh or frozen and thawed blackberries
15 ml/1 tbsp/1 sachet powdered gelatine
2 egg whites
fresh apple slices and blackberries, to decorate

sweet cider

vanilla essence

clear honey

eggs

blackberries

powdered gelatine

1 Peel, core and chop the apples and place them in a pan, with half the cider. Bring the cider to the boil, and then cover the pan and let the apples simmer gently until tender.

2 Tip the apples into a food processor and process them to a smooth purée. Stir in the honey and vanilla. Add half the blackberries to half the apple purée, and then process again until smooth. Sieve to remove the pips.

3 Heat the remaining cider until it's almost boiling, and then sprinkle the gelatine over and stir until the gelatine has completely dissolved. Add half the gelatine to the apple purée and half to the blackberry purée.

4 Leave the purées to cool until almost set. Whisk the egg whites until they are stiff. Quickly fold them into the apple purée. Remove half the purée to another bowl. Stir the remaining whole blackberries into half the apple purée, and then tip this into a 1.75-litre/3-pint/7½-cup loaf tin, packing it down firmly.

5 Top with the blackberry purée and spread it evenly. Finally, add a layer of the apple purée and smooth it evenly. If necessary, freeze each layer until firm before adding the next.

6 Freeze until firm. To serve, allow to stand at room temperature for about 20 minutes to soften, and then serve in slices, decorated with fresh apples and blackberries.

INDEX

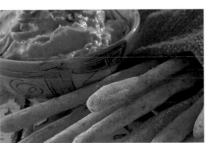

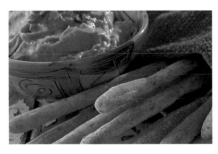